1 MONTH OF
FREE
READING

at
www.ForgottenBooks.com

By purchasing this book you are
eligible for one month membership to
ForgottenBooks.com, giving you
unlimited access to our entire
collection of over 1,000,000 titles via
our web site and mobile apps.

To claim your free month visit:
www.forgottenbooks.com/free171832

ISBN 978-0-332-43814-6
PIBN 10171832

REGULATIONS

FOR

THE GOVERNMENT

OF

THE UNITED STATES NAVY.

1865.

WASHINGTON:
GOVERNMENT PRINTING OFFICE.
1865.

NAVY DEPARTMENT, *April* 18, 1865.

The following Regulations are herewith established and published for the government of all persons attached to the United States Naval Service.

All Orders or Regulations from this Department in conflict with these are hereby revoked. All Circulars or Instructions from any of the Bureaus of this Department not in contravention with these Regulations are to be considered as still in force, and will be obeyed accordingly.

A rigid observance of these Regulations is required from all persons belonging to the Navy of the United States, and it is further now made their positive duty to report forthwith to the Secretary of the Navy any negligence, disobedience, or infraction thereof which may come to their knowledge.

GIDEON WELLES,
Secretary of the Navy.

CONTENTS.

CONTENTS.

REGULATIONS

FOR THE

NAVY OF THE UNITED STATES.

1864.

ARTICLE I.

Classification of Vessels.

What vessels are to constitute first, second, third, and fourth rates.

FIRST RATES.

1....Sailing ships of 2,000 tons and upwards.
Screw steamers of 2,500 tons and upwards.
Paddle-wheel steamers of 2,400 tons and upwards.
Iron-clad steamers of 3,300 tons and upwards.

SECOND RATES.

2....Sailing ships from 1,300 to 2,000 tons.
Screw steamers from 1,200 to 2,500 tons.
Paddle-wheel steamers from 1,000 to 2,400 tons.
Iron-clad steamers from 2,000 to 3,300 tons.
Purchased screw steamers of 1,400 tons and upwards.
Purchased paddle-wheel steamers of 1,500 tons and upwards.

THIRD RATES.

3....Sailing ships from 700 to 1,300 tons.
Screw steamers from 600 to 1,200 tons.
Paddle-wheel steamers from 700 to 1,000 tons.
Iron-clad steamers from 1,200 to 2,000 tons.
Purchased screw steamers from 700 to 1,400 tons.
Purchased paddle-wheel steamers from 900 to 1,500 tons.
Receiving ships.

Line and Staff Officers, with their relative Rank.

4....Sailing ships under 700 tons.
Screw steamers under 600 tons.
Paddle-wheel steamers under 700 tons.
Iron-clad steamers under 1,200 tons.
Purchased screw steamers under 700 tons.
Purchased paddle-wheel steamers under 900 tons.
Store and supply vessels.

ARTICLE II.

Line and Staff Officers, with their relative Rank.

5....Surgeons, Paymasters, Naval Constructors, Chief Engineers, Chaplains, Professors of Mathematics, Passed Assistant Surgeons, Secretaries, Assistant Surgeons, Assistant Naval Constructors, Assistant Paymasters, First Assistant Engineers, Second Assistant Engineers, Third Assistant Engineers, Clerks, Carpenters, and Sailmakers, are to be re⁻garded as Staff Officers, and all other officers of the service as Line Officers. The relative rank between the officers of these two classes is to be as follows:

6....*Assistant Surgeons* to rank with Masters.

7....*Passed Assistant Surgeons* to rank with Lieutenants.

8....*Surgeons* to rank with Lieutenant Commanders for the first five years after promotion; after the first five years, with Commanders : and after fifteen years' date of Commission, to rank with Captains.

9....*Surgeon of the Fleet* to rank with Captain.

10....*Assistant Paymasters* to rank with Masters.

11....*Paymasters* to rank with Lieutenant Commanders for the first five years after promotion; after the first five years, with Commanders; and after fifteen years' date of commission, to rank with Captains.

12....*Fleet Paymaster* to rank with Captain.

13....*Third Assistant Engineers* to rank with Midshipmen.

14....*Second Assistant Engineers* to rank with Ensigns.

15....*First Assistant Engineers* to rank with Masters.

16....*Chief Engineers* to rank with Lieutenant Commanders for the

Line and Staff Officers, with their relative Rank.

first five years after promotion; after the first five years, with Commanders; and after fifteen years' date of commission, to rank with Captains.

17.....*Fleet Engineer* to rank with the Captain.

18.....*Assistant Naval Constructors* to rank with Masters.

19.....*Naval Constructors* of less than twelve years' standing to rank with Lieutenant Commanders; of more than twelve years, with Commanders; and of more than twenty years, with Captains.

20.....*Chaplains* and *Professors of Mathematics* of more than twelve years' standing in their respective grades, to rank with Commanders.

Chaplains and *Professors of Mathematics* of less than twelve years, with Lieutenant Commanders.

21.....*Secretaries* with Lieutenants.

22.....*Clerks* with Midshipmen.

23.....*Carpenters and Sailmakers* with Gunners.

24.....The *Fleet Captain* to be called the "Chief of the Staff," and to take precedence of the Staff Officers of every grade.

25.....*Chiefs of Bureaus* of the Staff Corps to rank with Commodores, and to take precedence of each other, according to their dates of commission as Surgeons, Paymasters, Naval Constructors, and Engineers, and not according to the date of appointment as Fleet Officer or Chief of Bureau.

26.....*Fleet Staff Officers* to take precedence of Executive Officers.

27.....*All Executive Officers* to have authority and precedence over all Staff Officers, (except Fleet Staff Officers,) next to the Commander, while on board the vessel, or at the station to which they are attached.

28.....In processions on shore, on courts-martial, summary courts, courts of inquiry, boards of survey, and all other boards, Line and Staff Officers will take precedence according to relative rank.

29.....Temporary leaves of absence from station or ship, and reports of return, will be obtained from and made to the Commander or Executive Officer, as the Staff Officer may be senior or junior in rank to the Executive Officer, the latter being notified in the former case.

30.....The state-rooms opening into the wardroom country will be occupied, on the starboard side, by all the Line Officers borne upon the books, according to rank, commencing with the forward room.

31....The state-rooms opening into the wardroom country will be occupied, on the port side, by the Staff Officers, as follows: the forward room shall be occupied by the Senior Engineer, in charge of the engines, and if there be no such officer on board, then by the Paymaster, or Assistant Paymaster in charge of the Pay Department; the next room by the Surgeon, or Assistant, in charge of the Medical Department; the next room by the Marine Officer in charge of the guard; and all the rooms abaft this by Staff Officers, in the order of their rank. In flag-ships the Engineer, Paymaster, and Surgeon, in charge of their respective departments, shall occupy rooms conformable to the above rule, and all other officers entitled to rooms on the port side, according to their rank. All other rooms, not assigned by the Department, shall be occupied as the Commander-in-Chief may direct.

32....Officers duly appointed to act in a grade superior to their own shall, while so acting, be entitled to exercise command and to take precedence according to the date of their appointments.

33....No Staff Officer is to exercise command except in the corps or department to which he belongs, or to have, in consequence of his relative rank, any additional right to quarters, other than those assigned him by regulations.

34....When, from any circumstance whatever, the Commander-in-Chief of a fleet or squadron is rendered incapable of exercising command, the Line Officer of the fleet or squadron next in rank or seniority is to discharge his duties.

35....If the Commander-in-Chief of a fleet or squadron be killed in battle, the Line Officer on duty on board the flag-ship highest in rank or seniority, whether detailed as an aid of any kind to the Commander-in-Chief or otherwise, is to succeed him provisionally, and until the officer of the fleet or squadron next in rank or seniority to the Commander-in-Chief announces that he has taken command. It shall be the duty of any officer thus succeeding provisionally the Commander-in-Chief to inform the officer of the fleet or squadron next in seniority to the Commander-in-Chief, as soon as practicable, of the death of the latter. The flag of the deceased Commander-in-Chief is to be kept hoisted in its place until the enemy be out of sight or captured.

36....In case the Commander of a vessel should be rendered incapable of exercising command, or should die, the Executive Officer is always to succeed him in command until further orders, even although there may be officers on board, as passengers, higher in rank or seniority than himself; but in all cases where a Rear-Admiral, or a Commodore entitled to a broad pendant, appointed to a command or to perform any duty, is embarked on board a vessel of the Navy, as a passenger, by due authority, her Commander, if of lower grade or junior in rank, is to be amenable to his orders.

37.....Officers embarked as passengers on board a vessel-of-war, shall not be assigned to duty on board that vessel unless the exigencies of the service shall make such assignment necessary, of which necessity the Commanding Officer shall be the judge. When passengers shall be thus assigned to duty they shall have the same claim to command and quarters as if originally attached to said vessel.

38.....No officer can put himself *on duty* by virtue of his commission or warrant alone.

39.....Every person other than the Commanding and Executive Officers of a vessel, whatsoever may be his rank, shall regard the officer of the deck as the representative of the Commanding Officer, and shall recognize his authority as such in all matters pertaining to the management and police of the vessel which fall under his supervision.

40.....In the event of a riot, or quarrel between persons belonging to the Navy, it shall be the duty of the senior Line Officer present to suppress such disturbance, and if necessary to arrest those engaged in it, even though they be his seniors, or superiors in rank. And all persons belonging to the Navy who may be present shall render prompt assistance and obedience to the officer thus engaged in the restoration of order. Should there be no Line Officer present, the senior Staff Officer will exercise the same authority, and be entitled to the same obedience.

41.....Officers of the Line and Staff of the Marine Corps shall be regarded as belonging, respectively, to the classes of Line and Staff Officers of the Navy, and will take precedence according to their Army rank and as prescribed by the act approved July 16, 1862. Whenever Officers of the Line of the Navy and of the Marine Corps shall have the same assimilated rank and date, the Line Officer of the Marine Corps shall take precedence next after the Line Officer of the Navy, and before all Staff Officers who may hold the same relation.   Staff Officers of the Marine Corps shall take precedence of all Staff Officers of the Navy of the same assimilated rank and date.

42.... Officers of the Marine Corps are not to exercise command, either afloat or at a Naval Station, over others not of their own corps, unless specially authorized by the Commander of the vessel or station for a particular purpose, or when on guard, or in the performance of police duties.   But when serving on shore with a mixed detachment composed of sailors and marines, the Marine Officer will exercise command according to his relative rank and date of commission.

Section 2.

Petty Officers.

43.... The Petty Officers of the Navy shall be divided into two classes—*Petty Officers of the Line*, and *Petty Officers of the Staff*.

44.... The class of *Petty Officers of the Line*, and the order of rank, and of succession to command, shall be as follows :

   1. Boatswain's Mates.
   2. Gunner's Mates.
   3. Signal Quartermaster.
   4. Cockswain to Commander-in-Chief.
   5. Captains of Forecastle.
   6. Quartermasters.
   7. Cockswains.
   8. Captains of Main-top.
   9. Captains of Fore-top.
 10. Captains of Mizzen-top.
 11. Captains of Afterguard.
 12. Quarter-Gunners.
 13. 2d Captains of Forecastle.
 14. 2d Captains of Main-top.
 15. 2d Captains of Fore-top.
 16. 2d Captains of Mizzen-top.

Petty Officers.

45....All other Petty Officers, except the Master-at-Arms, shall be called Petty Officers of the Staff, and shall take precedence and have assimilated rank as follows :

    1. Yeomen.
    2. Surgeon's Stewards.
    3. Paymaster's Stewards.   To rank next after the Masters-
    4. Masters of the Band.   at-Arms.
    5. Schoolmasters.
    6. Ship's writers.

    7. Carpenter's Mates.
    8. Armorers.   To rank next after Gunner's
    9. Sailmaker's Mates.   Mates.

  10. Painters.
  11. Coopers.   To rank next after Captain of
  12. Armorer's Mates.   Afterguard.

  13. Ship's Corporals.
  14. Captains of Hold.   To rank next after Quarter-
  15. Ship's Cooks.   Gunners.
  16. Bakers.

46....The Master-at-Arms will be the Chief Petty Officer of the ship in which he shall serve. All orders from him in regard to the police of the vessel, the preservation of order, and obedience to regulations, must be obeyed by all petty officers and others of the crew. But he shall have no right to succession in command, and shall exercise no authority in matters not specified above.

47....*Petty Officers of the Staff* are not to exercise command except in the department to which they belong, or over those placed immediately under their control.

48....Precedence among petty officers of the same rate shall be established by the Commanding Officer of the vessel in which they shall serve.

49....Orderly Sergeants of guards of Marines, on board vessels of the Navy, shall rank next after Masters-at-Arms ; all other sergeants with Gunner's Mates ; and all corporals with Quarter-Gunners.

50....Non-commissioned Officers of Marines are not to exercise military authority or command over others not of the corps to which they belong, unless specially authorized by the Commander of the vessel for a particular purpose, or when on guard or police duties.

51.....When serving afloat, Petty Officers of the Navy shall take precedence of Non-commissioned Officers of Marines, holding the same relative rank; but when serving as troops on shore, the Non-commissioned Officers shall take precedence of Petty Officers of the same relative rank.

ARTICLE III.

SECTION 1.

Military Honors, Ceremonies, and Salutes.

52.....When the President of the United States shall visit a vessel of the Navy, he shall be received as follows: The yards shall be manned at the moment when the bow oars of the boat in which he is embarked shall be tossed; the men on the yards of the fore and main masts facing aft, and on those of the mizzen-mast, forward; all the officers of the vessel shall be arranged in line upon the quarterdeck, according to seniority, in full uniform. The full marine guard shall be paraded. The President shall be received at the gangway by the Admiral, Commodore, or Commanding Officer, and such other officers as he may designate to assist in the reception. When the President shall reach the deck, the flag or pendant usually worn shall be struck, and the American ensign displayed at the main. All officers and men on deck, the guard excepted, shall uncover their heads, the guard shall present arms, the drums shall give three ruffles, the band shall play the national air, and a salute of twenty-one guns shall be fired; the men on the yards shall lie in and lie down at the last gun. The same ceremonies shall be observed when the President leaves the vessel; the yards shall be manned as he crosses the gangway; at the last gun of the salute the men on the yards shall lie in and lie down, and the ensign at the main shall be struck. If other vessels of the Navy be present, they shall man their yards at the moment the ensign is displayed at the masthead of the one visited, and shall also fire a salute of twenty-one guns, unless otherwise directed by the senior

Military Honors, Ceremonies, and Salutes.

officer present. On passing such vessels, their sentinels shall present arms, the drums shall beat three ruffles, and the band shall play the national air.

53....The Vice-President of the United States, when visiting a vessel of the Navy, shall receive the same honors as have been prescribed for the President, except that the yards shall not be manned, and that there shall be but one salute of seventeen guns, which shall be fired when he goes on board ; and that the American flag shall not be displayed, unless the reception takes place abroad, in which case it shall be hoisted at the fore.

54....An ex-President of the United States, when visiting a vessel of the Navy, shall receive the same honors as those prescribed for the President, except the display of the American flag and the manning of the yards.

55....Members of the Cabinet, Justices of the Supreme Court, or Governors of States, when visiting a vessel of the Navy, shall receive the same honors as those prescribed for the Vice-President, except that the salute shall consist of fifteen guns.

56....A foreign sovereign, or the chief magistrate of any foreign republic, when visiting a vessel of the Navy, shall be received with the same honors prescribed for the President, except that the flag of his own country shall be displayed at the main, and the band shall play his own national air.

57....Members of a royal family, when visiting a vessel of the Navy, shall receive the same honors as would be paid to their sovereign, except that one salute only shall be fired.

58....Whenever a Minister appointed to represent the United States abroad, or a Minister of a foreign country, shall visit a vessel of the Navy, he shall be received by the Admiral, Commodore, or Commanding Officer ; the marine guard shall be paraded, and a salute of fifteen guns shall be fired.

59....A Chargé d'Affaires or Commissioner shall be received in the same manner, but the salute shall be thirteen guns.

60....A Consul General shall be received by the Commanding Officer, and saluted with nine guns.

61 ...A Consul shall be received by the Commanding Officer, and saluted with seven guns.

Military Honors, Ceremonies, and Salutes.

62....When a Rear-Admiral shall go on board his flag-ship to assume command, he shall be received by all the officers of the vessel in full uniform, and the crew arranged on the side opposite to that on which he enters ; the full marine guard to be paraded. He is to be met at the gangway by the Commanding Officer and such other officers as he may select ; the officers and men shall uncover their heads, the guard shall present arms, the drums shall give two ruffles, and the band shall play a march. When he orders his flag to be hoisted a salute of thirteen guns shall be fired. When he shall make a visit of inspection to any vessel of his fleet, the same ceremonies shall be observed ; the salute shall be fired immediately after he arrives on board.

63....When a Rear-Admiral relinquishes his command afloat, the ceremonies prescribed for his first reception shall take place at his departure. His flag shall be hauled down at the last gun of the salute.

64....A Rear-Admiral leaving his flag-ship with the intention of soon returning on board, shall be entitled to an officer's guard, which is to present arms as he passes in front of it, and the drums to give two ruffles. He is to be attended at the gangway by the Line Officer next in rank to himself on board, and all the Line Officers of his Staff, other than those who are to accompany him ; the officer of the deck and the junior officers of the watch will also be in attendance. The same ceremonies are to be observed on his returning on board. If absent at night, three lights are to be displayed perpendicularly at the peak. If Commander-in-chief, the toplight will also be shown.

65....When a Commodore is duly authorized by the Navy Department to hoist a broad pendant as Commander-in-Chief of a squadron, he is, on first going on board the vessel which is to carry his broad pendant, to be received in the same manner as prescribed for a Rear-Admiral, except that the salute is to be eleven guns. Whenever he shall make a visit of inspection to any other vessel of his command, the same ceremonies shall be observed ; the salute shall be fired immediately after he arrives on board.

66....A Rear-Admiral's flag, or a Commodore's broad pendant, shall not be hoisted on board any ship of his fleet or squadron, which he may visit for any purpose, without his special order.

67....When a Commodore duly authorized to hoist a broad pendant relinquishes his command afloat, the ceremonies prescribed for his first reception are to take place at his departure. The broad pendant shall be hauled down at the last gun of the salute.

68....A Commodore duly authorized to wear a broad pendant, when leaving his ship with the intention of soon returning on board, shal be entitled to the same honors as those prescribed for a Rear-Admiral, and the same are to be paid him on his return. If absent at night, three lights shall be displayed perpendicularly at the peak. If Commanding-in-Chief, the toplight will also be shown.

69....When the Commander-in-Chief of a fleet or squadron, or naval station, whether a Rear-Admiral or Commodore, duly authorized to wear a broad pendant, shall first visit a ship not belonging to his own fleet or squadron, he shall be received as if he were visiting a ship under his own command, but in no case shall a flag or broad pendant be hoisted.

70....Whenever a Rear-Admiral employed on shore, but not in command of a naval station, shall visit a vessel of the Navy on duty, he shall be received by the senior Line Officer present and the officer of the deck. The marine guard shall be paraded, and on the occasion of his first visit a salute of thirteen guns shall be fired.

71....If a Commodore, while in command of a single ship, be duly authorized by the Navy Department to wear a broad pendant, and to command a division or squadron, or if he be promoted to Rear-Admiral, his pendant or flag shall be saluted by his flag-ship when first hoisted, as already provided for.

72....When a Commodore, Captain, or any other officer is appointed to the command of a single vessel, he will, if she be at a navy yard and ready to be transferred to him, make, in company with the Commanding Officer of the yard, or some other proper officer or officers appointed by such Commanding Officer for the purpose, a thorough personal examination of her, and inform himself as to all her arrangements and preparations of equipment; after which the transfer is to be formally made in the presence of as many of her officers and crew as can be assembled, before whom his appointment is to be read; and then the vessel is to be placed in commission by hoisting her ensign and pendant. If the vessel is already in commission, he is, nevertheless' to examine her and inform himself as stated above, and to read to her officers and crew his appointment.

73....All commissioned officers other than Rear-Admirals and Commodores entitled to wear a broad pendant, when visiting a vessel of the Navy, shall be received at the gangway by the officer of the deck. The approach of all Commanding Officers shall be promptly reported to the officer in command. Warrant Officers shall be received by a Warrant.Officer of the watch.

74....Whenever the Commanding Officer of a vessel-of-war shall leave such vessel, he shall be accompanied to the gangway by the Line Officer next to him in rank, to whom he will deliver the temporary charge of the vessel; upon his return the senior Line Officer on board will receive him at the gangway to report anything of note that may have occurred during his absence. The officers of the watch will also attend at his departure and return. If absent at night, two lights shall be displayed perpendicularly at the peak.

75....When a Rear-Admiral or Commodore duly authorized to hoist a broad pendant, or any other officer, shall be ordered to command a shore station, he is to be received at the gate, or landing, by the officer whom he is to relieve and the Line Officer next in rank, by all the officers of the station in uniform, and by the marine guard with arms presented; the drums shall give two ruffles, if the officer be a Rear-Admiral or Commodore. At the moment the flag or broad pendant shall be hoisted it shall be saluted as for a Rear-Admiral, or Commodore commanding-in-chief. On relinquishing his command, like ceremonies shall be observed, and his flag or broad pendant shall be hauled down at the last gun.

76....Whenever the President of the United States, the Vice-President, an ex-President, or any other personage for whose reception afloat ceremonies have been prescribed in the foregoing articles, shall visit a naval station, he shall be received with the same ceremonies, so far as may be practicable.

77....Officers of the Army or Marine Corps, on visiting a vessel of the Navy, or naval station, shall be received agreeably to their relative rank with officers of the Navy.

78....When naval, military, or civil officers of a foreign nation visit a vessel of the Navy, or naval station, they may be received with the salutes herein prescribed for our own officers of the same rank.

79....In the reception of officers of the Army or Marine Corps not attached to the ship or station, an officer of equal rank, if there be any such on board, shall receive him at the gangway and attend him at his departure. Foreign Admirals or Commanding Officers shall always be received and attended in like manner, but the Commanding Officer shall always be present at the arrival and departure of a foreign Commanding Officer.

80....Any officer or other person may dispense with a salute, or other ceremonies provided for his reception, at his pleasure.

81....Side-boys are not to be employed at any reception, unless an accommodation ladder be not shipped; nor shall the side be piped, unless side-boys are to be piped over.

82....No officers of the Navy shall be saluted, other than Rear-Admirals commanding a fleet or station, Rear-Admirals on shore duty, or Commodores duly authorized to wear a broad pendant. When several officers entitled to be saluted may be assembled on board a ship, or at a naval station, on the same duty, but one salute shall be fired which shall consist of the number of guns to which the senior of such assemblage may be entitled. Return salutes shall be as follows: Between officers of equal rank, gun for gun. To an inferior by a superior: if the inferior be a Commodore duly authorized to wear a broad pendant, the number of guns already specified in preceding paragraphs. If a Commodore commanding a single vessel, nine guns; if a Captain or officer of less rank, seven guns.

83....No vessel of the Navy mounting less than six guns, nor any storeship or transport, is, on any occasion, to fire a salute. If necessary, in order to avoid giving offence, she may, however, fire a return salute; but no surveying vessel is ever either to fire or return a salute.

84....A vessel mounting more than six guns, ordered to join a fleet or squadron, is, on meeting the Commander-in-Chief, to salute his flag, and shall not again salute it while under his command, except he shall make a visit of inspection to such vessel.

85....The flag-ship only shall salute the flag of an officer appointed to command a fleet or squadron, on his assuming command and hoisting

Military Honors, Ceremonies, and Salutes.

his flag. Any vessel belonging to a fleet, or squadron, having already saluted the flag of the Commander-in-Chief, will not salute in the same fleet or squadron, the flag of any officer succeeding to the command of that fleet or squadron ; but all vessels entitled to salute on first joining a fleet or squadron will salute the flag of the Commander-in-Chief.

86.....When fleets, squadrons, or divisions meet, none but the officers commanding them are to salute.

87.....No salute shall be fired in the presence of a senior without his permission, except it be one rendered to such senior.

88.....On the Fourth day of July and the Twenty-second day of February, the national flag shall be displayed at the peak and at each mast-head, from sunrise to sunset, on board of every vessel of the Navy in commission, not under way; the jack shall also be hoisted forward ; at noon a salute of twenty-one guns shall be fired by all vessels permitted to salute. Vessels at sea shall fire a salute of twenty-one guns at noon, with the ensign flying at the peak. At naval stations the ensign shall be displayed from sunrise to sunset, and a salute of twenty-one guns shall be fired at noon.

89.....When a national anniversary to be celebrated occurs on a Sunday, all the ceremonies are to be deferred until the following day ; and in no case shall a salute be fired on Sunday, unless the failure to do so would give offence to foreign authorities ; but salutes may be returned on that day.

90.....If a vessel join a commanding officer who is entitled to a salute on Sunday, it is not to be fired until the following morning, immediately after hoisting the colors.

91.....All vessels of the Navy mounting ten guns or less shall use the smooth-bore howitzers in saluting. Vessels mounting more than ten guns shall use the smooth-bore heavy guns. Rifled guns must never be used for saluting, unless a vessel has no smooth-bore guns of any calibre.

92.....Commanding officers of vessels of the Navy, when in foreign ports, are to give timely information to the public authorities of such ports, and to the Commanding Officers of foreign vessels-of-war, of any anniversary or other event which it is intended to celebrate ; and should they fire salutes in honor of the occasion, the salutes are not to be re-

Military Honors, Ceremonies, and Salutes.

turned unless the failure to do so would give offence, but a message of acknowledgment and thanks is to be promptly sent to them and all others who may have publicly displayed any mark of honor, or respect, on the occasion.

93....In saluting any personage, whether civil, naval, or military, the ensign of his nation is not to be exhibited, if its display will involve a return of the salute.   When a salute shall be fired in honor of a visit from any public functionary, either to ship or shore, it shall be regarded as personal, and shall not be returned.   The same functionary shall not be saluted by the same vessel, at the same place, oftener than once in twelve months, except when it may be necessary in cases of foreign officials, or of naval or military officers who may have received advancement of rank.

94....Forts, castles, or cities of the United States are not to be saluted by any vessel-of-war of the United States.

95....When a foreign vessel-of-war, of a nation in amity with us, shall arrive in a port of the United States where there is a vessel of the Navy, or a navy yard, the Commanding Officer shall, without delay, send a proper officer on board to offer the usual civilities and any assistance in his power; but he is not to pay the first visit of ceremony, or give the first salute.   He is, however, to return either promptly, and the latter, gun for gun.

96....The Commanding Officer of any fleet, squadron, or vessel shall, on anchoring in any foreign port, pay the first visit to the Commanding Naval Officer of the station to which the port belongs, and to the civil authorities of the place, *provided* the usual offers of civilities shall have been made to him.

97....On the arrival of a vessel of the United States in a foreign port, her Commander is to inform himself as to the salutes and ceremonies usually given and observed, and be governed accordingly; and he is to pay all proper attention to its civil and military regulations. In saluting the place, he is to hoist its national ensign at the fore, and be assured that gun for gun will be given in return.   In countries having treaty stipulations with the United States in regard to salutes, Commanding Officers will be careful to conform strictly thereto.

98....Vessels of the United States shall salute vessels-of-war of other nations in foreign ports, or at sea, when commanded by Flag-Officers, on being assured of a return, gun for gun ; and when they themselves are saluted by foreign vessels-of-war, they are to give in return, gun for gun. The national flag of the vessel saluted shall be displayed at the fore.

99....Vessels of the Navy may participate in celebrating the national festivals of a country, while lying in one of its ports, by hoisting the ensign of that country at either the fore or main, as circumstances may require, and firing salutes ; and they may also participate in a similar way, while lying in a foreign port, in celebrating the national festivals of any other country in amity with ours besides the one to which the port belongs, if in effect invited so to do. In such cases, the colors shall be hauled down with those of the foreign ships, or forts, whose national festival is celebrated. And in case of foreign vessels-of-war lying in our ports and celebrating their national festivals, the Commander of the station, or senior officer present, may participate in the celebration, as provided for when lying in a foreign port.

100....Foreign officials visiting our ships and stations will receive the salutes and honors prescribed for persons of the same rank in the service of the United States.

101....Whenever any person for whom a salute has been provided in the preceding articles shall embark on board a vessel of the Navy for passage, he shall be entitled to the same salute as if he were visiting such vessel, and also to the same salute on disembarking.

102....Should it occur that any foreign official of high rank or distinction, whose reception has not been provided for in the foregoing paragraphs, should visit any vessel or naval station of the United States, he may be received with the salutes and honors assigned to him by his own country.

103....No salute is ever to exceed twenty-one guns ; all salutes must be fired between sunrise and sunset, and the national colors must always be displayed at the time. On the occasion of a visit by any person entitled to one salute, such salute shall be fired on his arrival on board, or at the station.

104....No vessel of the Navy is to lower her sails, or dip her colors to another vessel of the Navy ; but should a foreign vessel, or a merchant

Military Honors, Ceremonies, and Salutes.

vessel of the United States, dip her colors, or lower her sails, the compliment will be returned.

105....Cheers shall never be given as a compliment to any officer, or man, on joining a vessel of the Navy, or while attached to or being detached from her.

106....Vessels of the Navy are not to salute any functionary of the United States, in a foreign port, until the proper honors have been paid to the flag of the nation to which the port belongs.

107....The Commander of a squadron, on arriving at a foreign port, is to call in person and pay the first visit to the diplomatic functionaries of the United States thereat, whose rank is of and above that of Chargé d'Affaires ; and the Commander of a vessel of the Navy, on so arriving, is to so call and first visit the functionaries of our government thereat, whose rank is of and above that of Consul General. The Commander of a squadron, on so arriving, is to send a suitable officer to visit the consular officer, and tender to him a passage to the flag-ship ; and the Commander of a vessel of the Navy, on so arriving, is to send an officer, who is to visit the consular officer, and if he be of the rank of Consul General, to inform him of the presence of the ship and of the Commander's intention to visit him, unless the latter should find it convenient to make the visit at that time ; if of lower rank than Consul General, to offer him a passage to the ship.

108....Whenever any vessel of the Navy may be lying in a foreign port, or may enter such port, and foreign vessels-of-war of nations in amity with us may be at anchor there, or may enter, it shall be the duty of the Commanding Officer to render to such vessels all such civilities as may be customary, and to reciprocate fully all such as may be extended to himself.

109....Officers in boats not laden, nor engaged in towing, are, on meeting or passing other boats, to observe the following ceremonies as marks of respect, according as they may be under oars or sail ; and the officers to whom the salutes are made are to be careful to acknowledge them promptly by raising their caps : To a boat with the flag of a Rear-Admiral, or the broad pendant of a Commodore, boats with a narrow pendant are to lie on their oars, or let fly their sheets, and

2

boats without any pendants are to toss their oars, or lower their sails. In both cases officers in them are to salute by raising their caps. In the case of two boats meeting or passing, each with the same insignia of a Commanding Officer, the junior officer in rank or seniority is first to salute the other by raising his cap. Officers in boats meeting or passing their own immediate Commander in a boat with his pendant flying, are to salute him by lying on their oars, or letting fly their sheets and raising their caps; and in passing each other the salute of raising the cap is always to be mutually made, but first by the junior in rank or seniority. All officers inferior in grade to the Commanding Officer of another vessel than the one to which they belong, are, on passing him in a boat with his pendant flying, to lie on their oars, or let fly their sheets, and raise their caps; if equal in grade, but junior in seniority, they will salute by raising their caps. All juniors, though wearing a pendant, will first salute their seniors not in command by raising their caps, except the Commander of a vessel on passing one of the boats belonging to his own vessel, which will always salute as provided for above, even if a senior be a passenger in it. Cockswains steering boats are, whenever Commissioned Officers are saluted, to stand up and raise their caps; and whenever Warrant Officers are saluted, they are to raise their caps only. The officer and Cockswain of loaded boats, or of boats engaged in towing, shall salute a boat with the flag of a Rear-Admiral, or the broad pendant of a Commodore, by standing and raising their caps. On passing boats with a narrow pendant, or with Commissioned Officers on board, the Cockswain shall stand, and both he and the officer shall raise their caps. Boats containing superiors of other grades shall be saluted as already provided for. When boats are rowing in the same direction, an inferior is not to pass his superior in grade, unless he be on urgent duty, or authorized by the superior. When boats are pursuing opposite directions, the rule of the road, to prevent fouling, is that both should put their helms to port, circumstances permitting. When boats are approaching the same landing or vessel, an inferior is always to yield the way to a superior in grade. Boats about leaving the ship's side with inferiors are to give way in ample season to others approaching it with superiors. No boat is ever to be permitted to remain unnecessarily at a landing or gangway, or to be moored at the booms so as to interfere with boats coming to or leaving the gangway.

110....A sentinel at a gangway is to present arms to all officers coming on board or leaving the vessel, of and above the rank of Lieutenant Commander, and to carry arms to all other Commissioned Officers ; but neither this ceremony, nor that of piping the side, is to take place except during the hours when the colors should be displayed. And, after tattoo, all side lights but one may be dispensed with, except in the case of a visit or departure of a foreign officer.

111....All inferiors, in passing a superior, either afloat or on shore, or in addressing him on duty, shall raise their caps, and superiors are strictly enjoined to return such salutes in the same way. The fact that an officer is not on duty, nor in uniform, shall not be regarded as an excuse for any act of disrespect or omission of naval courtesy on the part of an officer towards a superior whose rank he knows. No personal feelings are to be allowed to interfere with official courtesy, or pleaded as an excuse for its neglect. All persons having occasion to address the Executive Officer, or the Officer of the Deck, on matters of duty, shall always raise their caps.

112....Every officer, or man, on reaching the quarter-deck, either from a boat or below, or on leaving it to go over the side, is to salute it by raising his cap, and this is to be acknowledged in return, and in the same way, by all the officers of the watch at hand.

113....On board vessels having an accommodation ladder shipped at each gangway, the starboard gangway is to be reserved for the use of the cabin and wardroom officers and their visitors ; the port gangway for all others. When one accommodation ladder only is shipped, it is to be used indiscriminately by all officers.

114....Officers and men are not to omit, on any occasion, to extend to officers of the Army of the United States, and to all foreign officers, the courtesy and mark of respect due to their rank, when passing in boats or meeting on shore.

Section 2.

Funeral Honors.

115....On the receipt of official intelligence of the death of the President of the United States, the senior officer present shall, on the

Funeral Honors.

following day, cause the ensign of each vessel under his authority to be hoisted at half-mast from sunrise to sunset, and a gun to be fired by his vessel every half hour, beginning at sunrise and ending at sunset. At naval stations the same ceremonies are to be observed.

116....On the death of a Commander of a fleet, squadron, or division, occurring at sea, the ensigns of all the vessels present, and the distinctive flag of command which he wore, shall be hoisted half-mast during the performance of the funeral ceremony, and on committing the body to the deep, the flag-ship shall fire as many minute guns as he was entitled to receive for a salute when alive, and finally, haul down his flag at the last one of these guns. If occurring in port, the ensigns and distinctive flag mentioned shall be hoisted half-mast during each day from that of his decease until sunset of the one on which the funeral service is performed, and, on sending the body to the shore, the number of minute guns indicated above is to be fired. The escort will fire three volleys of musketry over the grave.

117....On the death of a Commodore, or any other officer commanding a vessel, occurring at sea, the ensigns of all the vessels present, and the pendant of the vessel he commanded, shall be hoisted half-mast during the performance of the funeral ceremony ; and on committing the body to the deep, the vessel he commanded shall fire as many minute guns as he was entitled to receive from his superior as a return salute when alive. If occurring in port, the pendant of the vessel he commanded shall be hoisted half-mast during each day from that of his decease until sunset of the one on which the funeral service is performed ; and, on sending the body to the shore, all the vessels present are to half-mast their ensigns until sunset, and the number of minute guns indicated is to be fired. The escort will fire three volleys of musketry over the grave.

118....On the death of a Commissioned Officer, other than those already mentioned, occurring at sea, the ensigns of all the vessels present shall be hoisted half-mast during the performance of the funeral service ; and, if occurring in port, said ensigns are to be so hoisted during the time that the body is being conveyed to the shore, and until the return of the funeral escort to the ship. In either case, after

Funeral Honors.

the funeral services three volleys of musketry are to be fired by the full marine guard.

119....On the death of a Warrant Officer the ensigns of all the vessels present shall be hoisted half-mast during the performance of the funeral service when at sea, and, when in port, during the time that the body is being conveyed to the shore, and for one hour afterwards. In either case, three volleys of musketry are to be fired by a sergeant's guard of fourteen men.

120....On the death of a Staff Officer the same funeral honors are to be observed as those prescribed for a Line Officer of the same rank, except that the distinctive flag or pendant of the vessel is not to be hoisted half-mast, and that no minute guns are to be fired. If a Commissioned Officer, three volleys of musketry are to be fired by the full marine guard.

121....On the death of a Petty Officer, or other person of inferior rating, the ensigns of all vessels present shall be hoisted half-mast during the performance of the funeral service when at sea, and when in port, during the time that the body is being conveyed to the shore. In either case, three volleys of musketry are to be fired by a corporal's guard, consisting of ten men in the case of a Petty Officer, and of eight men in that of a person of inferior rating.

122....On the death of an officer, non-commissioned officer, or private of the Marine Corps, the funeral honors are to be regulated by his relative rank. In no such case are ships to half-mast their distinctive flags, or pendants, or to fire minute guns.

123....On the death of any officer, or other person belonging to the Navy, on shore, he will be entitled to the same funeral honors, so far as circumstances will admit, as though he had died on duty at sea. As a recognition of distinguished services, the Secretary of the Navy will, in all cases, order such additional honors as in his judgment may seem appropriate.

124....No vessel of a squadron other than that of the senior officer present, is ever to half-mast her colors until permission to do so has been obtained ; but whenever the vessel of the senior officer present has her colors at half-mast, all other vessels in sight are to follow motions.

125....Funeral honors are not to be paid before the rising nor after the setting of the sun.

Distinctive Flags of Officers.

SECTION 3.

Distinctive Flags of Officers.

126.....The flag of a Rear-Admiral is to be rectangular, plain and blue ; and it is to be worn at the mizzen. But if two or more Rear-Admirals in command afloat should meet, or be in the presence of each other, the senior only is to wear the flag of blue, the next in seniority is to wear it of red, and the other or others to wear it of white.

127.....No officer is to hoist a broad pendant except in command of a separate squadron, and by the authority of the Secretary of the Navy, and one so authorized is not to strike it until duly ordered, except on meeting with an officer of a different squadron or commanding a station, senior or superior to himself, wearing a narrow pendant.   When two or more officers entitled to wear broad pendants shall meet, or be in the presence of each other, the senior or superior in rank shall wear one of blue, the next in rank one of red, and the other or others to wear it of white.

128.....A Rear-Admiral, or any officer wearing a flag or broad pendant, commanding a fleet, squadron or division, may shift his flag or pendant from one vessel to another of those under his command, informing the Secretary of the Navy—or in case of a Divisional Commander, the Commander of the fleet or squadron—of the fact, and of the reasons which governed him, by the earliest opportunity.

129.....A divisional mark and the mark of a senior officer present are both to be triangular in shape, with a middle part of a different color from the rest, in the form of a wedge, the base occupying one-third the whole hoist or head, and the point extending to the extremity of the fly. For a first division it is to be blue, white, blue ; for a second division, red, white, red ; for a third division, white, blue, white ; and for a senior officer present, white, red, white.

130....Any officer not authorized to wear the flag of a Rear-Admiral, nor the broad pendant of a Commodore, who may be appointed by an express order to command a division of a squadron, shall wear a divisional mark of the size prescribed in the book of allowances, at the mast-head where the pendant is usually worn. And whenever two or more vessels of the Navy, in commission, away from a naval station, may be assembled, the senior officer present for the time being, when not already authorized to wear a mark or flag of higher significance, shall wear, in like manner, the mark of a senior officer until he may fall in with a superior, or senior officer in command.

131....No Divisional Commander is to wear the distinctive mark of one when separated singly from the squadron and station to which he belongs ; and no officer wearing such distinctive mark, or that of a senior officer present, is, in consequence thereof, to assume any additional title, to allow himself to be addressed by any other than his commission bespeaks, or to permit his vessel to be designated as a flag-ship.

132....Any officer commanding a vessel of the Navy, except one on board which a flag, broad pendant, divisional, or senior officer's mark may be worn, shall wear a narrow pendant at the main. This pendant is to be regarded not as an emblem of rank, but rather as significant of command, and that the vessel is of a public character.

133....All officers of and above the grade of Lieutenant Commander may wear at the bow of the boat in which they may be embarked a flag or pendant of the same character which they are entitled to wear at the mast-head of their respective vessels ; but no divisional flag, nor flag of a senior officer, shall be worn in the bow of boats.

134....The distinctive flag or broad pendant of a Commander-in-Chief, or of the Commander of a squadron, shall be worn only when he is actually in command of such squadron, nor shall it be worn by any vessel in a port of the United States during his absence from that port for a longer period than twenty-four hours. The senior officer present in such cases is, for the time being, to wear his distinctive mark, to issue all necessary orders, and to obey any directions that may have been, or may be, given to him by said Commander.

135....When the Commander-in-Chief of a fleet or squadron, in a foreign port, shall absent himself therefrom, and from the vessels under his authority, to remain away more than twenty-four hours, yet temporarily, his flag or pendant is not to be struck, but it is to be kept hoisted on board the vessel serving as his flag-ship, if either the officer commanding her or the Captain of the Fleet is next to him in rank ; otherwise it is for the time being to be hoisted on board the vessel commanded by the officer who may be next to him in rank, and such officer is to issue all necessary orders, and to carry out any instructions that may have been, or may be, given by said Commander-in-Chief.

136....No officer left temporarily in the place of a Commander-in-Chief is to assume, or to allow himself to be addressed by, any higher title than his commission bespeaks, nor is he, in his written communications, to subscribe himself otherwise than, after his rank, as the senior officer present.

137....Rear-Admirals in command of shore stations are to wear the distinctive flag to which they may be entitled, and to hoist it on board the receiving vessel; or, if there be no such vessel thereat, at any suitable place in the yard. Commodores in such command who have, by order of the Department, commanded a squadron, are to wear a broad pendant, and to so hoist it.

ARTICLE IV.

General Instructions.

138....The attention of all persons belonging to the Navy is particularly called to the laws for the government of the Navy, and to all general orders and regulations of the Navy Department which now exist or may be issued hereafter.

139....Hereafter every general order issued by this Department, or published by authority, will be read to the officers and crew by the Executive Officer on board of every naval vessel, at the first general muster subsequent to its receipt, and entered upon the ship's log. All officers are directed to preserve a copy of each general order and circular.

140....Although particular duties are prescribed for officers and others in the following instructions, yet it is to be distinctly understood that it is not intended to confine or limit them to those specified, but every person is enjoined to promote, by zeal and energy, the efficiency of the service.

141....Authority is to be exercised with firmness, but with kindness and justice to inferiors.

142....Officers will bear in mind that the authority to punish offences is strictly defined by law; no deviation therefrom will be tolerated.

General Instructions.

143.___All persons in the Navy are to be constant in attention to their duties, never absenting themselves therefrom without the consent of their immediate Commanding Officer, nor remaining out of the vessel to which they may belong during the night, after sunset, without express permission from the Commander of the vessel, or from the Commander-in-Chief of the fleet or squadron.

144.___Every officer or other person of the Navy shall treat with respect his superior, or any one having authority over him, and is required to set an example of morality, subordination, and devotion to duty.

145.___If any person in the Navy consider himself oppressed by his superior, or observe in him any misconduct, he is not on that account to fail in his respect to him, but he is to represent, through the proper channel, such oppression or misconduct to the proper authority. But in all cases such person will be held accountable if his representations should be found vexatious, frivolous, or false.

146.___If any person belonging to the Navy shall know of any fraud, collusion, or improper conduct on the part of any agent, contractor, or other person employed in matters connected with the naval service, he shall report the same, in writing, through the proper channel, to the proper authority; but he must, in all cases, specify the particular acts of misconduct, and the means of proving the same, for he will be held strictly accountable for any frivolous or vexatious charges he may present.

147.___If an officer receive an order from a superior contrary to any particular order of any other superior, or to instructions, or general orders from the Department, he shall respectfully represent, in writing, such contrariety to such superior, and if, after such representation, the superior shall still insist upon the execution of his order, it is to be obeyed, and the officer receiving and executing it, is to report the circumstances to the one from whom he received the original order.

148.___Every officer who shall divert another from any service upon which he shall have been ordered by a common superior, or require him to act contrary to the orders of such superior, or interfere with those under his command, must show to the Department, or to the officer under whose command he may be acting, that the public interest required the procedure.

General Instructions.

149....All orders countermanding a written order from a common superior shall be given in writing.

150....No person in the Navy shall, without the authority of his superior or Commanding Officer, exchange with another for the performance of any duty with which he may be charged.

151....When any officer, whether in command of a fleet, squadron, or single vessel, shall meet with his superior or senior officer, also in command, he shall visit him in person, show him his orders or instructions, and consider himself under his command for the time being. If he shall have received confidential orders, he is at once to inform his superior of that fact, and he must not be delayed in the execution of such orders by his superior *without an overruling necessity therefor*, of which the Department must be informed in detail, at the earliest possible moment; in all cases of such interference, the original instructions must be carried out as soon thereafter as practicable, and a full report upon the subject forwarded to the authority which issued such confidential orders.

152....Any officer who may be sent on detached duty, and who may arrive within the limits of a port or station commanded by an officer belonging to the same fleet or squadron, shall always communicate with such Commanding Officer, either in person or by letter, according as he may be junior or senior to such officer, before proceeding to execute any part of the duty with which he may be charged within such limits, unless otherwise directed by their common superior, or the position of such Commanding Officer, or other imperative circumstances would cause a delay prejudicial to the service. Such officer will always communicate with the Commanding Officer of the port or station before leaving it, in order that an opportunity may be afforded to send reports or despatches in case there should be no regular means of communication between him and the Commander-in-Chief or Navy Department.

153....Boats shall not be regarded as being on *detached duty* while engaged in the ordinary service of the ship to which they belong. Unless specially fitted for an expedition for which a regular detail of officers and men is made, or unless separated from the ship by unavoidable or unforseen circumstances, they shall be regarded as attached to

General Instructions.

her, and no officer in such cases shall assume authority on the ground that he is engaged on detached duty.

154.... When two or more vessels are in company, whether belonging to the same squadron or not, the senior officer present will regulate the motions of all.

155.... No deviation shall be made from the directions of the Navy Department in relation to the construction, repair, arrangement, armament, or equipment of vessels without its previous sanction, or in cases of absolute necessity occurring abroad, of the Commander-in-Chief, or in his absence, of the senior officer present, and then the nature of the alteration, effects produced, and costs are to be reported to the Department at the earliest moment practicable. Nor shall any change be made in the fixtures or furniture of officers' apartments without such sanction, and if made for private convenience, no article substituted for that allowed shall be removed, even though it may have been purchased by the officer desiring the change.

156.... Every officer is strictly enjoined to avoid all unnecessary expenditures of public money or stores, and as far as may be in his power, to prevent the same in others, and to encourage the strictest economy consistent with the interests of the service. All persons in the Navy are hereby held answerable for any wasteful or improper expense they may direct, authorize, or knowingly permit.

157.... No article of public stores is ever to be appropriated to the private use of any person not in distress, without the consent of the Navy Department, or the order of the senior officer present in command, who shall give to the Department early information of every case that may occur, together with the attending circumstances, and he shall, in every instance, be careful to take the best security for future indemnity to the government that the nature of it will admit.

158.... In all cases of real distress, gratuitous assistance is to be offered to the fullest extent practicable.

159.... Mechanics on board vessels on foreign stations may be allowed to repair vessels of the merchant service of the United States in cases where a refusal to do so would of necessity impose injurious delays or greatly increase expenses. For such services they may receive such compensation as may be properly offered and their Com-

General Instructions.

manding Officer may regard as fair and equitable. No officer in the Navy, however, is ever to claim or receive any compensation whatever for such services. Assistance may likewise be rendered to foreign vessels, on similar terms, when not attainable otherwise, by permission of the senior officer.

160....All persons employed in the Navy, or for naval purposes, are strictly prohibited from having any interest whatever in purchases or contracts for supplies of any kind for the Navy, or in any works pertaining to it, nor shall they receive, directly or indirectly, any emolument or gratuity of any kind from any contractor or other person furnishing supplies, nor act as agent or attorney for any such contractor or other person.

161....When the sun sets at or after six o'clock, tattoo shall be beat at nine o'clock in the evening, and the colors be hoisted at eight o'clock in the morning; and when it sets before six o'clock, the tattoo shall be beat at eight o'clock in the evening, and the colors be hoisted at nine o'clock in the morning. The colors shall be kept flying until sunset if the weather will permit, or the senior officer see no objection thereto. Whenever a vessel of the Navy shall get under way, or come to anchor, the colors shall be hoisted, though earlier or later, if there be light enough for them to be seen; also in passing, meeting, joining, or parting from any other of the vessels of the Navy; and unless there should be sufficient reason to the contrary, on falling in with any other vessel at sea, and in passing or approaching forts, castles, batteries, light-houses, or towns.

162....All lights and fires, except those necessary for the service of the vessel, or specially allowed by the Commanding Officer, or the lights used in the wardroom, steerages and forward officers' apartments, shall be extinguished at tattoo. The wardroom lights shall be extinguished at ten p. m., and all others at nine p. m , unless otherwise allowed in special cases by the Commanding Officer. The greatest caution is to be observed with regard to lights in any part of a vessel. No light shall be left unattended in any apartment, unless it be in a lantern properly secured. No uncovered light shall be used in any store-room or in the hold, nor shall spirit lamps, explosive oils, or friction matches be allowed on board any vessel of the Navy.

General Instructions.

163....In the execution of process issued by civil authority, appiicable to a person or to persons on board a vessel of the Navy, or in a navy yard, or other naval establishment, Commanding Officers, when legally required, are to afford facilities and active assistance within their respective commands.

164....Gambling is strictly prohibited on board vessels of the Navy and in navy yards, and all places and stations belonging to, or under the control of the Navy Department.

165....Should any officer of the Navy so far forget what is due to his own honor, and to that of the service of which he is a member, as to incur debts, especially upon a foreign station, without a reasonable expectation of discharging them, or should any officer leave any foreign port without paying, or providing for the payment of every debt he may have incurred, his conduct, when brought to the knowledge of his commanding officer, shall be reported by him to the Commander of the squadron, or the Secretary of the Navy, in order that such course may be pursued as the circumstances of the case may require.

166....Officers of the Navy not on duty, arc to keep the Department at all times advised of their address.

167....Officers, on being detached from duty, will immediately inform the Department of their intended place of residence, and notice must be given of any contemplated change before it shall have been made.

168....Officers will promptly acknowledge the receipt of orders, and also inform the Department immediately on their having reported in obedience to them.

169....All persons belonging to the Navy will conform strictly to such regulations for uniform as may be published from time to time; and every person is strictly forbidden to wear any dress, or decoration, other than that to which his grade clearly entitles him.

170....Officers on serving afloat, or travelling in foreign countries, shall communicate to the Commander-in-Chief of the squadron, or to the Secretary of the Navy, any information they may acquire that will be useful to the government of the United States.

171....Officers of the Navy, and all others in the employment of the Navy, are forbidden to give publicity to any hydrographical knowledge obtained, or discoveries or improvements in ordnance made during their service afloat.

172....In ports, whether home or foreign, and especially in communicating with foreign vessels, every boat is to carry the national ensign, unless otherwise ordered by the Commanding Officer.

173....All important orders to the officer of the deck, to be carried out during the night, whether given by the Commanding or Executive Officer, must be in writing.

174....No person in the Navy will upbraid another person in the Navy for refusing a challenge to fight a duel. Every person is enjoined to assist in the honorable adjustment of any differences that may occur. No disgrace can attach to any one for refusing a challenge, as such a course would be in obedience to law.

175....No person in the Navy shall use any language that may tend to render officers or others dissatisfied with any service in which they may be engaged, or upon which they may be ordered, or to diminish their confidence in, or respect for their superiors in command, or which may in any manner tend to weaken that subordination which is essential to the security and usefulness of the Navy ; and it shall be the duty of any officer who may hear any such language to suppress it, and report it immediately to the proper officer.

176....Combinations on the part of officers, or others, for the purpose of remonstrating against a superior, or his orders, or complaining of details of duty, or of service, are strictly forbidden. If an individual believes that he has cause to remonstrate or complain, he is at liberty to do so either in writing or personally ; but to combine with any other person to prefer or set forth a complaint against a superior is to be regarded as insubordinate and factious, and may be punished by a court-martial. No person is to delay obedience to an order for the purpose of remonstrating or complaining.

177....The practice of presenting swords, plate or other things of value, from inferior officers, or from crews, to their superior or commanding officer, in the way of compliment, and all votes, resolutions or testimonials, whether of praise or censure, from inferiors to superiors, are injurious to discipline, and are therefore strictly forbidden.

178....Written testimonials of the general or particular conduct of

General Instructions.

officers and others, are only to be given by their Commanding Officer, and in case of Commanding Officers themselves, by the Commander of the squadron. All such are to be addressed officially to the Secretary of the Navy, and forwarded to the Department for record and use. But in case of officers subject to examination, letters may be written by the head of the Department to which they may belong, which shall be forwarded to the Department through the usual channel of communication.

179....Testimonials, in writing or otherwise, between officers relative to the performance of their duties are prohibited.

180....No person belonging to, or in the employ of the Navy, shall accept any gift, or testimonial of any kind, from the workmen, or any other person or persons employed in any navy yard or other place under the control of the Navy Department.

181....Intelligence respecting any contemplated naval or military operations, descriptions of naval vessels or armaments, their destination, or the names of such as are under repair, or fitting for sea, or any other information whatsoever that can be used to the injury of the government by a public enemy, are prohibited from being given by any person in the naval service.

182....Discussions of military or naval movements by officers in the presence of their attendants, or any of the crew, are prohibited.

183....All publications, or communications in private letters, relative to military or naval operations, the movements of ships or of distinguished officers, or containing information of any kind or description that can be used by the public enemy, are strictly forbidden.

184....Publications relating to private transactions, or having in view the praise or censure of any person in the naval service, are prohibited.

185....In all matters liable to undergo investigation by court-martial, or otherwise, officers and others will be careful not to prejudge the case, or commit themselves by giving an oral or written opinion, until required to do so by the Department, or Commander-in-Chief of the squadron.

186....No officer will interfere personally in the arrest and management of intoxicated men more than may be absolutely necessary. The

General Instructions.

arrest should always be made by persons not above the grade of Petty Officers, and no more violence should be used than that required to restrain or confine them.

187.....The use of sheath knives on board ship is strictly forbidden. Jack-knives shall be worn with lanyards and in fobs.

188.....All officers of the Navy, not on duty, whose names are borne on the books of a naval station for pay, will, on the receipt of orders for duty, enclose a copy of the same to the Commandant of the station.

189.....And all officers returning from sea, under orders or permission from their Commanding Officer, will, immediately on their arrival in the United States, report in writing to the Department, enclosing a copy of the order or permission under which they return.

190.....An order or permission given by a Commanding Officer on a foreign station to an officer to return to the United States and report to the Secretary of the Navy, requires no more than that he should report, in writing, from the place of his arrival. No allowance for travel to the seat of government will be allowed, unless specially authorized by the Department.

191.....Duty on board a sea-going vessel of the Navy in commission, on board a practice ship at sea, or on board a coast survey vessel actually employed at sea, will be regarded by the Department as sea service.

192.....Officers of the Navy, while attached to vessels of the coast survey on sea service, will be entitled to sea pay.

193.....No order will be given to medical officers of the Navy to render professional aid to any person who is not attached to the naval service, or on board a ship-of-war. The Department will confide in their humanity to respond to any appeal for their assistance whenever the requisite aid cannot be obtained elsewhere. An exception may be made in favor of vessels in distress, when, if necessary to secure the requisite medical aid, the authority of the Commander may be interposed.

194.....Steam vessels shall not be hired to tow any United States vessels in or out of port unless circumstances should require it for their safety, or when the full use of all their own means may not be able to prevent injurious delays when ordered on special or urgent service.

General Instructions.

195....Steamers-of-war of the Navy are never to be used for towing vessels, unless when necessary for aiding in battle, or to engage therein; or to enter or depart from a port during a calm or other impediment; or to relieve them in distress at sea.

196....No officer or man attached to a squadron on the west coast of Africa will be permitted to be on shore before sunrise or after sunset, or to sleep there at night; this rule to apply not only to the continental coast, but to the Cape de Verde islands. No United States vessel will ascend or anchor in any of the African rivers except upon imperative public service. Boat excursions up rivers, or hunting parties on shore, are forbidden. Vessels, when possible, will anchor at a reasonable distance from shore; far enough not to be influenced by the malaria floated off by the land breeze. Convalescents from fever and other diseases, when condemned by medical survey, are to be sent to the United States with the least possible delay. When the general health of a ship's company shall be reported as impaired by cruising upon the southern or equatorial portion of the coast, the earliest possible opportunity will be given them to recruit, by transferring the ship, for a time, to the Canaries, or other windward islands of the station. Boat and shore duty, involving exposure to sun and rain, is to be performed, so far as the exigencies of the service will permit, by "Kroomen" employed for that purpose. All possible protection from like exposure is to be afforded to the ship's company on board; and the proper clothing and diet of the crew, as well as the ventilation and care of the decks, will be made a frequent subject for the inspection and advice of the medical officers.

197....All "slush" which may not be required for the use of the vessel, or the messes of the men, shall be sold, and the proceeds paid over to the paymaster, who shall receive, expend, and account for the same, under the direction of the Captain, for the following purposes, viz: For premiums to the Captains of guns who shall fire most accurately at a target when exercising with ball; to men making the best shots with small arms; for musical instruments and music, exclusive of that for the band; for furnishing rough clothing for the cook and his assistants, and for the Captain of the hold.

198....When any barrels or packages in which provisions or other

3

General Instructions

articles have been received on board shall have been emptied, they shall, if they cannot be returned to a navy yard, be disposed of to the best advantage to the public service. If sold, the amount received for the same shall be paid to the paymaster, and reported and accounted for by him in the same manner as other public moneys ; and all articles so sold, and the amounts paid to the paymaster, shall be entered in the log-book.

199 ...Whenever any articles from a vessel of-war may be sold abroad, it is strictly enjoined that all the port regulations, or custom-house laws referring to such articles, shall be rigidly complied with.

· 200....Ships-of-war will take pilots only when it is deemed necessary, and pay them such rates as the ,laws of the States respectively authorize. Pilots will not be called on board until the ship is ready to proceed to sea, and will be paid only from that time. In coming from sea, the pilot will be discharged the moment his services are no longer absolutely necessary. Coast pilots may be employed when approved by the Secretary of the Navy, or the Commander-in-Chief of a squadron. Their pay is to be governed by the direct decision of the Department. During the stay of a pilot on board, he shall be furnished with a cot or hammock, and bedding, and a suitable place be appointed for his sleeping. He will take his meals at the ward-room table, or in such other mess as the Commanding Officer may direct.

201....All mail matter conveyed by vessels of the Navy is to be delivered immediately after arrival in port to the postmaster of the place.

202....The families of officers, or of other persons, are not allowed to reside in national vessels, nor to become passengers therein, unless by the assent of the Secretary of the Navy.

203....Women are not to be taken to sea from the United States in any vessel of the Navy, without permission from the Secretary of the Navy ; nor when on foreign service, without the express permission of the Commander-in-Chief of the fleet or squadron, or of the senior officer present, and then only to make a passage from one port to another.

204....No seaman or other sea-faring man, not being a citizen of the United States, shall be admitted, or received as a passenger on board of any public vessel of the United States in a foreign port, without permission in writing from the proper officers of the country of which such eaman, or sea-faring man may be a subject or citizen.

General Instructions.

205....No vessel of a squadron is to take any person on board as a passenger, without the express direction or permission of the Commander-in-Chief, or of the senior officer present.

206....The law in relation to distilled liquors on board vessels of the Navy, does not include ale, beer, wine, or other liquors not distilled.

207....Card playing is not to be permitted on board of any vessel of the United States.

208....The practice of bringing home, in the public vessels of the United States, various animals, such as horses, asses, mules, and other quadrupeds, formerly authorized by the Department, is hereby strictly prohibited.

209....When gold, silver, or jewels shall be placed on board any vessel of the Navy for freight or safe-keeping, the Commander of the vessel shall sign bills of lading for the amount, and be responsible for the treasure. The usual percentage shall be demanded from the shippers of the treasure, and its amount shall be divided as follows : One-fourth to the Commander in-Chief of the squadron to which the vessel may belong ; one-half to the Commander of the vessel ; one-fourth to the navy pension fund. But in order to entitle the Commander-in-Chief of the squadron to receive any part of the amount, he must have signified to the Commander of the vessel, in writing, his readiness to unite with him in the responsibility for the care of the treasure. When a Commander-in-Chief of a squadron does not participate in a division of the amount, then two-thirds of the whole of it shall inure to the Commander of the vessel, and the remainder to the navy pension fund.

210....Sunday must be observed on board of all vessels of the navy, and at all stations and navy yards, in an orderly manner, by officers and men. All labor or duty will be reduced to the measure of strict necessity. The religious tendencies of officers and men are to be encouraged, and suitable times and places will be assigned for Divine worship. It is hoped that the religious rights of Christian sailors will at all times, receive due regard from all commanding officers and otherl in authority.

211....No officer of the Navy will, by virtue of any assimilated rank or otherwise, claim or exercise any command over any part of the land forces of the United States on shore ; nor will he permit the assumption of authority or command by any officer of the Army over any vessel, or other part of the force under his orders. Co-operation with the Army is strictly enjoined whenever it may be requested, if, in the opinion of the officer in command, his force and other circumstances will permit.

212....All Officers of the Line, when on duty, from the grade of Rear-Admiral to Lieutenant Commander, inclusive, will be addressed by their proper title. The word "Captain" will be used only in reference to, or when applied to, the officer holding that rank, and all Line Officers below the rank of Lieutenant Commander, whether commanding or not, will be addressed either by the title of their grade, or as Mr. Officers of the Marine Corps above the rank of 1st Lieutenant, will be addressed by their military title, brevet or lineal ; of and below that rank by their title, or as Mr. Officers of the Staff will be addressed by their titles, or as Mr., or as Dr., as the case may be.

ARTICLE V.

APPLICATIONS—QUALIFICATIONS—EXAMINATIONS—APPOINTMENTS AND PROMOTIONS—RATINGS AND DISRATINGS.

SECTION 1.

Applications and Qualifications.

213....Applications of candidates for admission into the Naval Academy, must conform to the regulations of that institution, which contain all the information necessary, together with a description of the requisite qualifications.

214.... All applications for admission into the Navy, in any capacity, can be made to the Secretary of the Navy, at any time, by the candidate himself, or by his parent, guardian, or any friend. No application will be considered unless strictly in accordance with the following rules. The registry of a name will give no assurance of permission to be examined, as the Department reserves to itself the right of selecting for examination those whom it may consider most likely to be of service to the country.

215....All applications must state the age, birth-place and residence of the candidate, who must also furnish certificates of his moral and physical qualifications. - An applicant for the office of Assistant Naval Constructor, must furnish, in addition to the foregoing, evidence showing that he is a shipwright by profession, that he has been engaged in that business, and must present the certificate of the persons with whom the business was learned, and those by whom he has since been employed. (See form No. 16, appendix.)

216....No person will be appointed to any commissioned or warranted office in the Navy until he shall have passed a physical and a professional examination, except Chaplains and Professors of Mathematics, who are not required to undergo the latter. The physical examinations shall precede the professional, and if a candidate should be declared physically unfit, he will not be examined otherwise. The passing of an examination must not be considered as giving any assurance of appointment, as the Department reserves to itself the right to select those persons of the highest attainments, in case there should be more candidates than vacancies.

217....A candidate for the appointment of Master's Mate, must be of sober and correct habits ; he must be not less than eighteen, nor more than thirty-five years of age ; he must have been at sea before the mast, or as an officer, at least five years. The recommendation by Commanding Officers, of Petty Officers or men, for zeal or gallantry, may entitle them to examination.

218....A candidate for a Boatswain's appointment must be of sober and correct habits ; he must be not less than twenty-one, nor more than thirty-five years of age ; he must have been at least seven years at sea, and have served one complete year of that time as a Petty Officer in the Navy ; he must be a thorough, practical seaman, and understand the rigging of ships according to regulations, and the cutting and fitting of the same ; also, the weighing, catting, fishing, securing and transportation of anchors, and the working of cables ; the erection and securing of shears, the handling of purchases, the masting of ships, the securing of yards, and be able to write sufficiently well to keep a rough account of stores.

219....A candidate for a Gunner's appointment must be of sober and correct habits ; he must be not less than twenty-one, nor more than thirty-five years of age ; he must understand the fitting and

Applications and Qualifications.

arrangement of magazines, light-rooms, passages and shell-rooms ; the stowage and preservation of ammunition, fire-works, and ordnance stores generally ; the proportion of powder for guns of every class, the method of making and filling cartridges, the construction, strapping, filling and fusing of shells, the application of fuses of all kinds, and the use of fire-works ; also, the making of cartridges for small arms, of wads, both junk and grommet ; the fitting of gun-gear, the details and use of gun carriages of all kinds, the securing and transportation of guns, the use of gun-sights, and the exercise established by regulations ; he must also be able to write sufficiently well to keep a rough account of stores, and to make up his returns as required in the ordnance ledger.

220....A candidate for a Carpenter's appointment must be of sober and correct habits ; he must be not less than twenty-one, nor more than thirty-five years of age ; he must be a good shipwright, understand caulking, the fishing of masts and yards, and the quality and strength of timber ; also, how to unship and hang a rudder, to construct and hang a jury-rudder, and be able to write sufficiently well to keep a rough account of stores.

221....A candidate for a Sailmaker's appointment must be of sober and correct habits ; he must be not less than twenty-one, nor more than thirty-five years of age ; he must be a good workman in his line of business ; be capable of draughting, and understand thoroughly the cutting and making of sails, awnings, hammock-cloths, boom-covers, and windsails for a vessel-of-war, and be able to write sufficiently well to keep a rough account of stores.

222....A candidate for an appointment as Third Assistant Engineer must be not less than nineteen, nor more than twenty-six years of age ; he must be of moral character and correct habits ; he must have worked not less than eighteen months in a steam-engine manufactory, or else have served not less than that period as an engineer on board a steamer provided with a condensing engine, and have secured a favorable impression of the director or head engineer as to his ability ; he must be able to describe and sketch all the different parts of the marine steam-engine and boilers, and to explain their uses and mechanical operation, the manner of putting them in operation, regulating their action, and guarding against danger.   He must be well acquainted with arithmetic, rudimentary mechanics, mensuration of surfaces and solids, write a fair, legible hand, and have some knowledge of the chemistry of combustion and corrosion.

223....A candidate for the office of Assistant Naval Constructor must be not less than twenty-four, nor more than thirty-five years of age ; he must be of good, moral character, have an accurate knowledge of arithmetic, of the nature and use of logarithms ; be able to resolve a simple algebraic formula into numbers ; be acquainted with the primary elements of geometry, descriptive geometry, mensuration, naval architectural drawing, and laying off on the mould-loft floor, and with practical building.

224....A candidate for the office of Assistant Paymaster must be not less than twenty-one, nor more than twenty six years of age, except as provided for under the act approved April 1, 1864. His moral and mental qualifications, as well as his fitness for the office he solicits, especially as to the mode of receiving and issuing provisions, clothing and small stores, of keeping the required accounts, of making returns and reports agreeably to the prescribed general instructions, of making out the accounts of officers and men, calculating rates of exchange, and deducing the relative value of United States and foreign coins, weights and measures, will be subjects of rigid investigation.

225....A candidate for the office of Assistant Surgeon must be not less than twenty-one, nor more than twenty-five years of age. His moral, mental and professional qualifications, will be decided upon by the board.

226....An applicant for the position of Professor of Mathematics must be not less than twenty-one, nor more than thirty-five years of age. He must be of good moral character, and must satisfy the Department of his ability to perform all the duties required of that grade of officers.

227....An applicant for the office of Chaplain must be not less than twenty-one, nor more than thirty-five years of age. He must be a regularly ordained minister of some religious denomination, and of unimpeached character.

228....No person shall be appointed a Secretary who is under twenty-one years of age ; nor shall any person be appointed a Clerk who is under eighteen years of age. The officers who may appoint Secretaries or Clerks, will be responsible for their moral character and fitness for the duties they are to perform.   No person shall be appointed to either of these offices who may have been dismissed from the Navy for any misconduct.

SECTION 2.

Examinations.

229....At stated or convenient periods, boards will be ordered for the examination of candidates for appointment or promotion, who will be duly informed of the time and place of meeting.   Before proceeding to the examination of any candidate for appointment, the medical officers who may be ordered for the purpose will furnish to'the board, to examine professionally, a certificate of the physical fitness of each candidate who may pass the examination ; and also a list of those who may be found to be physically unfit for the service.   No person will be passed by the medical board who is not free from physical defects, and all obvious tendency to any form of disease which would be likely to interfere with a prompt and efficient discharge of duty.   In the case of an Assistant Surgeon, the board of examiners will scrutinize his physical qualifications, and will make a separate report in each case, *direct* to the Department, to be placed on file with his testimonials.   The board to examine professionally, having received the certificate of the physical fitness of the candidate, will proceed to examine him on all the required qualifications ; it will grant certificates to those who may be found duly qualified, numbering them in succession in the order of relative merit, beginning with *one* to the best qualified.   It will, besides, report to the authority convening them, at the close of a session, the result of all their investigations, and forward all the documentary evidence they may have received in relation to the capacity and fitness of parties.

230....The board of Naval Surgeons will assemble annually, and usually about the close of the lecture season.   In no case admitting of a reasonable doubt will it report favorably, as the health and lives of the officers and men of the Navy are objects too important to be intrusted to ignorant, or incompetent persons.

231....Boards for the examination of candidates for appointment or promotion shall be composed as follows.   For a Master's Mate, of three

Line Officers, one of whom shall be of, or above the rank of Lieutenant Commander. For a Boatswain or Gunner, of three Line Officers, one of whom shall be of, or above, the rank of Lieutenant Commander, and one shall be of the grade in which the applicant desires an appointment. For a Carpenter or Sailmaker, of two Line Officers, one of whom shall be of, or above, the rank of Lieutenant Commander, and of one Staff Officer of the grade in which the applicant desires an appointment. For Engineer Officers, of not less than three Chief Engineers. For Medical Officers, of not less than three Surgeons. For Assistant Paymasters, of not less than three Paymasters. For Assistant Naval Constructors, of not less than three Naval Constructors, and one Professor of Mathematics.

232....Candidates who may exhibit the highest degree of practical experience and professional skill will be given a preference, both in admission and promotion.

233....No qualified candidate will be held over for appointment more than one year. If not appointed within that time, it will be necessary for the candidate to be re-examined, when he will take position, if successful, with the class last examined.

234.... Any person who shall fail to present himself for examination, after having obtained permission, shall be considered as having forfeited his right to be examined, and any officer who shall fail to present himself, after having been ordered so to do, (unless for reasons satisfactory to the Department,) shall be dropped from the list.

235.... Any Assistant Surgeon who, after examination, shall be reported by the board as not qualified for promotion, shall be dropped from the list of officers of the Navy.

236....If an officer should fail to pass a first examination, and be granted an opportunity to present himself a second time, he will, in case of success, have his position on the register designated by the board, subject, however, to the decision of the Department. But if he should fail in the second examination, he shall be dropped from the Navy list.

237.... Any officer who may have been absent from the United States on duty, or have been excused by the Department from attending at the time when others of his date were examined, will, if not rejected at a subsequent examination, be entitled to the same rank with them, and if, from any cause, his relative seniority cannot be assigned, he shall retain his original relative position on the register. In order, however, that the relative position of officers of the same date who may be examined for promotion at different times may be more readily determined, a majority of the members of the board will be selected, if practicable, from those who served on the next preceding board.

238....No allowance will be made for the expenses of persons undergoing examinations for appointments, as the latter are indispensable prerequisites to appointment. An exception to this rule will be made in the case of candidates for admission to the Naval Academy, who, if successful, will be allowed their actual necessary travelling expenses.

239....Any person producing a false certificate of age, time of service or character, or making a false statement to a board of examination, will be dropped immediately

SECTION 3.

Appointments and Promotions.

240....Any person having passed an examination will be eligible to an appointment. Appointments will be made as vacancies may occur, in the order of merit as reported by the board. Every person on receiving an appointment from the Department to any office in the Navy, will forward a letter of acceptance immediately to the Department, together with the oath of allegiance duly signed and certified. (See appendix, form No. 17.)

241....No officer shall, when within the jurisdiction of the United State, unless authorized by the Secretary of the Navy, appoint any person not holding a commission or warrant in the Navy to perform the duties of a commissioned or warranted officer, nor give to any commissioned or warranted officer any acting appointment. An exception to this rule will be found in the fourth section of the act to provide for the appointment of Assistant Paymasters, approved July 17, 1861.

242....No officer other than the Commander-in-Chief of a fleet or squadron, shall give any *acting appointment*, except as provided for in the

Appointments and Promotions.

last paragraph; nor shall any such acting appointment be issued unless a lasting vacancy should occur in the established complement of a vessel of the Navy, which cannot be filled from supernumerary officers on board other vessels of the fleet or squadron, and in such case it shall be in writing, and be subject to revocation by himself, or by his successor, or by the Secretary of the Navy. In the case of a vacancy by death on board any vessel absent from the United States, and acting singly, the Commanding Officer may issue a *written order* to supply the deficiency, which shall continue in force until the vessel falls in with the Commander-in-Chief, or arrives in the United States.

243 ....Temporary vacancies on board vessels not within the United States, occasioned by the continued indisposition of officers, their absence on duty, or inability to perform it, may be filled by a written order from the Commander-in-Chief, or senior officer present, to other officers of the fleet, squadron, or vessel, who will perform the duties of such sick, absent, or incompetent officers, until their return to duty, or until further orders be received from competent authority. All such orders may be revoked by the officer from whom they issued.

244 ....No Commanding officer of a vessel which may be ordered to sail from the United States, or which may be separated from the Commander-in-Chief of the fleet or squadron to which such vessel belongs, shall issue any order to fill vacancies among offices which existed and could have been reported to the Navy Department in time for orders to be issued to other officers before sailing, or to the Commander-in-Chief before the separation occurred.

245 ....All *acting appointments* and *orders* directing an officer to perform duties higher than those of his proper grade, must specify the vessel on board which he is to act, and in case of subsequent removal to another vessel, a new appointment or order must be given, except when the original shall have issued from the Navy Department.

246 ....Officers conferring acting appointments, or giving orders to fill vacancies, will promptly inform the Department of such transactions, and of the reasons which governed them. In no case will the established complement of the vessel be exceeded. If an acting appointment or order to perform duties belonging to a higher grade be revoked, the reasons for the revocation must be immediately reported to the Department.

Appointments and Promotions

247.... An officer holding an *acting appointment*, will wear the uniform of the grade to which he is appointed, and will annex the title of his acting rank to his official signature; but when holding only an *order* to perform the duties of a higher grade, he will not change his uniform nor his official designation.

248.... All officers of, and above, the grade of Lieutenant Commander, when commanding or acting as Captain of the Fleet, shall be allowed to appoint a clerk.

249.... Every officer entitled to a secretary or clerk may appoint or discharge him. But the appointment or discharge of a clerk by any officer not in command shall be subject to the approval of the Commander of the vessel; the latter, however, will not refuse his approval except for good and sufficient reasons, which he will state in writing to such officer. No secretary or clerk shall be entered upon the muster roll of any vessel, nor be entitled to any pay, until he shall have accepted his appointment by letter, in duplicate, binding himself therein to be subject to the laws and regulations for the government of the Navy, and the discipline of the vessel so long as his appointment may continue. One of these letters in duplicate shall be transmitted immediately to the Department by the officer conferring the appointment, together with the oath of allegiance, the other copy of the letter of acceptance shall be preserved by that officer. In the case of any clerk appointed by an officer not in command, the letter of acceptance sent to the Department must bear the approval of the Commander of the vessel. The acceptance of an appointment as secretary or clerk shall be understood as binding such person to serve with the officer who appointed him until regularly discharged, or until the return of such officer to the United States.

250.... Masters-at-arms and Yeomen will be appointed by the Commander of the vessel; Surgeon's stewards and nurses will be appointed by the Surgeon, and Paymaster's stewards by the Paymaster; but all such appointments must bear the approval of the Commander of the vessel. They will be entered on the ship's books after having been found physically qualified, have taken the oath of allegiance, and have signed an agreement (form No. 18, appendix) to serve faithfully for the cruise, to be amenable to the laws and regulations of the service and discipline of the vessel, and to be subject to discharge in case of misbehavior, in any port, foreign or domestic, without claim for passage money, the fact of misbehavior to be established by a summary court-martial, appointed by the Commander of the vessel. This agreement must be executed in duplicate, one copy of which, approved by the Commander of the vessel, together with the oath of allegiance, shall be forwarded to the Department, and the other copy shall be retained by the Commander of the vessel. The physical examination of Surgeon's stewards and nurses will be made by the officer appointing them. Masters-at-arms, Yeomen, and Paymaster's stewards will be examined by the Surgeon of the vessel or of the station. The Petty Officers named in this paragraph, together with the Orderly Sergeant of Marines, shall be allowed to mess separately on the berth-deck.

251....The Surgeon of every vessel of the Navy may appoint, for duties connected with the medical department, a steward, and on board every vessel commissioned for sea-service, he may appoint one nurse, when the complement is less than (200) two hundred, and when it is (200) two hundred and over, two nurses. Nurses will be allowed on board receiving-ships, in numbers proportionate to the necessities of the case. Their compensation is provided for in the article on "allowances."

252....No Paymaster, nor Assistant Paymaster, shall be allowed a clerk in a vessel having the complement of one hundred and seventy-five (175) persons, nor less, excepting in supply steamers and store-vessels. Stewards may be appointed in all vessels having a complement of twenty persons and over.

253....Whenever an officer may be appointed Commander-in-Chief of a fleet or squadron, he will be allowed to nominate to the Department an officer not below the grade of Commander to serve as Captain of the Fleet, and such other officers of lower grade as he may wish to have on his personal staff, who, if allowed by the Department, will be in addition to the complement of the flag-ship.

254....The Commander-in-Chief of a fleet or squadron, in the case of a vacancy occurring on a foreign station, may *order* the senior Surgeon of the squadron to perform the duties of Surgeon of the Fleet, unless from disability, or other good cause, it be found necessary to select another of the same, or of a lower grade, for the purpose.

255....No officer whatever is to order into service or to appoint to duty any officer who is on leave of absence or furlough, or make any change in the distribution or arrangement of officers established by the Secretary of the Navy, except in cases of emergency, and then he shall report his acts to the Department without delay.

256....If an officer be promoted while in command of a vessel on foreign service, he is not, on that account, to be removed from his command until instructions be received from the Secretary of the Navy.

257....As a general rule, Ensigns, Masters, Lieutenants, or Lieutenant Commanders will not be nominated for promotion to the next higher grade until they shall have performed as such, respectively, at least two years sea service, exclusive of coast survey service.

258....Masters who have not been promoted from Ensigns, are not to be considered eligible to further advancement, except under extraordinary circumstances.

259....Hereafter no officer will be promoted to the grade of Lieutenant, until he has served one year as Master, one year as Ensign, and at least one year as Midshipman after leaving the Naval Academy.

260....Any person having served six months at sea under an acting appointment as Boatswain, Gunner, Carpenter, or Sailmaker, may be eligible to a warrant bearing the same date as his acting appointment, provided the Commanding Officers under whom he may have served shall have certified favorably as to his merits.

261....No person will receive a warrant as Master's Mate unless he shall have served at least one year at sea under an acting appointment, and the Commanding Officers under whom he may have served shall have certified favorably as to his merits.

262....Candidates for promotion to the grade of Second Assistant Engineer, must have served at least two years at sea as Third Assistant Engineer on board of a naval steamer; favorable testimonials must have been received by the Department from the Commanding Officers and senior Engineers under whom they may have served. They must also pass, before the board appointed to examine them, a thorough examination upon the subjects prescribed for Third Assistant Engineers, and, in addition thereto, be able to explain properly the principles, peculiarities, and uses of the different kinds of valves and valve-gear applied to marine steam-machinery; the construction, principles, peculiarities, and uses of the various apparatus for working steam expansively; the construction of the various marine boilers commonly used, together with their attachments, uses of the same, and the reasons therefor; the causes of derangement in the operation of air and feed pumps and feed pipes, and how to prevent and remedy them; the chemistry of boiler scale, the means of preventing it, and the mode of removing it; the construction, principles, peculiarities, and uses of the different kinds of surface condensers; how to calculate the loss by "blowing off," with the sea-water in the boiler at a given concentration; the principles of, and the manner of using, the various instruments for determining the water's concentration, and the method of graduating them; the theory of using steam expansively, together with the limits and modifications imposed by practice, and the necessary calculations connected therewith; the construction and mode of applying the indicator, and the interpretation of its diagrams; the construction and principles of the various steam and vacuum gauges, and the causes of their derangement; and besides, they must have a thorough knowledge of rudimentary mechanics, be well versed in the elements of geometry, including descriptive, and be well acquainted with the practical building and repairing of steam-machinery.

263.....Candidates for promotion to the grade of First Assistant Engineer, must have served at least three years at sea as Second Assistant Engineer on board of a naval steamer; favorable testimonials must have been received by the Department from the Commanding Officers and senior Engineers under whom they may have served. They must also pass, before the board appointed to examine them, a thorough examination upon the subjects prescribed for Second Assistant Engineers, and, in addition thereto, be able to explain properly the whole subject of fundamental mechanics, and the theory of the steam-engine, the use of logarithms and the solution of a simple algebraic equation. They must further satisfy the board that they possess a competent knowledge of the first six books of Euclid's Elements, of plane trigonometry, of descriptive geometry, of conic sections, and of the strength of materials, and the influence of form in connection therewith; that they are capable of furnishing a working drawing of any piece of steam machinery, superintending its construction, and determining its adaptation for the use intended; and that they have a general knowledge of the theory, laws, and construction of the various kinds of paddle-wheels and screw propellers in use.

264....Candidates for promotion to the grade of Chief Engineer, must have served at least two years at sea as First Assistant Engineer on board of a naval steamer; favorable testimonials must have been received by the Department from the Commanding Officers and senior Engineers under whom they may have served. They must also pass, before the board appointed to examine them, a thorough examination upon the subjects prescribed for First Assistant Engineers, and in addition thereto, they must satisfy it that they are well versed in mechanical philosophy, the physical laws of steam, applied mechanics, the theory of the steam-engine, and likewise in the construction, principles, and the laws of action of various types of marine governors, paddle-wheels, and screw propellers, and in all the necessary calculations relating to these. Furthermore, they must satisfy the board that thay are thoroughly acquainted with the various kinds of paddle-wheel and screw propeller engines, able to point out their respective advantages and disadvantages, to design and erect the same, and to proportion them to a given vessel, for a given speed, with a given propelling instrument; that they are thoroughly versed in the strength of materials, in the theoretical laws governing form, the limits and modifications imposed by practice, and the reasons connected therewith; that they are familiar with the different kinds of boilers, their respective advantages and disadvantages, and able to properly proportion and construct the same for supplying a given power under given conditions; and that they do understand so much of chemistry as is involved in the laws of combustion and corrosion, and the metallurgic operations connected with steam-engineering.

265....When, in the opinion of the Department, the wants of the service require a greater number of Engineers of any grade above that of Third Assistant than can be obtained by regular promotion, candidates presenting themselves for admission will have to undergo the the same examination as that prescribed for the grade to which they may aspire; and with regard to subsequent promotion, the same length of sea-service prescribed as necessary to advancement from one grade to another will be required. But all persons so appointed to the grade of Second Assistant Engineer must be between the ages of twenty-one and twenty-eight; all to the grade of First Assistant Engineer, between twenty-five and thirty-two; and all to that of Chief Engineer, between twenty-eight and thirty-five.

266....Assistant Surgeons, after five years' service in the Navy, at least two years of which shall have been passed on board a public vessel of the United States at sea, shall be entitled to an examination for promotion. Testimonials of correct deportment and habits of industry from the Surgeons with whom they have been associated on duty must have been received by the Department, and they shall present to the board a journal of practice, or case-book, in their own handwriting. They are expected to be familiar with all the details of duty specified in the "Instructions for the Government of Medical Officers."

267....Candidates for promotion to the grade of Paymaster must satisfy the examining board of their competency to perform the various duties of Paymaster. They must be well acquainted with all laws and regulations relating to the duties and responsibilities of the position they aspire to. They must have a good theoretical and practical knowledge of book-keeping, and the law and practice of exchange, the value of foreign coins as compared with those of the United States, and the weights and measures of foreign countries; and they must have a sufficient knowledge of the Spanish and French languages to enable them to transact the business of their departments in those languages. But the acquaintance of these languages is not to be exacted until two years after the promulgation of this regulation. They must produce satisfactory testimonials from the Bureau of Provisions and Clothing and from the Fourth Auditor's Office that their accounts have been well kept and promptly rendered, and that their returns have been properly and seasonably made.

268....Candidates for promotion to the grade of Naval Constructor must have been at least five years in the service as Assistant Naval Constructors; they must pass, before the board appointed to examine

4

them, a satisfactory examination in Euclid's Elements, algebra, with its application to geometry, plane trigonometry, conic sections, descriptive geometry, mechanics, strength of materials; calculation of displacement, of stability, of centre of gravity, of centre of effort, and other matters relating to the theory of naval architecture, as well as the practice in building ships of wood and of iron.

Section 4.

Ratings and Disratings.

269....On a crew being transferred from a receiving vessel to a vessel of the Navy intended for sea-service, the officer ordered to command her is' to select and have rated from such crew the different Petty Officers allowed by the Department for one of her class, except such as are eligible to appointment.

270....In the event of a vacancy occurring among the appointed Petty Officers, if a suitable person can be found among the crew of the vessel, the Commanding Officer may *rate* such person, and cause him to perform the duties appertaining to the vacant situation. . The rating of such person will not discharge him from his enlistment, however; but in case that it should be revoked, he will return to his former rate on the ship's books.

271....No enlisted person shall be transferred from any quarter to any vessel, navy yard, station, or hospital, with the rating of a Petty Officer.

272....No Petty Officer, or person of inferior rating, shall ever be disrated by the Commander of a vessel, unless he shall have received his rating from that Commander; and this shall be done for good and sufficient cause only, which must be stated in the log. But any Commanding Officer transferring his command shall previously reduce all persons who may have been rated by himself to the rates they held at the time of joining his ship, and his successor shall appoint them immediately to the same rates. In case, however, of the death of any Commanding Officer, his captivity, or any other circumstance which may vacate his command, all ratings established by himself shall also be vacated, subject to re-establishment by his successor, as provided for

Ratings and Disratings.

above, except those of such persons as a Commander is allowed to take with him from one ship to another, who shall not be reinstated, unless such successor shall fail to bring with him other persons to fill their situations. If not reinstated, the Cockswain shall resume the rate he held on joining the vessel, and the steward, cook, and one other person of inferior rating, shall be regarded as having fulfilled their enlistment, and be entitled to their discharge if they desire it, unless they enlisted for the ordinary duties of deck-hands, in which case they shall resume their former rates and serve their full time.

273....No person having enlisted in any particular rate shall be reduced to a lower rate, except by order of the Department, or to carry out the sentence of a court-martial, except as provided below for firemen and coal-heavers.

274....No person, about to be discharged from a vessel going out of commission, or transferred and sent home to be discharged, shall be disrated by reason of such discharge or transfer, but his rate, whatever it may be, shall be expressed on the face of his discharge or transfer for that purpose.

275....Whenever a change of rating takes place an order in writing will be given by the Commander of the vessel to the Paymaster, stating the change of rate and the time from which it is to date; but no such order shall be given in one quarter to take effect in a preceding quarter.

276....Should any fireman or coal-heaver be reported by the senior Engineer of the vessel for neglect of his duty, or inability to perform it, from other causes than sickness, or injury received in line of duty, the Commanding Officer of the squadron, or, in his absence, the Commanding Officer of the vessel to which such fireman or coal-heaver belongs, may, if he deems it necessary, direct another person to perform them during the continuance of such neglect or disability, or until the place is supplied by a person of the proper rating, and the person so appointed shall receive the pay of the situation which he may thus fill. But the Commanding Officer shall, when it is practicable, direct second class firemen to succeed or supply the places of the first class; and the coal-heavers, if qualified, shall take the place of the second class fireman in preference to other persons. The pay of such reduced fireman or coal-heaver is provided for under the head of allowances.

The Commander-in-Chief of a Fleet or Squadron.

ARTICLE VI.

GENERAL DUTIES OF LINE OFFICERS.

SECTION 1.

The Commander-in-Chief of a Fleet or Squadron.

277....When an officer shall be appointed Commander-in-Chief of a fleet or squadron, he shall, as early as possible, inform himself of the state and condition of the vessels, and the qualifications and characters of the Commanding and other officers placed under his command, so that he may be able to select for any special service the officer best qualified to perform it.

278....If the fleet or squadron is to be equipped under his own direction, he will use every exertion to forward the work, and will make weekly reports to the Department of its progress, or the cause of any delay, should it occur. If the work of equipment should be carried on at a navy yard not under his command, he will, nevertheless, keep himself informed of its progress, and make such suggestions to the Commanding Officer as may occur to him, so that when the vessels are put in commission no delay may ensue by reason of alterations or additions. As soon as the vessels are transferred to him, he will use all diligence in preparing them for sea, and will report to the Department the time when they will be ready to sail.

279....Should any deficiencies or defects be discovered which would render any vessel or vessels unfit for the service for which they are destined, or would impair their efficiency, he will represent the same immediately to the proper bureau.

280....Immediately before sailing for foreign service, he will cause reports to be made to the proper bureaus of the length of time for which the fleet is provided with provisions and stores ; and he must, thereafter, give them such information as will enable them to forward supplies in time to prevent the necessity of disadvantageous purchases abroad.

281....He will at all times keep the fleet or squadron in the most perfect condition for service that may be practicable.

The Commander-in-Chief of a Fleet or Squadron.

282....He will strictly enjoin upon all Commanding Officers of vessels to take the greatest care of stores, and to practice the utmost economy in their expenditure.

283....He shall direct frequent examinations of the hospitals and hospital ships, and will require from the examining officers written reports of their state and condition, and cause every attention to be paid to the comfort of the sick.

284....All requisitions must receive his approval before the articles will be furnished, unless the vessels should be separated so as to render it impracticable, and in such cases the requisitions must be approved by the senior officer present, and copies transmitted to the Commander-in-Chief by the earliest opportunity. He will require every officer who may approve a bill for supplies to furnish him immediately with a copy of it, together with the reasons for the purchases.

285....He shall forward quarterly a copy of every bill for purchases made abroad to the proper bureau, with a statement of the reasons which rendered the purchases necessary.

286....In ports where there is no regular agent of the United States, he will direct the Paymaster of the fleet to make all necessary purchases on the most advantageous terms; the articles shall be selected by an officer belonging to the department for which they are required. If vessels should be separated from the Commander-in-Chief, the senior officer present will direct the Paymaster of the vessel for which articles may be required to make the purchases.

287....He will exercise the vessels of the fleet or squadron, whenever circumstances will admit, in performing the various evolutions that are essential to order and safety, and particularly those which it may be necessary or useful to adopt in presence of an enemy.

288....He will cause the boats of the squadron—manned and armed—to be frequently assembled, inspected, and exercised in fleet manœuvring, and in the evolutions for landing or embarking from the shore, and for boarding the vessels of an enemy.

289....He is required to make a semi-annual inspection of each vessel under his command, according to the form given in the Ordnance Instructions. He will also inspect them at other times, as frequently as he may deem necessary, and will hold their Commanding Officers to a strict accountability for proper attention to the order, discipline, efficiency, and cleanliness of their vessels, to the laws and regulations, and to the instructions of the Department, and he shall be careful that the ship bearing his flag or broad pendant be a proper example to others.

290....He will be attentive, when in battle, to observe the conduct of all under his command ; he will correct any errors that he may discover, and will make a report to the Department of every occurrence, and of the conduct of his subordinates.

291....He will require the Commanding Officers of the vessels of his fleet or squadron to forward reports from themselves their Executive Officers, and, if a steam vessel, from the senior Engineer in charge, of every event which may occur in action, and of the services performed by their respective vessels, giving to every person concerned the praise or censure justly due to him.

292....He will also require reports from the Commanding Officers, addressed to the Department, of every important service performed by the ships under their command, accompanied by diagrams, in all cases in which they are applicable, showing every particular which may tend to give clear information concerning the event.

293....He shall forward to the Department, by the first opportunity, the reports and diagrams mentioned above, and retain copies of them for future use or reference.

294....Should he find cause to transfer or suspend any officer under his command, he shall, in such case, transmit to the Secretary of the Navy, by the earliest conveyance, his reasons for the same.

295....He shall issue general orders regulating the extent of leave of absence which may be granted to officers and men to visit the shore by the Commanding Officers of vessels ; but no officer shall be allowed to be absent on leave from the vessel to which he belongs, when in squadron, more than twenty-four hours without the written permission or authority of the Commander-in-Chief.

296....He shall make to the Secretary of the Navy quarterly reports of the professional skill and attainments of all Commanding Officers of squadrons, divisions, and vessels under his command, and also of the order and efficiency in which they keep their squadrons, divisions, and vessels ; and if an unfavorable report is made, the officer shall be furnished with a copy of it.   (See form No. 25, Appendix.)

The Commander-in-Chief of a Fleet or Squadron.

297.....He will forward the quarterly reports of the number and rates of the crews of the vessels under his command, and the expiration of their service, as furnished by the Commanding Officers.

298.....He shall correspond regularly with the Secretary of the Navy, keeping him informed of his proceedings and of the state, condition, and probable wants of the vessels under his command, and of all other important information within his knowledge relative to the service on which he may be employed, or to any foreign naval force employed upon the station or in its vicinity.

299.....He shall forward to the Secretary of the Navy monthly returns of the condition, distribution, and employment of the vessels of the squadron.

300.....At the termination of his command, he will transmit to the Secretary of the Navy a list of all the numbers of his correspondence with the Department, and shall furnish duplicates of all such as the Secretary shall inform him have not been received.

301.....He will forward to the Navy Department any suggestions or plans for the improvement of public works in navy yards, or in the construction, equipment, or arrangement of vessels of war, or upon any subject connected with the Navy, which he may deem important to the interests of the United States, accompanying the same with plans and estimates of their cost, when practicable.

302.....When a vessel of a squadron is to return to the United States, he shall withdraw all provisions and stores not necessary for her passage home, and transfer to her invalids and all persons whose terms of service have expired, or are about to expire, unless the public interest should require their detention.

303.....He shall not resign his command without the previous consent of the Secretary of the Navy, unless a medical survey shall certify that the state of his health renders it absolutely necessary.

304.....When he shall, for any cause, resign or transfer his command, he shall deliver to his successor accurate copies of all unexecuted instructions and orders, taking receipts for the same, together with all information relating to the squadron or the service, which may be useful to him.

305.....Should he die, or leave his station permanently from any cause, before being relieved by a successor appointed by the Navy Department, the officer of the fleet or squadron then succeeding in order to the command shall exercise the powers and authority of Commander-in-Chief, until otherwise directed by the Secretary of the Navy. Any officer who shall have succeeded to the command-in-chief as just mentioned shall discontinue to exercise the powers and authority thereof immediately on receiving official information of the arrival, within the limits of the station, of the officer duly appointed Commander-in-Chief of the fleet or squadron, without waiting either to meet with or to receive an order directly from such officer.

306....He will examine and carefully compare all orders for general police which may be prepared by the Commanders of vessels, and modify them when necessary, to secure uniformity in executing the duties of the fleet or squadron.

307....He will direct the course to be steered by all vessels present under his command.

308....If, from any circumstance, he shall deem proper to take the immediate command of the ship in which he sails, he will cause the fact to be entered on the log.

309....He will see that the commanding officers of steam vessels strictly observe the orders in regard to the expenditure of coal, and the use of sails.

310....On arriving within the limits of his station on foreign service, he is to place himself in communication with the diplomatic agents of the government of the United States thereabouts, and he is to afford them, on his own responsibility, such aid and co-operation in all matters for the benefit of the government as they may require, and as he may judge to be expedient and proper.

311....He shall cause a quarterly inspection to be made by the fleet engineer, or, in his absence, by some other competent engineer, of the steam machinery and boilers of the steam vessels under his command, and shall require from him a report in duplicate, one of which reports shall be forwarded to the Bureau of Steam Engineering, and the other shall be retained by himself for future reference. No proposed alterations or additions to the machinery are to be included in the list of defects; on those points special reports must be made, stating their probable cost and the time necessary for their execution. Should it occur that the inspection of any vessel cannot be made as often as once in a quarter, he must report the fact and the circumstances rendering it impossible.

Section 2.

Commanders of Squadrons under a Commander-in-Chief, and Commanders of Divisions.

312....Whenever a fleet may be organized into squadrons, or squadrons and divisions, their respective Commanders will be responsible to their immediate Commander for the efficiency, discipline, and management of the vessels composing their squadrons or divisions.

313....All reports, returns, and requisitions will be forwarded in accordance with the routine prescribed in the article on "Correspondence."

314....The Commander of a squadron or division may correct, by signal or otherwise, any mistake or negligence of vessels of another squadron or division, when it is probable that it cannot be distinctly seen by the Commander of the squadron or division to which they belong. In battle he is carefully to observe the conduct of all vessels that may be near his own, so that, if required, he may report that of each.

315....If a Commander of a squadron or division should, during battle, perceive any vessel of a squadron or division commanded by an officer inferior or junior to himself, evidently avoiding battle, or not doing his duty, he shall make proper signals to him, or take such other measures as the case may require, and give the earliest information of his proceedings to the Commander-in-Chief, and to the Commander of the squadron or division to which the vessel may belong.

316....Commanders of squadrons and divisions shall inspect the vessels under their command as often as once in a quarter ; and they will make written reports to the Commander-in-Chief of their efficiency, discipline, and preparation for battle.

317....Whenever the Commander-in-Chief shall not declare his intention of manœuvring the fleet in detail, it shall be the duty of the Commanders of squadrons and divisions to make all the signals which may be necessary to regulate the movements of their squadrons or divisions to carry into execution any general evolution, or to preserve any prescribed position which may have been ordered by the Commander-in-Chief.

318....After battle they will forward to the Commander-in-Chief the reports of the officers commanding vessels, required by paragraph 291, accompanied by full remarks of their own.

SECTION 3.

Fleet Captain.

319....The Fleet Captain is to assist the Commander in-Chief in the various details and arrangements for the management of the fleet or squadron, and for maintaining it in the most efficient condition; and, to this end, he is to be embarked on board the same vessel with the Commander-in-Chief, and subject only to his orders and directions.

320....He shall keep a journal of the proceedings of the fleet or squadron, noting in general terms every circumstance of importance that may pass under his observation.

321.....He shall also keep a register of all orders issued by the Commander-in-Chief, or by his authority, and of all signals that may be made in the fleet or squadron, noting the day and hour when the former were received or transmitted, and when the latter were made. (See forms Nos. 5 and 6, appendix.)

322....He shall take care when officers are called on board to receive verbal orders, that they note in an order book, which they must bring for that purpose, the substance of the order given.

323....He will immediately report to the Commander-in-Chief any neglect or disobedience of the orders of the Commander-in-Chief.

324....In order to expedite the administrative duties of a fleet or squadron, the following reports, returns, &c., will be transmitted by commanding officers to the Commander-in-Chief, through the Fleet Captain, who, after examination and indorsing them with such remarks as may appear to him expedient, will place them before the Commander-in-Chief for his information, and, if necessary, for his action or decision. Reports of state and condition of ship ; reports of defects ; applications for refitting or repairs ; requisitions for money, stores or provisions ; all periodical returns ; applications for leave, transfer, or discharge ; applications for surveys ; and, in general, all reports connected with the equipment, efficiency, and state of the vessels. All reports of the operation of their commands, the execution of their orders, or of the discipline of their vessels, commanding officers will transmit direct to the Commander-in-Chief.

SECTION 4.

Fleet Lieutenant.

325....The Fleet Lieutenant, and such other officers as may be appointed to serve on the personal staff of a Commander-in-Chief, are to act as his aids, and will assist the Fleet Captain in his duties.

326....Should there be no Fleet Captain, the duties prescribed for that officer will be performed by the Fleet Lieutenant.

SECTION 5.

Officers Commanding Vessels.

327....When an officer shall be appointed to the command of a vessel he shall join her forthwith, unless a particular day be designated for him to do so by the appointing authority ; and, on joining her, he is to examine and ascertain her state and condition, and inform himself of the character and qualifications of the officers placed under his command.

328....If the vessel be still under the charge of the Commanding Officer of the navy yard, he will be attentive to her repair and equipment, and report to such Commanding Officer any defects or deficiencies which, in his opinion, require further attention. He will be particular in his examinations and reports at the time when it may be proposed to transfer the vessel entirely to his charge, so as to prevent any subsequent complaints in relation to neglects or deficiencies in the repairs or equipments.

329....He will exercise no authority or control over the repairs or equipments of the vessel before she is delivered into his charge, nor over the officers and mechanics of the navy yard, unless with the assent or direction of the Commanding Officer of the yard.

330....When appointed to the command of a vessel, he shall be furnished with a statement of her condition and her presumed or ascertained qualities, by the Commandant of the navy yard, or by the previous Commander, if the vessel be already in commission, and with drawings and plans showing the dimensions of the ship, arrangements and stowage of the holds, store-rooms, magazines, shell-rooms, shot-lockers, &c.

331....When a vessel shall be transferred by the Commanding Offi· cer of a navy yard to him for service, he shall use every exertion to complete the arrangements that may be necessary for her efficient employment at sea, and shall report weekly to the Secretary of the Navy her condition, progress of repairs, and any deficiency of officers or men, for the information of the Department.

332....After assuming the command he will be held responsible for the whole conduct and good government of the officers and others belonging to the vessel, according to the laws and regulations for the government of the Navy, and must himself set an example of respect and obedience to his-superiors, and of unremitting attention to his duties.

333....When a ship shall have been put in commission, a general muster of the officers and crew shall be had for the purpose of verifying the descriptive lists, of ascertaining that the name of every man is correctly registered, and that every one has the exact uniform dress prescribed by regulations; the full dress is not to be worn during war. The Executive Officer, Surgeon, and Paymaster shall be present at such muster, and any discrepancy in the descriptive lists, or error in the transfer roll, shall be then corrected, and a certificate of such correction, approved by the Commanding Officer, shall be transmitted by him to the Department, to the rendezvous where the man was shipped, and the receiving ship from which he was transferred. On the receipt of such certificate the necessary corrections will be made.

334....He will see that a note is made upon all accounts, transfer ·

and descriptive lists, and on all shipping articles, and enlistment returns, against the name of every person who may come under the seventh section of the act approved February 24, 1864, for enrolling and calling out the national forces.

335.... He shall not exceed the number of men allowed in any rating except to make up for a deficiency in some superior rating, or by the express authority of the Secretary of the Navy, or the Commander-in-Chief of a squadron on foreign service.

336.... Should he deem it necessary to issue other orders for the general police of the vessel than those contained in the Laws and Beg-ulations for the Navy, he will prepare such and submit them to the Department, or to the Commander-in-Chief if serving in a squadron, for approval or modification.

337.... He shall have the officers and crew stationed for the perform-ance of their different duties, and shall exercise them as frequently as other duties will permit before going to sea ; and shall cause the quarter, watch, fire, and other station bills, to be fairly made out and hung in some conspicuous place, where all persons on board may have access to them.

338.... In all matters connected with the preparation of his vessel for battle, and the exercise of his crew at quarters, he shall follow care-fully such instructions as have been or may be issued by the Bureau of Ordnance and approved by the Secretary of the Navy.

339.... He shall require each of the Lieutenants, Masters, and Ensigns, belonging to the vessel, to procure a good sextant or octant, and some approved work containing the usual tables for ascertaining the ship's place from observations for latitude and longitude, that, in case it should be necessary to place any of them in charge of a prize or other vessel, they may have the necessary means of navigating her.

340.... He will impress upon the men under his command the im-portance of providing, by allotment tickets, for their families during their absence from them, and will see that the tickets of those who avail themselves of the privilege are duly forwarded as provided for in the article on allotments. •

341.... When approaching any vessel of war at sea, he shall take care that the vessel under his command is so far cleared for action as to guard against any possible danger from surprise.

342....He will, when acting singly, hold a semi-annual inspection of his ship according to the form given in the Ordnance Instructions, and forward his report to the Bureau of Ordnance by the first opportunity.

343....He may, at his discretion, require the Line Officers under his command to make frequent observations and calculations for determining the latitude and longitude, and the variation of the compass, and report the results to him, and he will encourage the officers under his command to improve themselves in every branch of nautical science.

344....Whenever a Commander is removed from one vessel to another, he may take with him his clerk, Cockswain, one officers' steward, one officers' cook, and one person of inferior rating.

345....He shall deliver to the officer appointed to succeed him in command all signal books, and the originals or attested copies of all unexecuted orders which he may have received, for which he must take receipts in duplicate, sending one copy through the proper channel to the Navy Department. He will leave with his successor in command a complete muster book, and expense book, duly audited and signed by him to the time of his resigning his command. He shall leave with his successor a report of the qualities of the vessel according to such forms as may be prescribed, together with every other information which he may deem serviceable to her Commander, and he will forward a similar report to the Navy Department whenever he is removed from or resigns the command of a vessel. Whenever he is removed from or resigns the command of a vessel, he will furnish the officer succeeding him in the command with a list of the names of such of the crew who enlisted for three years as may be deemed worthy of an honorable discharge.

346....Should he find it necessary to go into a port not designated or permitted by his instructions, he will make no unnecessary stay, and will report the cause of the necessity and of any delay that may occur.

347....Should a vessel be separated from a fleet or squadron to which it belongs, the Commander must show, in the most satisfactory manner, that such separation was not caused by any neglect of his, and that he had complied strictly with all instructions which may have been given for his government in case of such separation.

Officers Commanding Vessels.

348....He will facilitate any examination which it may be the duty of any custom-house officer of the United States to make on board the vessel he commands.

349....The Captain or Commanding Officer of a vessel, in which the Commander-in-Chief, or the Commander of a squadron or division, (not commanding-in-chief,) shall be embarked, will be particularly careful to conform strictly to all orders he may receive from such superior officer respecting the management of the vessel, the sail to be carried, and all matters which may regulate or influence the movements of the vessels of the squadron ; and such superior officer will communicate all his orders which may relate to the vessel in which he is embarked immediately to the Commanding Officer of such vessel, unless the urgency of the case should require an order to be given directly to the officer of the deck, in which case the Commanding Officer of the vessel is to be immediately notified.

350....He shall cause some competent person among the Petty Officers, or persons of inferior rating, to instruct the boys of the ship in reading, writing, and arithmetic.

351....He will not permit any boy who shall have been shipped to serve until he is twenty-one years of age, to act as a waiter upon any person.

352....He shall cause vacancies among Petty Officers and seamen to be filled from the ship's company, if persons qualified be found on board, in preference to those from other ships.

353....He shall cause the ordinary seamen, landsmen, and boys to be instructed in steering, heaving the lead, knotting and splicing, in rowing, in the use of the palm and needle, and generally in other duties, such as bending and reefing sails, &c , that they may become qualified for the rating of seamen and Petty Officers.

354....He shall have a liberty book kept, in which shall be recorded the names of such of the crew as may have been granted liberty on shore, specifying the length of leave, the time of the return, and the condition and conduct of each man on his return to the ship.

355....He will cause a conduct book to be kept by the Executive Officer, in which the names of all Petty Officers and persons of inferior rating shall be entered, with remarks from time to time on the conduct of each, and a record made of any fact or circumstance that may aid him in preparing proper discharges at the end of the cruise.

356....He is to keep a remark book, in which he is to note all usefu information regarding the places he may visit, stating, in every case, their latitude and longitude at least, and, as occasions may allow him to ascertain them, the variation of the compass, the prevailing winds and currents, the dangers in approaching the various anchorages, and the means of avoiding such dangers ; the supplies, particularly of water, provisions, and spars, which the said places can afford, and, generally, every other information regarding them which may be deserving of notice, and shall, when practicable, cause surveys to be made by the officers under his command, and shall make reports to the naval bureaus on the subjects appropriate to each, and at the conclusion of his cruise the remark book shall be sent to the Navy Department.

357....In case of shipwreck, or any other disaster whereby the ship may be lost, the Commander, with the officers and men, shall stay by her as long as possible, and save all they can. He shall particularly endeavor to save the muster, pay, and receipt books, and other valuable papers.

358....If shipwrecked within the United States, he shall, after doing all in his power to save the public property, repair, as soon as practicable, to the nearest navy yard or station, and, in all cases, make the earliest possible report to the Navy Department.

359....He shall, in cases of shipwreck without the United States, lose no time in returning to the fleet or squadron to which he may belong, or, if acting alone, to the United States, with his officers and crew, to effect which he may dispose of the property saved, or draw bills, as he may deem most advantageous to the public interests.

360....Should the Commanding Officer of a vessel be compelled to strike his flag, he is to take especial care to destroy all signals and papers the possession of which by an enemy might be injurious to the United States, and he will keep them so prepared, with weights attached to them, that they will sink immediately on being thrown overboard.

361....In every case of the loss or capture of a vessel of the Navy, it is hereby made the duty of her Commander to cause immediately

Officers Commanding Vessels.

the officers of divisions to ascertain carefully the loss of clothing and bedding sustained by their men, and to report to him, in writing, the result of their investigation. These reports, drawn up in a uniform way, and signed by himself and those officers respectively, he is to submit, without delay, to the Navy Department.

362....In the event of loss of accounts occurring from the loss or capture of a vessel of the Navy, he will order the Paymaster to open fresh ones with the survivors, commencing them from the date of the disaster, and giving to each person the rate he held at the time the accounts were lost; and these accounts, so made out, are to accompany the survivors on their being transferred to a vessel or station, the Paymaster of which is to govern himself by them in making payments or issues, until he receives further instructions concerning them from the Navy Department, or the Fourth Auditor of the Treasury.

363....When, from the loss of a vessel, or from any cause, the descriptive lists of the crew are lost, it shall be the duty of the Commanding Officer to make application for such descriptive lists to the Bureau of Equipment and Recruiting, forwarding, with his letter of application, a list containing the names and rating of the crew at the time of their enlistment.

364....He will, in forwarding his report of the qualities of the vessel, and at other times, if he deems it important, suggest any alterations which, in his opinion, would render the vessel more efficient, or improve her qualities in any particular, and the probable expense attending such change.

365....He will preserve discipline, and prevent any irregularities which might give just cause of offence to the inhabitants of the country where his vessel may be, and any violations of the laws or port regulations.

366....He shall make a report to the Commander-in-Chief of the squadron, or to the Secretary of the Navy, if cruising alone, of all passengers carried in the vessel under his command, assigning his reasons for having them on board.

367....All orders received by a Commanding Officer applicable to others under his command or authority are to be promptly communicated. No delay will be tolerated, except in cases of palpable necessity.

368....The Commanding Officers of vessels falling in with each other are, whenever practicable, to compare signal books, general orders, and circulars, in order to possess themselves of any changes or alterations that may have been made, and of information to the latest date. They will suggest to the Department any necessary signal or word not to be found in the books.

369....Immediately on arriving in port, the Commander of a vessel is to submit to the Commander-in-Chief, or to the senior officer present, requisitions in triplicate for deficiencies on board the vessel under his command; but he is to be particularly careful that every article embraced is really needed, and that the quantity mentioned is not excessive.

370....On arriving in port or at a naval station, to be refitted or repaired, the Commander of such vessel is not to permit the stores belonging to any department of her to be landed without previous authority from the senior officer present. In the United States this authority is not to be granted without the sanction of the Navy Department.

371....Every Commander of a vessel of the Navy shall report to the Chief of the Bureau of Construction and Repair, immediately on its occurrence, every instance of the vessel under his command touching on a shoal or rock, or sustaining any injury to the lower masts, hull, or bowsprit, with all the circumstances attending the accident, and his opinion as to the probable injury sustained, and at the termination of his cruise he will send duplicates of all such reports made during the cruise to that bureau.

372....In all cases of collision resulting seriously, Commanding Officers are to report the facts to the Commander-in-Chief of the squadron to which they are attached, or, if acting singly, to the Secretary of the Navy.

373....In the event of a collision between a vessel of the Navy and a merchant vessel, so serious or under such circumstances as not to admit of immediate repair with the resources at hand, and, therefore, likely to involve damages, the Commander of the naval vessel is, if

Officers Commanding Vessels.

possible, at once to order a board of three officers, (one of whom, when practicable; to be a carpenter,) to ascertain all the attending circumstances, injuries received, probable amount of damages, and report to him, in triplicate, accordingly ; and he is then, without delay, to forward to the Navy Department one of these triplicates, and to furnish the master of the merchant vessel with one of them. The remaining one he is to retain for any future reference that may be necessary. When repairs have been effected on the spot, a suitable certificate of the fact is to be taken from the master of the merchant vessel, and forwarded to the Navy Department.

374....Commanders of public vessels-of war are not to suffer their vessels to be searched by any foreign power under any pretext, nor any officers nor men to be taken out so long as they have power of resistance. If force be used, resistance must be continued as long as possible. If overcome, they are to yield their vessel, but not their men without the vessel.

375....When not acting under the orders of a superior officer, they will be governed by the regulations for Commanders-in-Chief, so far as they may be applicable to their situation.

376....Commanders of vessels on foreign stations may receive on board distressed sailors of the United States without reference to the established complement. If, on the usual examination, they be found fit for the service, they may be enlisted for such period as may be judged expedient, not exceeding three years ; but if not so found, or if unwilling to enlist, they may be entered as supernumeraries, for passage and rations, provided they bind themselves to be amenable, in all respects, to the Laws and Regulations for the Government of the Navy. Such persons, however, are not to be so received, enlisted, or entered, without the authority of the senior officer present, and Commanders concerned are to keep the Commander-in-Chief of the fleet or squadron fully informed of all transactions with regard to them.

377....They shall take care that no merchant seamen be received on board on a foreign station, as prisoners, under charges preferred against them, unless the witnesses necessary to substantiate such charges accompany them, or some equally certain means are adopted to insure their appearance on the arrival of the prisoners at the place where they will be handed over to the civil authorities.

378.....Commanders of vessels violating or departing from their orders or instructions at the request of a consul, or any other person, must do so on their own responsibility, and will be held to a strict account by their superiors.

379.....They shall make to the Honorable Secretary of the Navy, through the Commander-in-Chief, a full report of any action, chase, or important movement in which the vessels they command may be engaged, and will also furnish diagrams illustrating the positions and movements of the vessels, the direction of the wind, the bearing, dis- tance, and outline of land should any be in sight, and all information which may tend to throw light on the occurrence. They will also be careful to mention all such as may distinguish themselves as defined by the act of December 21, 1861, and recommend them for medals ; and will, after an action, require from the Executive Officer and officers commanding divisions, reports of the general conduct of those under their observation. (*See paragraphs* 291, 318.)

380.....In case of the death, desertion, or capture by an enemy of any person belonging to the Navy, it shall be the duty of the Com- mander of the vessel, upon the books of which the name of such per- son may be borne, to cause his effects to be collected and delivered to the Paymaster for safe-keeping, together with an inventory of the same, to be signed by two mess mates, if they belonged to an officer, or if they belonged to any other person, by the officer of his division. He shall, also, in addition to the usual official report of the death of any person, on board the vessel under his command, cause information of the same to be forwarded to the nearest relative, or friend of the deceased, if the address of such relative or friend can be obtained.

381.....Whenever an officer may be relieved from command, he shall, before the transfer be effected, make a thorough inspection of the ship in company with his successor, and cause the crew to be exercised in his presence. He shall point out any defects, and account for them, and explain fully any peculiarities of construction or arrange- ments. A statement, in triplicate, of the inspection shall be drawn up, and if satisfactory, shall be signed by the officer succeeding to the command. If not satisfactory, the latter shall state in what particular it is not so, and the officer relieved shall make such explanations as he may deem necessary, each over his own signature. One copy of this statement shall be forwarded to the Secretary of the Navy, and one shall be retained by each of the Commanding Officers.

SECTION 6.

Officers Commanding Steam-Vessels.

382....When an officer shall be appointed to the command of a steam-vessel, he is to observe carefully the following directions, in addition to those prescribed in the next preceding section, relating to "Officers Commanding Vessels."

383....He is to use all possible diligence to make himself acquainted with the principles and construction of the engines, the intention and effect of the various parts of the machinery, the time the engines were constructed, the repairs they may have undergone, the period when the last repairs were made, and when the vessel last received new boilers.

384....As a material saving in the consumption of fuel may be produced by reducing the engine power, without reducing essentially the speed, and as occasions for this exercise of economy may frequently occur, he is to make himself acquainted with the principle and effect of the expansion of steam, and to require that the expansion gear should at all times be brought into play when the engines are not worked up to their full power.

385....In order to ascertain the capabilities of the ship under his command, he is, as soon as he proceeds to sea, to make careful and repeated trials by using the steam expansively, under every variety of wind and weather, draught of water, and other circumstances, so as to be able at all times to apply the principle of expansion, according to the nature of the service on which he may be engaged, and to calculate with accuracy the number of days the ship can be under steam without being obliged to put into port for fuel.

386....Except for experiments ordered, (and which will be necessary only when the information cannot be obtained from reports of the performances and capabilities of the ship on former occasions,) he is

Officers Commanding Steam-Vessels.

most carefully to avoid getting up, or keeping up the steam, in any case where the use of the sails alone would enable him to perform, in a satisfactory manner, the duty on which he is engaged. For the slightest neglect of this part of his instructions he will be held rigidly responsible.

387....As to the use of sails, either with or without the use of steam, or as to moderating the steam when running head to wind and sea, each Commanding Officer must be guided by his own judgment, but with the understanding that he must be prepared to justify every expenditure of fuel for steaming purposes, if cal'ed upon to do so. His judgment will necessarily be based upon a consideration of the urgency and nature of the service to be performed, of the wind and weather, and upon the difficulties of the navigation, and the qualities of the vessel ; but he is to take care, first, that steam is not used at all when the service can be equally, or nearly, as well performed without it; secondly, that sail is never dispensed with when it can be employed to advantage to assist the steam ; and, thirdly, that full steam power is never employed, unless in chase, or absolutely necessary, the cause for which must be reported to the Department in writing.

388.... He is carefully to inform himself of the usual daily consumption of coals, and to obtain all information in regard to the most economical and efficient use of the engines and their appendages.

389....To prevent accidents by spontaneous combustion, he is to order the greatest care to be observed that the coals are not taken on board when wet, and that when on board they are kept as dry as possible. When a fresh supply is received, he is to direct that those remaining in the coal-bunkers be, as far as practicable, so stowed as to be used first.

390....He is, before leaving the port where the vessel was fitted, to cause all the spare gear belonging to the engines and machinery to be taken on board, and he is to land no part of it at any port where he may touch, without the written authority of the Commanding Officer of the station, or of the Commander of the squadron to which he belongs.

391....Whenever he joins his Commanding Officer after separation, or when he arrives at any port where there is a superior officer in com mand, he shall report the number of hours the vessel was under steam and under sail, and the circumstances which rendered the use of steam necessary.

392.... When practicable, he shall, before going to sea, cause the boilers to be filled with *fresh* water.

393.... He will direct the Engineer to have the flues, chimneys, and boilers cleaned whenever it may be necessary, and when repairs or cleaning are required for the engines or boilers, they are to be made, as far as practicable, by the engineers, firemen, and coal-heavers of the vessel.

394.... He shall take care that the proper lanterns, to prevent collision at sea, be kept in good order and always lighted at night, except when it may be expedient to conceal all lights.

395.... He is to have the force-pumps, hose, and all other means for extinguishing fires, kept constantly in order and ready for immediate use ; and he is to require the utmost care to be taken at all times in the storage of stores, the use of lights and fires, and in the adoption of all other precautionary measures to prevent danger from fire.

396.... He shall examine the steam-log daily, and if satisfied of its correctness, sign it every month, or oftener, should the vessel in the mean time arrive at any port.

397.... The Commander of the vessel shall transmit to the Bureau of Steam Engineering, by the first safe opportunity after the close of the months of March, June, September, and December, a fair copy of the steam log-book for the preceding quarter, and whenever a steamer is placed in ordinary, for the period which has not been previously transmitted.

398.... He will require the steam-engineers to conform to the orders of the officer of the deck for the time being ; but they are not, except in cases of great emergency, to be ordered to perform other duties than those immediately connected with the preservation, repair, management, or supplying of the engines and their dependencies.

399.... He will cause the engineers, firemen and coal-beavers, to be arranged in watches, and, when on watch, they are to be under the immediate direction of the senior engineer of the watch, and are not to be ordered on other duties than those connected with the engines, boilers and their dependencies, except in cases of emergency; and then the engineer on duty is to be informed, that he may adopt all necessary precautions.

400....He will cause the senior Engineer to submit for his approval, watch, fire, quarter, and cleaning bills, showing the specific duties of the engineers, firemen, and coal-heavers.

401....He will require the senior engineer on board to examine daily the engines and their dependencies, and all parts of the vessel which are occupied by them, or by stores for their use, and to report them to the Executive Officer for inspection ; to make immediate report, should any defect or danger be discovered ; to give timely notice to the Commander of the vessel of the probable wants of his department, and whenever articles are received for it, to carefully examine if they are of proper quality, and report any which, in his opinion, may be objectionable.

402....He will make such regulations with regard to leave on shore that the ship will never be left without the services of an experienced engineer. He will cause a full engineer watch to be kept constantly whenever the fires are lighted, and take care that one engineer at least, with a suitable number of firemen and coal-beavers, are always on watch, even though the ship may be at anchor and the fires hauled.

Section 7.

Executive Officer.

403....The Line Officer next in rank to the Commander of the vessel shall be the Executive Officer.

404.... He will at once make himself acquainted with all the arrangements and equipments of the vessel, and report to the Commanding Officer any defects he may discover.

405....He shall, under the direction of the Commander, have the superintendence of the general duties to be performed, and of the police, to such extent as the Commander may authorize or prescribe.

406....He shall have the quarter, watch, fire, and station bills made out and kept complete according to the orders which he may receive from the Commander, and see that copies of them, and of the laws and

Executive Officer.

regulations, are so disposed that all persons may readily refer to them for information.

407....He shall examine the vessel daily, and report to the Commander the result of his inspection.

408....He shall never absent himself from the vessel without the permission of the Commanding officer ; nor will he ever leave her in the absence of the Commanding Officer, except on urgent public duty.

409....He shall not be required to keep a watch, unless circumstances, in the judgment of the Commander of the vessel, should render it necessary.

410....When the Commander of the vessel is not on deck, he may advise and direct the officer of the deck in the working and management of the ship ; and if, in his judgment, circumstances should make it necessary, he may take charge of the deck, stating his reasons for so doing to the Commander.

411'....He will exercise authority over all officers, and see that they vigilantly perform their duties, and that they conform to all orders for securing uniformity in the mode of executing them.

412....He shall inform himself of the capacity of each man on board, and of the stations they may have previously filled, that he may station them to the best advantage.

413....In case of fire, or any other occurrence that may place the ship in danger, he shall exert himself to maintain order ; and if it should become necessary to abandon the vessel, he shall, under the direction of the Commanding Officer, see that the sick and wounded are first cared for.

414....Whenever all hands are called for any particular duty, exercise, or evolution, he shall take charge of the deck.

415....He shall require from the Boatswain, Gunner, Carpenter, and Sailmaker, reports of the state of the vessel in their respective departments, at eight o'clock in the evening, and at morning quarters.

416....He shall, at eight o'clock in the evening, report the condition of the vessel to the Commander, and receive any orders he may have for him.

417....He shall immediately report to the Commander any defect or deficiency that may come to his knowledge, and which may in any manner endanger the safety or impair the efficiency of the vessel.

418....He is to correct, as far as his power extends, all abuses; and if he observes, or has knowledge of, any violation of the Laws and Regulations for the government of the Navy on the part of any person whomsoever, he is not to exercise any discretion in the matter, but to make immediate report to the Commander.

419....He shall, under the direction of the Commander, control the expenditure of all stores in charge of the yeoman, and examine weekly the reports of receipts and expenditures; and, upon being satisfied of their correctness, will approve and send them to the Commander.

420....Whenever the magazine is to be opened for receiving or discharging powder, he shall see, in person, that all the prescribed precautions against accidents are rigidly observed.

421....In the absence of the Commander, he is to act in his stead, but is not to alter or change any of his regulations.

422....He shall cause a convenient locker to be prepared, in which the keys of the holds and all storerooms shall be hung up, except those which the Ordnance Instructions require to be kept in the charge of the Commander of the vessel; it shall be his duty to see that all such keys are hung up at sunset, and that they are not taken away during the night without his knowledge, and that the keys of no storeroom are ever taken out of the ship.

423....He shall keep at hand a breaker of water, and a supply of provisions sufficient for the support of the crew of each quarter-boat for one week, which will be placed in the boat whenever there is a probability of separation from the ship, by fog or otherwise. The boat sails shall be kept in readiness for immediate use. If it shall be necessary to send a boat from the ship at sea, he shall be careful that she is provided with a compass.

424....He shall, when the number of officers will permit, assign one to each boat, whose duty it shall be to command the boat when required for special service, and who will be responsible that the arms, equipments, and crew, are in order and ready for service.

425....He will keep a correct muster-roll of the crew, and a descriptive list, and he will have charge of the liberty and conduct books. He will superintend the messing of the crew, and in case of any changes involving the issue of provisions, he will cause the Paymaster to be duly informed.

426....He will see that the officers keep correct copies of the watch, quarter, fire and station bills ; that the officers of divisions keep correct clothes-lists of the men under their command ; and that they instruct them faithfully in their duties.

427.....If from any cause he should be rendered incapable of perform-ing his duties, they will devolve upon the Line Officer next below him in rank.

SECTION 8.

Lieutenants, Masters, and Ensigns.

428....Lieutenants, Masters, and Ensigns, are the Watch and Divi-sion Officers.

429....They will punctually and zealously execute all orders they may receive from their Commanding or other Superior Officer, and, as far as in their power, see that all on board, who are subordinate to them perform with diligence and propriety the several duties assigned them. They are to be attentive to the conduct of the ship's company ; to prevent all profane, abusive, and improper language, all disturbance, noise and confusion ; and to report to the Executive Officer those whose misconduct they may think deserving of punishment. They will con-form to the manner of performing duty adopted by the Executive Officer.

430....On taking charge of a watch, an Officer is to make himself well acquainted with the position of the vessel with reference to all other vessels in sight, and to any land or danger that may be near, and with all orders that remain unexecuted. He shall hold no conversation with any one, except on duty, nor engage in any occupation which may distract his attention. He is to see that the men on deck are kept on the alert and attentive to their duty ; that the look-outs are kept at their several stations and are obviously vigilant ; that each sail set is kept properly spread and trimmed ; and every precaution is observed to prevent accidents from squalls. Throughout his watch he is to be careful that the vessel is properly and duly steered ; that a correct account is kept of her way and leeway ; and that the courses and distances, together with every occurrence of importance and interest, and accident resulting in loss of any kind, are plainly and legibly entered on the deck-log, which log he is to sign at the conclusion of his remarks, with his initials, on the termination of his watch.

431.....He is to see that the subordinate officers of the watch are in their stations and attentive to their duties, and that they muster the men on deck when the other men are relieved from it, and as often afterwards as he may judge necessary.

432.....He is to be careful, at night, that the required lights are kept burning and are properly trimmed, and, in fogs, that the required signals are sounded. In approaching and passing vessels he is to be governed by the regulations for preventing collisions.

433....He is promptly to inform the Commanding Officer of all strange vessels that may be discovered ; of any land, shoal, rock, or danger that may be made ; of all changes of wind or weather ; of all alterations of canvas or steam by the Commanding Officer of the squadron or division to which the vessel may belong ; and, generally, of all occurrences worthy of notice.

434....He is never, on his own authority, to carry sail or steam so as to endanger spars or machinery ; nor, when the Commanding Officer is on deck, is he ever to alter either without first consulting him.

435....He is never to change the given course without orders from the Commanding Officer, unless it may be necessary to do so to avoid danger, and then he shall report to him without delay.

436.....On the discovery of a strange sail at night, or in a fog, during war, he is, besides sending at once to inform the Commanding Officer of the fact, to have made immediately every preparation for action that circumstances will allow.

437.....At night he is to take care that the Master-at-Arms, ship's Corporal, or non-commissioned officer of marines detailed for the purpose, on watch, is particular in going the rounds and visiting every accessible part of the vessel below the spar deck, every half hour, in order to see that no irregularities are occurring among the crew ; that all prisoners are safe and in their places ; that no improper lights are burning ; that no smoking after hours is taking place ; and reporting to him accordingly. He will also take care that an officer of the watch go the same rounds at least as often as twice during his watch. And besides, he is to cause the pumps to be sounded twice, or oftener, during his watch, and a Gunner's Mate or Quarter Gunner to examine the security of the battery as frequently, and have the reports with regard to both examinations made to him.

438....He is not to make any signal without orders from the Commander, unless to warn vessels of some danger ; but he will see that everything is in readiness to make them by day or by night.

439....He shall always have his side-arms either on the person or at hand ; a trumpet shall be carried at sea, and a spy-glass in port. During wet weather he may wear a water-proof coat and cap.

440....He shall give his attention that all officers, or others, coming on board or leaving the ship, shall receive the marks of respect to which they are entitled.

441....No boat is to be allowed to leave the ship or come alongside without the knowledge of the Officer of the Deck. When boats or tenders come alongside with provisions, water, or stores of any kind, he is to see them cleared without delay, and that no prohibited articles are brought on board ; and that all articles which may be ordered to be sent out of the vessel are carefully and properly put on board the vessel or boats which are directed to receive them.

442....When boats leave the ship he shall be particular to see that they have their proper crews, suitably clothed, and that no man not belonging to a boat shall take the place of one who does, without the authority of the Executive Officer.

443....He shall take care that a strict and accurate account is taken of all stores received on board, or sent from the vessel during his watch, and see that those which are received are delivered in charge of the proper officer, and that the number or quantity received or sent from the vessel is correctly entered on the log-slate.

444....He shall never cause the engines of a steam vessel to be stopped, without first slowing them, nor to be worked at full speed until the vessel has first gathered way, except in cases of great emergency.

445....He will see the conductors, life-buoys, heaving lines, and drift leads ready for service, and that a boat is always ready for lowering.

446 ....A Lieutenant, Master, or Ensign, when called or sent on board the vessel of the Commander-in-Chief, Commander of a squadron, or Commander of a division, to receive orders, is to take with him an order book, and insert therein the orders that may be given to him.

447 ....An Officer commanding a division of guns and men on board a vessel is to be held responsible for its efficiency in all respects. Besides keeping the guns in constant condition for action, and the men well trained to their use agreeably to the Ordnance Instructions, he is to give his personal attention to the cleanliness and good appearance of the men ; to the examination of their clothing and bedding, and to the making out requisitions to supply their necessary wants at stated periods ; to the issuing of clothing to them, and to their converting materials drawn from the paymaster to the purpose for which they were required ; to observe that their clothing is neatly made, marked, and kept in good order, and to keep correct clothes lists. In inspecting clothing, it is to be done by calling a gun's crew at a time, and also in making out requisitions.

SECTION 9.

Navigator.

448 ....The Line Officer next in rank to the Executive Officer shall be the Navigator.

449 ....He shall, at sea, ascertain and report daily to the Commanding Officer the vessel's position at meridian, and make such other reports of position, variation of the compass, &c., as the Commanding Officer may require.

450 ....He is to have charge of, and must account for, all nautical instruments, books, charts, national flags, and signals.

451 ....He shall frequently examine the compasses, time glasses, log and lead lines, and thus see that they are constantly in proper order for service.

452 ....He shall examine the charts of all coasts which the vessel may visit, and note upon them any errors which he may discover, and

Navigator.

inform the Commanding Officer of the same, who shall report them to the Navy Department.

453....When the vessel may be approaching any land or shoals, or entering any port or harbor, he shall be very attentive to the soundings, and he shall at all times inform the Commander of any danger to which he may think the vessel exposed, whether under charge of a pilot or not.

454....He shall have charge of keeping the ship's log-book, and shall see that all particulars are duly entered in it, according to such forms as are or may be prescribed, and he shall, immediately after such entries, send it to the watch officers, that they may sign their names at the end of the remarks in their respective watches while the circumstances are fresh in their memories, and he shall take it to the Commanding Officer for his inspection immediately after noon of each day.

455....There shall be entered on the log-slate and log-book, with minute exactness, the following particulars :

1. The name and rank, or rating, of all persons who may join or be discharged from the vessel ; all transfers, deaths, and desertions ; the names of all persons made prisoners by an enemy, and of all absent without leave ; the names of all passengers, with times of coming aboard and leaving ; the direction of the wind, state of the weather, courses steered, and distances sailed ; the time when any particular evolution, exercise, or other service was performed ; the signal number of all signals made, the time when, and by what vessels, and to what vessel they were made ; the nature and extent of all public punishments inflicted, with the name and crime of the offenders ; the rating and disrating of Petty Officers ; the result of all observations made to find the ship's place, and all dangers discovered in navigation.

2. The grounding of the ship, and the loss of or serious injury to boats, spars, sails, rigging, and stores of any kind, with the circumstances under which they happened, and the extent of the injury received.

3. A particular account of all stores received, from whom received, or by whom furnished, and the department for which they were received.

4. A particular account of all stores condemned by survey, or converted to any other purpose than that for which they were originally intended.

5. A particular account of all stores lent, or otherwise sent out of the vessel, and by what authority it was done.

6. All the marks and numbers of each cask or bale, which, on being opened, is found to contain less than is specified by the invoice, or than it ought to contain, with the deficiency found.

7. Every alteration made in the allowance of provisions, and by whose order.

8. The employment of any hired vessel, her dimensions in tonnage, the name of the master or owner, the number of her crew, how or for what purpose employed, by whose order, and the reasons for her employment.

9. The draught of water, light and loaded, as furnished at the navy yard ; and always on going into or leaving port the ship's draught is to be taken and entered on the log.

456....After the log has been signed by the officers of the watches no alteration shall be made therein, except to correct some error, or supply some omission, and then only with the approbation of the Commanding Officer, and upon the recollection of the officer who had charge of the watch in which the alteration or addition is proposed, who shall then sign the same if satisfied of its correctness.

457....The navigator shall deliver to the Commanding Officer of the vessel, signed by himself, and, after careful comparison, certified to be correct, a fair copy of the log-book, every six months, to be transmitted by the first safe opportunity to the Bureau of Navigation.

458....The original log-book shall be kept by the vessel until she is paid off, when it shall be placed in charge of the Commanding Officer of the yard, and by him transmitted to the Bureau of Navigation.

459....Besides the log-book, he is to keep a remark-book, in which all the hydrographical information he can obtain is to be carefully inserted, as well as a description of the instruments he may employ in any of the observations hereafter mentioned. He is to determine as

Navigator.

accurately as he can the various particulars relating to navigation of every place which the vessel may visit, entering the results in his remark-book, under the following heads :

    1. Latitude.

    2. Longitude.

    3. Variation of the compass.

    4. Time of high water immediately following new and full moon.

    5. Rise and fall of the tides at springs and neaps.

    6. Prevailing winds.

    7. Periods of the year at which the wet and dry seasons prevail, if any.

    8. Seasons at which hurricanes prevail.

    9. The temperature of the chronometer room at the time observations are taken.

The particular spot at the place visited, to which the latitude and longitude refer, is to be carefully noted ; also, the number and nature of the observations, and the means by which they were made, whether the artificial or sea horizon was used ; and with reference to the longitute, if obtained with chronometers by means of meridian distances from another place, he is to state the number employed, their general character, the age of the rates used, or the interval since which they were last rated, with the longitude he has assumed of the place measured from. He is to observe the variation of the compass by amplitudes or azimuths, at least once every day, whether at sea or in port, excepting only when refitting in harbor. The azimuth compass is to be always placed, when practicable, in the same precise situation amidships, marking the point where each of the tripod legs stands ; and he is to take care that the direction of the ship's head at the time of observation shall be recorded, as well as the difference between the standard or azimuth and the steering compasses, by which precaution alone can the real course of the ship be regulated. These variations are to be daily inserted in columns at the end of his remark-book, along with the ship's place and the direction of her head at the time of observation. The local attraction is to be determined before the ship leaves

6

Navigator.

---

the United States, as well as after any material change of latitude, and is then to be tabulated by him for every point of the compass, so that the corrections on each course may be readily applied in working the ship's reckoning. In all places he is to ascertain the direction and velocity of the currents, the set and strength of the tides, with the limits of their rise and fall, and the time of high water of the tide which immediately follows the periods of the new and full moon. He is to describe as particularly as he can the appearances of foreign coasts, pointing out the remarkable objects by which they may be distinguished, so as to render a stranger certain of recognizing his land fall. He is to apply for boats to sound and survey any shoals or harbors which have not been correctly laid down in the charts, and the results are to be projected on a large and intelligible scale. In his remark-book he is carefully to note all inaccuracies in any of the charts supplied to the ship. He is frequently to present this remark-book to the Commander for examination, and on the first of January, in every year, he is to deliver to him a correct copy of it, accompanied by all the charts, plans, and views of the coasts and headlands which he has made during the past year, all of which the Commander will transmit by the first safe opportunity to his Commander-in-Chief to be forwarded to the Department.

460....Every vessel, before sailing, shall be furnished with a skeleton chart embracing her probable cruising ground, on which he shall lay down her track and daily run during the whole time of her absence, which chart shall be transmitted to the Bureau of Navigation at the end of the cruise.

461....He shall keep a book, in which he shall make all calculations connected with the navigation of the vessel. No erasures shall be made, but the book shall be a complete record of all observations, computations and results, with the dates upon which the observations and computations were made. At the end of the cruise this book shall be sent to the Bureau of Navigation by the Commander of the vessel.

462....He is, if ordered to a vessel before a stowage is commenced, to superintend, under the direction of the Commanding Officer of the yard, or Commander of the vessel, as the case may be, the stowage of the ballast, water, provisions, and all other articles.

463....In stowing provisions he shall take care that the oldest be

Navigator.

stowed so that they may be first issued, breaking out and restowing those already on board if necessary for that purpose, unless otherwise directed.

464.... When the stowage of the hold shall be completed, he shall make an entry on the log-book, specifying particularly the quantity and arrangement of the ballast, the number, size, and disposition of the tanks and casks, and of the quantity and stowage of provisions and other stores.

465.... Accurate plans must be made of the stowage of the hold, which he shall insert in the log-book; and if any material change should afterwards be made in the stowage, the change must be noted, and new plans be inserted in the log book.

466.... If the hold should be stowed at a navy yard, or private establishment, under the direction of the Commander of the vessel, he will furnish the latter with plans and descriptions for transmission to the Commandant of the yard, or the Bureau of Construction.

467.... He is to visit the hold daily, and cable tiers and chain lockers weekly, or oftener if necessary, and see that they are kept clear and in as good order as circumstances will admit.

468.... He shall exercise a particular supervision of the anchors and cables; he shall see that they are properly secured at all times, that the cables are distinctly marked, and that all necessary arrangements are made for getting under way, anchoring, mooring, unmooring, slipping, or shifting parts of one cable to another; for this purpose he will see that the shackle-pins can be removed readily.

469.... He will be careful to prevent any waste or improper expenditure of fuel or water, and he is to report daily, when at sea, to the Commanding Officer, the quantity of each expended in the last twenty-four hours, and the quantity remaining on hand.

470.... Should he be removed or suspended, he shall sign the log-book and deliver it to his successor, taking his receipt for the same, and for all other articles under his charge, and shall deliver to the Commander a fair copy of the remark-book, made up to the day of his removal or suspension.

471.... He shall not keep watch, except required to do so by order of the Commander of the vessel.

SECTION 10.

Midshipmen.

472.... Midshipmen, while at the Naval Academy, will be governed by the rules of that institution.

473.... If ordered to a cruising ship, they shall provide themselves with a sextant or octant, an approved treatise upon navigation, one on marine surveying, and with blank journals.

474.... They are daily to ascertain the position of the ship when at sea, by observations, and dead reckoning, and send the same to their Commanding Officer.

475.... They are to keep journals in such forms as may be prescribed, which they will present to the Commanding Officer for inspection, on the first day of every month, and they will at all times embrace every opportunity of acquiring useful information which may be applicable to their profession as seamen and officers.

476.... They shall attend regularly to the means of instruction which may be provided for them.

477.... They will not be granted leave to go on shore unless their journals are kept up, and they have copies of the watch, quarter, fire, and station bills, of separate quarter bills for their divisions, and they shall have given proper attention to their duties.

SECTION 11.

Boatswain and Gunner.

478.... They must, with the Yeoman, carefully examine all the articles belonging to, and all stores received for, their respective departments, and see that they are of good quality, that they agree in quantity with the invoice or bill sent with them, and that they are in good order, and must make immediate report to the Executive Officer of any defect or deficiency which they may discover.

479.... They are responsible for all articles of their departments not in the immediate charge of the Yeoman, and particularly for the careful preservation of all tools or implements issued by the Yeoman for the use of their departments. They will retain for survey all of these that may become worn out, or otherwise ren ered unfit for further use, as their responsibility with regard to them will not cease until they have been formally disposed of by survey.

480.... They shall request a survey upon all stores which may be injured, or become unfit for service, in their respective departments, and such as the surveying officers condemn shall be expended, preserving a copy of the survey as a voucher; but if the survey shall direct articles to be converted to some other use, they shall be charged accordingly, and expended in the same manner as any other stores.

481.... They shall be particularly watchful, and make immediate report to the Executive Officer of any neglect or misconduct which they may discover in the Yeoman, or person having charge of their stores.

482.... When a ship is about to be dismantled, they are to be careful that all the articles belonging to their respective departments are properly secured and tallied, with their name and quantity, whether "serviceable," "requiring repairs," or "unserviceable," and that all precautions are taken to prevent their being in any manner injured. They will only receive credit according to the receipt given for them by the Navy Storekeeper, or other person into whose charge they may be delivered, or according to the report of the surveying officers, duly appointed, and they will attend the survey which may be made, to ascertain the quantity of stores so returned by them, and will be called upon to account for any deficiency that may be found to exist.

483.... They are to report daily, at morning quarters and at 8 p. m., to the Executive Officer, the state of all things in their respective departments.

484.... The Boatswain is to be generally upon deck in the day, and at all times both by day and night when any duty shall require all hands to be employed. He is, with his mates, to see that the men go quickly upon deck when called, and that when there they perform their duty with alacrity.

485.... He is, every day, before 7½ a. m., and as much oftener as may be desirable, according to the service the ship is employed on, to examine the state of the rigging, to ascertain whether any part be chafed, or likely to give way, and to report to the Officer of the Deck the state in which he finds it. He is, at all times, to be careful that the anchors, booms and boats be properly secured ; and he is to be very attentive to have ready a sufficient number of mats, plats, nippers, points, and gaskets, that no delay or inconvenience may be experienced when they are wanted.

486....He shall be particularly careful that the masts of the ship are not crippled or strained in setting up the stays and rigging, and that the masts retain the same angle with the keel after the stays and rigging are set up that they did when they were only wedged.

487....He is to be very attentive when working up junk that every part of it is converted to such purposes as may be ordered.

488.... When the ship is preparing for battle, he is to be very particular in seeing that everything necessary for repairing the rigging is in its proper place, that the men stationed to that service may know where to find immediately whatever may be wanted.

489.... Besides the duties assigned to the Gunner in the "Ordnance Instructions," he is to have charge of the anchor-buoys and life-buoys, to see that they are at all times in good order, and the latter ready to be dropped into the water at a moment's warning.

490....He is to report to the Navigator for entry in the log-book, after an action, or after any exercise in which powder, or powder and shot are used, the quantity of each expended, and is to sign the entry in attestation of its correctness.

491....He is responsible for the good condition of everything pertaining to the guns and their equipments, magazines, shell rooms, shot and shell, small-arms, &c., and he is to satisfy himself that they are constantly in good order and condition.

SECTION 12.

Master's Mates.

492....The duties of this classs of officers will be such as the Commander of the vessel may direct ; when capable, they may be detailed as mates of decks, holds, and the like.

ARTICLE VII.

GENERAL DUTIES OF STAFF OFFICERS.

SECTION 1.

Fleet Engineer.

493....When a Chief Engineer is detailed to discharge the duties of Fleet Engineer, he will be attached to the flag-ship. His duties will be as follows :

1. To exercise a general supervision over all the engineers of the fleet or squadron.

2. To acquaint himself with the different kinds of engines in use in the squadron, and to take care that all means are used to keep them in the highest state of efficiency.

3. To make, under the orders of the Commander-in-Chief, frequent inspections of machinery, and to decide upon all ordinary repairs.

4. To recommend surveys when the imperfections or accidents are serious, and to make reports where carelessness is suspected.

5. To see that every vessel is provided with the necessary tools, stores, and spare parts of machinery, and that every engine and boiler is cared for properly.

6. To examine the coal used, and report to the Commander-in-Chief if there is any falling off in quality, or any undue dampness liable to produce spontaneous combustion.

7. To see that the coal is properly stored at the different depots, and that there is at all times a sufficient quantity on hand to meet the probable wants of the squadron.

8. To make frequent reports to the Commander-in-Chief of the condition of the engineer's department of every vessel in the squadron, and to bring to the notice of the Commander-in-Chief such engineers in charge as may be distinguished for the faithful performance of their duties.

9. To examine all returns and requisitions made by the engineers of the fleet or squadron, and to forward them promptly, with such remarks as he may deem necessary.

10. To recommend to the Commander-in-Chief such measures as will, in his opinion, promote efficiency, economy, and uniformity in his department of the service.

11 And, finally, to perform such other duties relating to his position as shall be assigned to him by the Commander-in-Chief.

Section 2.

Chief Engineer.

294....A Chief Engineer, on being ordered to a ship, will make himself acquainted with all parts of the machinery and boilers, the coal-bunkers and store-rooms; he will examine carefully all parts of the machinery and everything pertaining to it, and report to the Commanding Officer anything that is defective.

495....He will cause the assistant engineers, on their joining the vessel, to become familiar with all the cocks, valves, pipes, and the different parts of the machinery and boilers.

496....He will see that he has the requisite amount of stores, of good quality, on board, and that they are stored away in good condition.

497....He will provide a supply of oatmeal, to be issued to the firemen and coal-heavers, without charge, at such times and in such quantities as the Commanding Officer may direct.

498....He will keep a strict account of, and be responsible for, the expenditure of the coals, stores, duplicate pieces, and all articles in the engineer department; and he will examine each day's expenditure and approve it by his signature.

499....He will make out the watch, quarter, fire, and cleaning bills for the engineer department, assigning to each person his proper station and duty, and submit the same to the Commander of the vessel for his approval and signature, which bills shall then be hung up in some conspicuous place where all persons in the department may refer to them. He will see that the prescribed duties are performed in a proper manner, and will report all neglect of duty or other breech of discipline in the fire or engine-room to the executive officer.

Chief Engineer.

500....He will see that the fires are never lighted, nor hauled after being lighted, without the consent of the Commanding Officer ; and that the engines are never turned, after being stopped, except in obe‑ dience to signal, or by permission of the Officer of the Deck.

501....He will report to the Commander any accident or defect that may occur to the machinery, boilers, or their dependencies, and at meridian of each day report the quantity of coals consumed, the revolu‑ tions made by the engines, and the average revolutions per minute for the last twenty-four hours ; also, the quantity of coal remaining on hand ; and if at any time in his judgment the machinery is driven too hard, or undue strain put upon any of its parts by stress of weather, motion, or position of the vessel, he will report the same to the Com‑ mander, noting such report, and the causes for it, in the steam-log.

502....He shall make a daily personal examination of all parts of the vessel occupied by the engines and their dependencies, and will report them ready for inspection to the Executive Officer at such times as may be directed by the Commander of the vessel.

503....He shall, at the setting of the watch in the evening, report the condition of the engines, boilers, and their dependencies, to the Commanding Officer, and receive from him any orders he may have to give him for the night.

504....He will exercise a vigilant supervision over every part of the steam department, and see that it is kept in good order ; he will be particular that the steam-pumps, hose, and other means for extinguish‑ ing fire, are ready for immediate use ; that the water in the boilers is not carried to an improper density ; and that the coals and stores are used to the greatest advantage.

505....He shall afford every facility, and encourage in every way the Assistant Engineers to improve themselves in their profession, and at the en of a cru se. or on heir leaving the ship, he will address to the Secretary of the Navy a lette stating the deportment, character, and qualifications as an Engineer, of each.

506....He will examine the bunkers each time the ship arrives in port, or oftener, to see if the amount of coals correspond with the log, and if any discrepancy appears, he will report the same immediately to the Commander and note it on the log.

Chief Engineer.

507....He will, on the discontinuance of steaming, with the permission of the Commanding Officer, clean and repair, at once, the engines and their dependencies.

508....He will cause the Firemen to be instructed so as to qualify them for managing the engines and dependencies with safety, in case accident, or other causes, should prevent the attendance of the Engineer.

509....He will cause the temperature of the coal-bunkers to be ascertained twice in each watch, and have the result reported to the Officer of the Deck at the expiration of the watch.

510....Whenever a distilling apparatus is fitted on board a steamship, he is to take charge of it, and will be held responsible for its being kept in proper repair and condition.

511....A steam-log is always to be kept when the vessel is moved by steam, which log is to be signed in the column of remarks by the Engineers of the repective watches at the expiration of their watch, and at noon of each day by the Senior Engineer of the vessel The steam log-book is to be handed to the Commander of the vessel daily by the Senior Engineer on board. At the end of each quarter he shall send to the Commanding Officer of the vessel a fair copy of the steam log-book, certified by his own signature.

512....He will take the utmost care in the arrangement of stores, the use of lights and fires, and the adoption of every precautionary measure to prevent the danger from fire to which steamers are so much exposed.

513....He will carefully note in the steam-log the draught of water of the vessel and immersion of the bucket-boards just before going to sea, and on arriving in port, and frequently when receiving coal and other stores.

514....The Chief Engineer of the vessel will make a quarterly report to accompany the quarterly synopsis of the steam-log, (appendix, form, No. 2,) in which he will detail the breakage or other casualties of the machinery, the causes thereof as far as he may be able to ascertain with certainty, the time expended in repairing them and in adjusting the machinery, and whether done by his department on board or by workmen from the shore. He will also give his opinion of the present condition of the machinery, mentioning particularly the cylinders and their valves, the main journals, the connecting-rod journals, the steam bearings, the pumps, the condensers and boilers, and the paddle-wheels or screw, to which he will add his observations as to their sufficiency and efficiency. In the event of any experimental machinery being on board, or any horse machinery, or unusual arrangement, he will particularly describe it and its mode of action, and give the results therefrom and his opinion on its merits. He will state the maximum speed of the vessel under steam alone, in smooth water, that can be sustained for twelve consecutive hours, with the machinery in its existing condition, and give the necessary data in connexion therewith, such as the boiler pressure, number of revolutions of the engines per minute, vacuum in the condenser, number of holes of throttle-valve open, point of cutting off steam, temperatures, pounds of coal consumed per hour, number of tons of coal on board the vessel, indicated horse-power, &c. He will state the number of engineers, of first and second class firemen, and coal-heavers attached to the vessel, and also the number of tons of coal that the bunkers will contain. He will add such observations on the machinery and vessel as his experience may suggest, with a view to their correct appreciation and value. A copy of the tabular synopsis and of the report is to be pasted into each quarterly steam-log, and another is to be forwarded, through the prescribed channels, to the Bureau of Steam Engineering.

SECTION 3.

Assistant Engineers.

515..... When there is no Chief Engineer on board, the duties assigned to him will devolve on the senior Assistant Engineer.

516.... Assistant Engineers are at all times faithfully and zealously to carry into prompt execution all orders they may receive from the Engineer Officer in charge on board, or others their superiors; and they are to be especially careful in the management of the engines, boilers, and their dependencies; to adhere strictly to the directions of the Engineer in charge, and to report to him instantly on discovering anything going wrong about them.

Assistant Engineers.

517....When the engines are in operation, the Engineer of the watch will execute promptly all orders he may receive from the Officer of the Deck, though he must be careful in so doing that no risk of injury is incurred. Should he receive an order which, in his judgment, would involve dangerous consequences, he will immediately send his reasons for his opinion to the Officer of the Deck and inform the senior Engineer, who will at once refer to the Commanding Officer for instruction.

518....He will make hourly reports to the Officer of the Deck whether the engines and their dependencies, the force-pumps, hose, and all other means for extinguishing fire, are in good order, and that the pumps and hose are ready for immediate use. Should anything occur to require a change in the orders under which the Engineer is then acting, or should special attention be required to any object in order to insure safety or more efficiency, he will report the same to the Officer of the Deck immediately.

519....Should it be necessary from any cause to stop the engines suddenly, he will report the fact to the Officer of the Deck ; if not possible to do so in time before stopping them, he will report afterwards his reasons therefor and the probable length o. time they will be stopped. He will also inform the Chief Engineer immediately.

520....He will note hourly on the steam-log all the information which the columns in it require, and place in the column of "remarks" full information of the state of the weather and sea, and all accidents to or defects in the engines or their dependencies, the manner of their working, the quality of the coal, and any other circumstances which may be useful for determining the powers and qualities of the vessel and the engines under the various circumstances to which they may be exposed.

521....He will be particularly careful to prevent the waste of coals, oil, tallow, and all other stores in the Engineer's Department.

522....In the absence of the senior Engineer Officer belonging to the vessel, the one remaining on board highest in rank or seniority is to be held responsible for the good order of the engine-room, and for the proper discharge of all the duties connected therewith.

Section 4.

Surgeon of the Fleet.

523....In addition to the duties prescribed by law, and by the "Instructions for the government of medical officers," the Surgeon of the Fleet will be required :

1. To inquire into the practice of all the Surgeons or persons acting as such in the fleet or squadron to which he may be attached, and will report to the Commander-in-Chief any neglects which he may discover.

2. To suggest to the Commander-in-Chief and Commanding Officers of vessels, for their consideration and decision, the most proper measures for preventing or checking disease, or for promoting the comfort of the sick or wounded.

3. When required by the Commander-in-Chief to specify those vessels which may appear, from the state of the health of the crews, least fit for active service, or most in want of refreshments.

4. To keep a medical journal of the health of the fleet or squadron, from which he shall report to the Medical Bureau.

5. After an engagement to require a report of killed and wounded from the Surgeons of all the vessels engaged, which he will imbody in a general report and forward it to the Commander-in-Chief.

Section 5.

Surgeons.

524.....The Surgeon or the senior Medical Officer ordered to a vessel will, in addition to the duties prescribed in the "Instructions for the government of medical officers," examine the dispensary, medical store-rooms, and sick bay ; to see that every preparation is made for the reception of stores and medicines, and for the proper care of the sick and wounded In case of any defect in the arrangements he will report it immediately to the Commanding Officer.

Surgeons.

525.... The sick bay, dispensary, and medical store-rooms are under his immediate charge. He will see that they are kept in proper condition, and will report them daily for inspection to the Executive Officer, at such times as the Commander of the vessel may direct.

526.... He will be particularly attentive to the comfort and cleanliness of all patients under his professional care.

527.... He will report to the Commanding Officer daily the names and condition of the sick, according to such forms as may be prescribed, and will, at the same time, suggest any measures he may deem important for the health of the crew, and will cause to be deposited daily in the binnacle a list of the officers and other persons whose condition requires that they should be excused from duty.

528.... He will take every precaution to prevent the introduction or progress of any infectious disease, and make immediate report to the Commander of any probable danger from or the appearance of any such disease.

529.... He is carefully to examine the crew, as soon as practicable after joining the ship, for the purpose of reporting to the Commanding Officer any necessity that may exist for vaccination, which, if possible, is to be performed before the sailing of the vessel.

530.... He will be allowed to his exclusive use a convenient store-room for the preservation of articles in his charge, and will, upon application to the Commanding Officer, be allowed proper persons, in addition to the established attendants, should they be necessary, to assist in the care of the sick and to perform other services for their comfort.

531.... He is at all times to have in readiness everything necessary for the relief of the wounded.

532.... On the probability of an engagement he will cause a sufficient number of tourniquets to be distributed to the officers in different parts of the ship, and see that all persons stationed with him, and such others as may be designated, are instructed in the proper mode of using them.

533.... He will cause the boats attending the ship with articles of food for sale to be examined, and if any contain articles the use of which would, in his opinion, be injurious to the crew, he will represent the same to the Commanding Officer.

534....The journal of his daily practice shall be subject to the inspection of the Surgeon of the Fleet, and be forwarded, as directed, for correspondence and other reports, to the Chief of the Bureau of Medicine and Surgery at the expiration of the cruise.

535....Whenever any person on board shall receive any wound or injury which may probably entitle him to make application for a pension, he shall report the same to the Commander, in writing, before the person be removed or discharged from the vessel, that a proper survey may be held and certificate issued, according to such form as may be prescribed by the Pension Office.

536....When practicable such persons who may be sent to a hospital or a hospital vessel are to be accompanied by a medical officer, and the Surgeon will send with them a statement of their diseases or injuries, with a synopsis of treatment, according to such forms as may be prescribed by the Bureau of Medicine and Surgery.

537....He shall inspect the provisions for the crew, and report to the commanding officer when he may discover any that are unsound. Also, he will cause the purity of the water to be tested before it is received into the tanks, and he will make known to the commanding officer any want of care or cleanliness in the preparation of food for the crew, or any instance of personal neglect with regard to it, of which he may be cognizant. In fine, everything which may come to his knowledge as conducive to, or militating against, the general health and comfort of the ship's company, he will make known to the commanding officer.

538....After battle, he shall make out in duplicate a careful report of killed and wounded, one copy of which he will send to the commander of the vessel, and the other shall be forwarded, through the proper channel, to the Surgeon of the Fleet.

Section 6.

Passed and Other Assistant Surgeons.

539....They shall perform all the professional duties which may be required from them, and conform to the instructions which may be given by the Surgeon of the vessel to which they may be attached, and will be unremitting in their attentions to the comfort and cleanliness of the sick, and exact from those under their direction a rigid performance of their duties.

540....Assistant Surgeons, whether passed or otherwise, shall attend personally, to see that medicines are properly weighed or measured, and labelled for distribution to the sick.

541....In the absence of the Surgeon, the passed or other Assistant Surgeon, oldest in commission, is to perform all the duties of the Surgeon.

SECTION 7.

Fleet Paymaster.

542....When a Paymaster is detailed to discharge the duties of Fleet Paymaster, he will be attached to the flag-ship.   His duties will be as follows:

1. To exercise a general supervision over all the Paymasters of the fleet or squadron.

2. To keep an account of the stores on board the store vessels of the squadron, and at depots on shore within the limits of the Commander-in-Chief's command

3. To receive and classify the returns and requisitions of Paymasters of store vessels and depots, as well as of all other vessels of the squadron, and to receive, examine, and forward to the Department, Bureau of Provisions and Clothing, and Fourth Auditor of the Treasury, all returns and reports required to be made to them, taking care that the returns shall be in proper form, and accompanied by the required vouchers.

4. To keep the Commander-in-Chief informed of the quantities and condition of the Paymaster's stores in the fleet or squadron.

5. To distribute promptly the orders, circulars, and decisions of the Department, Bureau of Provisions and Clothing, Fourth Auditor of the Treasury, and Commander-in-Chief, in all matters relating to his department.

6. To draw all money for the fleet or squadron except in cases

of actual necessity when vessels are absent from the flag-ship, and to pay out the same on the requisitions of the different vessels duly approved by the Commander-in-Chief.

7. To make such recommendations to the Commander-in-Chief as will, in his opinion, tend to promote efficiency, uniformity, and economy in his department of the service.

8. And, finally, to perform such other duties relating to his position as shall be assigned to him by the Commander-in Chief.

All returns and requisitions made by the pay officers of the fleet or squadron are to pass through his hands, unless from his absence injury to the public service will ensue by delay.

SECTION 8.

Paymasters.

543....The Paymaster when ordered to a vessel will, in addition to the duties prescribed in the " Instructions for the government of Inspectors in charge of stores, Naval Storekeepers, Paymasters, and Assistant Paymasters," and in the "Rules in regard to the transaction of business at the office of the Fourth Auditor," carefully examine the bread-rooms, store-rooms and issue-room, and report immediately to the Commanding Officer any defect in their arrangement or construction that he may discover.

544....He will make requisitions for money, and for such provisions, clothing, small stores, and other articles as may be needed ; but such requisitions are at all times to be subject to the approval of the Commanding Officer of the vessel, and the revision and approval of the senior officer present in command.

545....When he shall present a requisition for money, for the approval of his Commanding Officer, or such Commanding Officer shall direct him to prepare a requisition for his approval, the Paymaster shall present a statement of the amount of public money then in his possession ; and the Commanding Officer shall not direct or approve a requisition for a larger sum than may appear to be necessary for the public interests, in addition to such unexpended balance as may have been reported already on hand.

546....If a requisition of a Paymaster for money require the approval of an officer superior or senior to his immediate Commanding Officer, it is hereby made the duty of such superior or senior to exact of the Commanding Officer of the vessel or navy yard to which the Paymaster may belong, a written statement of the amount of money reported to be in the hands of the Paymaster, and also specifying the particular objects and amounts under their appropriate heads of appropriation for which the money is wanted.

547....In all cases where a Paymaster shall have received, or shall have been duly authorized or directed to pay over, any public money without the previous knowledge or sanction of his immediate Commanding Officer, it shall be the duty of such Paymaster to report forthwith to his Commanding Officer the amount so received or paid, and the authority under which he acted.

548....No money which may be placed in charge of a Paymaster by order of, or authority from, his commanding or other superior officer, or of the Treasury or Navy Department, is to be used or paid away by him without the sanction or approval of either his immediate Commanding Officer, the Commander of the squadron or station to which he belongs, the Fourth Auditor of the Treasury, the Second Comptroller of the Treasury, or the Secretary of the Navy.

549....Whenever provisions or any other articles for which the Paymaster is responsible, are sent out of the vessel, he will procure from the Commander an order in writing, that proper account of and receipt for them may be taken.

550....He shall report to the Commanding Officer any articles which may be received in his department that he may think of improper quality, deficient in quantity, or requiring additional means for their preservation.

551....He shall make no changes upon the muster-roll of the vessel unless he shall receive information from the Commanding Officer of the promotion, resignation, dismissal, or death, or an order for the discharge, transfer, or change of rating, of any person borne upon it.

552....The accounts of men transferred will be made out in conformity to the regulations of the Treasury Department, and must accompany the men. They are to be sent by the Paymaster making the transfer to the Paymaster of the vessel, navy yard, or station to which the transfer is made, who will, after comparing them, receipt one copy and return it to the Paymaster who made the transfer, as a voucher for the settlement of his accounts. The transfer of accounts must in all cases be made through the Commanding Officers.

553....One copy of all bills or accounts is to be left with the officer who approves the same, to be transmitted to the department; but duplicates or triplicates of all such bills or accounts, after their approval by the proper officers, and payment by the Paymaster, are to be left in the possession of the Paymaster making the payment, as they are necessary vouchers for the settlement of his accounts, and for the safety of his sureties.

554....The Paymaster will only issue clothing and small stores and money to Petty Officers and persons of inferior ratings, in such quantities or sums, and at such times, as shall be directed in writing by the Commanding Officer; and all issues made shall be receipted for, or certified to, at the time, in the presence of a commission or warrant officer, and the receipts be witnessed or certified by him.

555....Whenever it is absolutely necessary upon foreign stations to purchase clothing, he shall take care that the articles be, as nearly as possible, of the same kind and quality as those furnished by the United States; and no more shall be purchased than shall be sufficient to meet the existing exigency.

556....When articles are furnished packed in bales, packages, or casks, for preservation, which cannot be opened without injury, they need not be opened to ascertain their contents, but the Paymaster will receipt for them according to their marks. And whenever they shall be opened it shall be in the presence of an officer, and their contents then compared with the invoice, and, if found to vary from it, a survey shall be held to authenticate the facts.

557....Articles of clothing which shall be found damaged by regular survey may be valued by the surveying officers, and issued by him in the same manner as other clothing, at the reduced prices fixed by the surveying officers.

Paymasters.

558....The messes of the ship's company may, with the approbation of the Commanding Officer, relinquish one complete ration in a mess of eight, and two in messes of not less than fourteen persons, for not less than three months, unless sooner detached, or unless their terms of service should expire in less than three months ; and they may receive the established value in money from the Paymaster when in port, at such times (not oftener than once a month) as the Commanding Officer may direct.

559....He shall not pay money to any person in debt to the United States, except for stopped rations.

560....He shall make no change in the daily allowance of provisions, except by the written order of the Commanding Officer.

561....He shall make monthly reports to the Commanding Officer of all expenditure of provisions, and quarterly reports of the expenditures of money, clothing, and small stores in his department, and of the quantity of each kind remaining on board, and the length of time for which there is a supply.

562....He shall draw and negotiate all bills of exchange, in conformity with such instructions as the Secretary of the Navy may give upon the subject.

563....He shall report quarterly, or oftener, if required, to the Commanding Officer of the vessel, the expiration of service of the men which will occur in each subsequent month in each rating, giving the number only in each rating.   (Form No. 20, Appendix)

564....Having received the effects of any officer, or other person who may have died, deserted, or been captured, together with an inventory of the same, he shall carefully preserve them until directed by the Commanding Officer to deliver them to the owner, his heirs, or representatives, or to sell by public auction the effects of deserters, or persons who may have died in debt to the United States.

565....When the stores on hand will admit of it, without an undue reduction of any article, he will, when ordered by the Commanding Officer, issue to officers' messes such articles of the public stores as they may require for their own use on board ship, at ration prices, whenever such articles bear exorbitant prices in the market, or cannot otherwise be obtained.

566....Whenever a Pay Agent shall be authorized to make advances of pay to officers bound on a cruise, it shall be the duty of the Paymaster of the vessel to furnish to such Agent, as his guide, a correct list, signed by himself and approved by the Commanding Officer, of all the officers entitled to an advance of pay, which list must exhibit their names, rank, and yearly pay.

567....Where there is no Pay Agent, travelling expenses incurred by an officer under an order of the Navy Department, or senior Commanding Officer, shall be paid by the Paymaster upon the order of the Commanding Officer of the station.

568....The Paymaster shall furnish clothing and small-stores to marines when embarked, upon a requisition signed by the Commanding Officer of the Marine Guard, and approved by the Commanding Officer of the vessel.

569....He will furnish to the Paymaster of the Marine Corps a statement of the account of any marine whose name is borne upon his books, who may die, desert, or be transferred to a shore station.

570....When attached to a receiving vessel, he shall receipt for all recruits considered fit for service, and certify that he has charged to them, respectively, the amounts rendered as advance by the Recruiting Officer.

571....He shall preserve as vouchers all orders given by Commanding Officers of receiving vessels to furnish clothing or small-stores to persons indebted to the United States.

SECTION 9.

Assistant Paymasters.

572....Assistant Paymasters, in the discharge of their duties, are to be governed by the Instructions to Paymasters.

SECTION 10.

Chaplains.

573....The Chaplain is to perform divine service and to offer prayers when duly requested by the Commanding Officer.

574....He is, with the consent of the senior Medical Officer, to visit the sick and afford them consolation.

575....He is to instruct in the principles of the Christian religion the boys and such other persons as the Commander of the vessel may commit to his care.

576....Should there be no schoolmaster on board, he is to apply to the Commanding Officer to detail an intelligent and well-disposed person of the crew to instruct, under his direction, the boys of the vessel, in reading, writing, and the elementary rules of arithmetic ; and he is frequently to examine the boys, and report from time to time to the Commanding Officer those whom he may find to be diligent and well-disposed, in order that they may be suitably encouraged and rewarded.

577....He is to make to his Commanding Officer, on the first of January, April, July, and October, a report of the duties performed by him during the previous three months, and also a condensed report of the kind at the end of the cruise.

Section 11.

Professors of Mathematics.

578....If ordered to duty on board ship, the Professor of Mathematics is carefully to attend to the tuition of the Midshipmen, should any be on board, and such others as may be placed under his instruction by the Commanding Officer, and will report weekly to the latter their attendance, proficiency, and conduct.

579....He shall present to the Commanding Officer, made up to the last days of March, June, September, and December, reports of the attendance and proficiency of those whom he has instructed, for transmission to the Secretary of the Navy.

Section 12.

Carpenters and Sailmakers.

580....The Carpenter and Sailmaker are to regard the general instructions contained in the paragraphs relating to Boatswains and Gunners as applicable to themselves.

Carpenters and Sailmakers.

581.... When the vessel is at sea, the Carpenter is every day, before half-past seven a m., and as much oftener as may be desirable, according to the service the ship is employed on, to examine the masts and yards, and to report to the Officer of the Deck their state.

582.... In ships of two or more decks, he is frequently to examine the lower deck ports, to see that they are properly lined; and when they are barred in, he is to see that they are all properly secured.

583.... He is to be particularly careful in keeping the pumps and hose in good order, always having at hand whatever may be necessary for their prompt and efficient use.

584.... He is to keep the boats, ladders, and gratings in as good condition as possible, always reporting to the Executive Officer every damage they may sustain as soon as he discovers it.

585.... He is to keep always ready, for immediate use, shot-plugs, and every other article necessary for stopping shot-holes and repairing other damage in battle.

586.... He is frequently to examine the sides and decks of the ship, and will report to the Executive Officer when caulking is required.

587.... When the ship is going into port, he is to prepare as correct an account as possible of the defects of the hull, masts, and yards of the ship, and the repairs she may stand in need of.

588.... The Sailmaker is, every day, before half-past seven a. m., and as much oftener as the service on which the ship is employed may render desirable, to examine the sails in use, and report to the Officer of the Deck their condition.

589.... Before the sails are received on board, he is to examine them carefully, and report to the Executive Officer, should he discover any defects   He is to examine the sail-rooms frequently, to see that the sails are kept perfectly dry and free from vermin. He is to keep the sails properly tallied, and so stowed that he may be able to find easily any one wanted. When sails are to be landed, he is to see that they are dry, well made up, and tallied.

ARTICLE VIII.

PETTY OFFICERS AND CREW.

SECTION 1.

Yeomen.

590....The Yeoman shall receipt and be responsible for all stores in the Boatswain's, Carpenter's, and Sailmaker's departments, and for all such in the Gunner's department as may be placed under his charge in the general store-room.

591....He shall see that all the regulations respecting lights in the store room are strictly observed, and that every precaution is taken to guard against fire or other accidents ; and must never suffer private stores of any kind to be kept in the store-room without written orders to that effect from the Commander.

592....He shall keep the accounts, according to the forms which are or may be prescribed, of all receipts, expenditures, conversions, or transfers of stores in the respective departments, specifying the time and place, and the person from whom the articles were received, and to whom and for what purpose they were delivered, and, if converted to other purposes than those for which they were received, by whose order.

593... He shall present the accounts of receipts and expenditures weekly to the Executive Officer of the vessel for examination.

594....He shall exhibit the abstract expense-books to the Commanding Officer within the first week of each month, that he may cause the same to be compared with his own, and, if found correct, the Commander shall approve the same, as a voucher for the Yeoman's accounts.

595....He shall, when a ship is to be paid off, or placed in ordinary, present to the Commander his expense-books, to be returned into the Navy store, and an abstract statement of the total quantities of the respective articles which may have been received and expended in each year during the cruise, and which may then remain on hand, or have been returned into store, as shown by his expense-books; and the Commander shall forward the same to the proper bureaus of the Navy Department, and shall state whether the quantities reported by the Yeoman's expense-books correspond with the quantities actually on hand, or returned into store, as ascertained by survey; and, if there should be any difference, he will note the same; and, if in his power, will state the probable cause of such difference.

596 . . . . Unless ordered by the Secretary of the Navy, the Yeoman shall not receive more than three-fourths of his pay until the stores in his charge shall have been examined and found correct.

Section 2.

Masters-at-Arms.

597 . . . . The Master-at-Arms, being the Chief of Police, must exercise a strict surveillance over the conduct of the crew, particularly when upon the berth-deck. When there is no officer in charge of the berth deck, he will be considered in charge, and must be obeyed accordingly; he will superintend the berth deck messes, maintain order and cleanliness, and report to the Officer of the Deck any violation of the regulations which may come to his knowledge; he will see the mess-bills made out on the last day of each month.

598 . . . . He is to keep an account of the offences committed by, and punishments awarded to, Petty Officers and persons of inferior ratings, and, at 9 a. m. daily, to furnish the Commanding Officer with a report of persons confined for misconduct, stating their offences, manner, and date of confinement.

599 . . . . In case of fire, of going into action, or of any sudden danger, he shall release any of the crew who may be confined, and will instantly report to the Executive Officer that they are so released.

600 . . . . He is to see the hold and all store-rooms locked at the appointed hour, and that no lights are left therein; and, on returning the keys, to report the same to the Executive Officer.

601 . . . . He is to see that all fires, and the officers' and ship's company's lights are extinguished at the proper hour; and that during the night no lights are permitted, except those authorized by the Commanding Officer.

602.... He, together with the Ship's Corporals, will be particularly vigilant in preventing the smuggling of liquor into the ship, and in examining boats or lighters to ascertain that no improper articles are either brought on board or carried away from the ship, and that none of the crew leave the vessel in them without due authority.

603.... When the magazine is about to be opened, he is to see that all required fires and lights are properly extinguished, and to report them so to the Officer of the Deck; and, at the same time, he is to notify the Marine Officer in charge of the guard that the magazine is about to be opened, so that the necessary directions may be given to sentinels to prevent the use of improper fires or lights until it is closed.

604.... He is, at all general musters of the crew, to account for absentees as their names are called.

605.... Immediately upon the death, desertion, or capture of any of the crew, he will secure all their property, and, after the inventories are made out, deliver the same to the Paymaster; and, should any of the crew absent themselves without leave, he will take charge of their effects, till otherwise ordered by superior authority.

606.... Ship's Corporals are to be subordinate to the Master-at-Arms, and assist him in the performance of his duties. In the absence of the Master-at-Arms, the senior is to discharge his duties.

SECTION 3.

Petty Officers Generally.

607.... The Petty Officers are required to exhibit a good example of subordination, alacrity, and cleanliness, and to aid their superiors to the utmost of their ability in maintaining order and discipline.

608.... They will be allowed such indulgence as the duties of the ship, and the nature of the service upon which she is engaged, in the judgment of the Commanding Officer, will permit.

SECTION 4.

Persons Inferior in Rating to the Petty Officers.

609.... All other persons composing the crew are hereby enjoined to yield, on all occasions, a willing, cheerful, and prompt obedience to those placed over them; to be especially attentive to their stations and the instructions they may receive; to avoid difficulties with each other, and departures from regulations; to be always tidy about their. persons and effects; and, in a word, to contribute all in their power to promote order and harmony.

ARTICLE IX.

PRESERVATION AND SAFETY OF THE VESSEL.

Section 1.

The Commander.

610.... The Commanding Officer will ascertain that the spare spars, sails, tiller, and other spare articles of importance, are of the proper size and ready for use.

611.... He shall never allow the vessel under his command to be left without one of the three, and in roadsteads or exposed situations, one of the two, senior officers, including himself; nor shall he grant leave of absence to any officer at any time when it will interfere with exercise, or otherwise retard the public interests, or render it necessary to place the deck in charge of an officer inferior in rank to those designated for the purpose. Unless in cases of absolute necessity, the charge of the deck is not to be intrusted to any other officer than one of those to whom it is regularly given.

612.... On approaching land or anchorage of any kind, he shall be careful to have the cables bent in due time.

613.... When going into any port or harbor, or approaching shoals or rocks, whether with or without a pilot, he shall cause regular soundings to be taken; and he shall have the leads frequently used whenever the vessel is on soundings.

614.... Upon all occasions of anchoring he is, if possible, to select a safe berth, and have the depth of the water and the quality of the ground examined for at least three cables' length around his vessel, in places that are not known, or where he is a stranger, and have such bearings and angles noted in the log-book as shall enable him to recover an anchor in case it should be necessary to slip a cable.

615 .... He will cause the chain cables to be carefully guarded against corrosion, and have them inspected once a quarter.

616 .... He shall take care that the lightning conductors are kept at all times ready for service, and that the wire boarding-netting of his ship is always in the most serviceable condition.

617 .... He shall see that the meteorological observations are taken and recorded as per form in log-book ; and on indications of the approach of gales or hurricanes, he shall cause hourly, or more frequent, observations of the barometer and sympiesometer to be made, and every change in the force and direction of the wind recorded.

618 .... He is to take every precaution against fire, and to establish general regulations for the duties to be performed by the officers and men, should one occur. He is not to allow lights to be used on the orlops, or in the holds or store-rooms, except in safe lanterns ; nor lights to be kept in officers' state-rooms, except the officer himself is present ; nor are friction matches, or any other substance or liquid, susceptible of easy or spontaneous ignition, to be on board in the private possession of any one. He is never, on any pretence, to allow varnishes or any inflammable liquid to be drawn off from any package or cask anywhere, but on the gun-deck, by daylight.

619 .... He will not permit smoking in the ward-room, steerages, cockpit, or any part of the berth deck; but he will designate such places for smoking as will be best for the comfort of the officers and crew, having due regard to the safety of the vessel and her discipline.

620 .... He will permit a lighted lantern to be hung up in a suitable place during meal hours, and after evening quarters until tattoo, or the setting of the watch, from which pipes or cigars may be lighted. No pipes or cigars shall be lighted at the galley or on the berth deck.

621 .... He shall cause all lights and fires, other than the lights in light rooms, to be extinguished whenever it is necessary to receive or discharge powder ; and all not absolutely necessary are to be extinguished whenever the magazine is opened for any general purpose. On all occasions of handling or passing powder the utmost precautions are to be taken to guard against accidents.

622 .... The magazine is never to be opened without the knowledge and consent of the Commanding Officer for the time being.

623....He will be careful that the vessel is kept well caulked, particularly about the bitts, water-ways, and other parts liable to be strained. He will cause this work to be done as far as practicable, by the carpenters and caulkers of the vessel.

624....He shall keep a night order book, in which shall be entered all orders given to the officer of the deck for his government during the night.

625....If, while sailing in squadron, he shall find that the course directed to be steered is leading the ship under his command or any other ship into danger, he will give notice to the Commander-in-Chief and to the ship endangered.

626....When in command of an iron vessel, he will take every opportunity of examining the bottom of such vessel, and be very careful that the plates are cleaned and coated with preserving composition as often as may be necessary, or opportunity may offer for so doing ; and he is to see that no injury be done by corrosion to the rivets or other parts, and that no copper articles be allowed to rest on the bottom in contact with the iron.

627....He shall cause every "notice to mariners" that may appear during his cruise, and that contains, from an authentic source, any information relating to his cruising ground, whether with regard to errors of charts, to the discovery of new dangers, or to the condition or position of lights, buoys, or beacons, to be copied in a book kept for that purpose, and to be embodied on the chart to which the information contained in such "notice" relates. He shall also compare his list of charts with that of every other public vessel, more recently from the United States, with which he may meet, for the purpose of procuring copies, tracings, or notes of any new charts or other hydrographical information that the latest publications may afford. At the end of the cruise such note books, tracings, copies, and memoranda must be returned by him to the Chief of the Bureau of Navigation.

SECTION 2.

Rules to Prevent Collisions.

628....From and after September, 1864, the following rules and regulations, for preventing collisions on the water, are to be strictly

Rules to Prevent Collisions.

observed in the Navy, with the understanding, however, that the exhibition of any light on board a vessel of the Navy may be suspended whenever, in the opinion of the Secretary of the Navy, the Commander-in-Chief of a squadron, the senior officer present, or the commander of a vessel acting singly, the special character of the service may require it—as in blockading, &c.

629....ARTICLE 1. Preliminary.

                Rules concerning lights.

      ARTICLE 2. Lights to be carried as follows.

      ARTICLE 3. Lights for steamships.

      ARTICLE 4. Lights for steam tugs.

      ARTICLE 5. Lights for sailing ships.

      ARTICLE 6. Exceptional lights for small sailing vessels.

      ARTICLE 7. Lights for ships at anchor.

      ARTICLE 8. Lights for pilot vessels.

      ARTICLE 9. Lights for fishing vessels and boats.

                Rules concerning fog-signals.

      ARTICLE 10. Fog-signals.

                Steering and sailing rules.

      ARTICLE 11. Two sailing ships meeting.

      ARTICLE 12. Two sailing ships crossing.

      ARTICLE 13. Two ships under steam meeting.

      ARTICLE 14. Two ships under steam crossing.

      ARTICLE 15. Sailing ship and ship under steam.

      ARTICLE 16. Ships under steam to slacken speed.

      ARTICLE 17. Vessels overtaking other vessels.

      ARTICLE 18. Construction of articles 12, 14, 15, and 17.

      ARTICLE 19. Proviso to save special cases.

      ARTICLE 20. No ship, under any circumstances, to neglect proper precautions.

630....ARTICLE 1. In the following rules every steamship which is under sail, and not under steam, is to be considered a sailing ship ; and every steamship which is under steam, whether under sail or not, is to be considered a ship under steam.

631....ARTICLE 2. The lights mentioned in the following articles, and no others, shall be carried in all weather between sunset and sunrise.

Rules to Prevent Collisions.

632....ARTICLE 3. All steam vessels when under way shall carry—

(*a*) At the foremost head a bright, white light, so fixed as to show an uniform and unbroken light over an arc of the horizon of twenty points of the compass, so fixed as to throw the light ten points on each side of the ship, viz: from right ahead to two points abaft the beam on either side, and of such a character as to be visible on a dark night, with a clear atmosphere, a distance of at least five miles.

(*b*) On the starboard side a green light, so constructed as to throw an uniform and unbroken light over an arc of the horizon of ten points of the compass, so fixed as to throw the light from right ahead to two points abaft the beam on the starboard side, and of such a character as to be visible on a dark night, with a clear atmosphere, at a distance of at least two miles.

(*c*) On the port side a red light, so constructed as to show an uniform, unbroken light over an arc of the horizon of ten points of the compass, so fixed as to throw the light from right ahead to two points abaft the beam on the port side, and of such a character as to be visible on a dark night, with a clear atmosphere, at a distance of at least two miles.

(*d*) The said green and red side lights shall be fitted with inboard screens, projecting at least three feet forward from the light, so as to prevent these lights from being seen across the bow.

633....ARTICLE 4. Steamships, when towing other ships, shall carry two bright, white masthead lights, vertically, in addition to their side lights, so as to distinguish them from other steamships. Each of these masthead lights shall be of the same construction and character as the masthead lights which other steamships are required to carry.

634....ARTICLE 5. Sailing ships under way, or being towed, shall carry the same lights as steamships under way, with the exception of the white masthead lights, which they shall never carry.

635....ARTICLE 6. Whenever, as in the case of small vessels during bad weather, the green and red lights cannot be fixed, these lights shall be kept on deck, on their respective sides of the vessel, ready for instant exhibition, and shall, on the approach of or to other vessels, be exhibited on their respective sides in sufficient time to prevent collision, in such manner as to make them most visible, and so that the green light shall not be seen on the port side, nor the red light on the starboard side.

Rules to Prevent Collisions.

To make the use of these portable lights more certain and easy, they shall each be painted outside with the color of the light they respectively contain, and shall be provided with suitable screens.

636....ARTICLE 7. Ships, whether steamships or sailing ships, when at anchor in roadsteads or fair-ways, shall, between sunset and sunrise, exhibit, where it can best be seen, but at a height not exceeding twenty feet above the hull, a white light in a globular lantern of eight inches in diameter, and so constructed as to show a clear, uniform, and unbroken light, visible all around the horizon, and at a distance of at least one mile.

637....ARTICLE 8. Sailing pilot vessels shall not carry the lights required for other sailing vessels, but shall carry a white light at the masthead, visible all around the horizon, and shall also exhibit a flare-up light every fifteen minutes.

638....ARTICLE 9. Open fishing boats and other open boats shall not be required to carry side lights required for other vessels, but shall, if they do not carry such lights, carry a lantern having a green slide on the one side and a red slide on the other side; and on the approach of or to other vessels, such lantern shall be exhibited in sufficient time to prevent collision, so that the green light shall not be seen on the port side, nor the red light on the starboard side. Fishing vessels and open boats when at anchor, or attached to their nets and stationary, shall exhibit a bright white light. Fishing vessels and open boats shall, however, not be prevented from using a flare-up in addition, if considered expedient.

639....ARTICLE 10. Whenever there is a fog, whether by day or night, the fog signals described below shall be carried and used, and shall be sounded at least every five minutes, viz:

(*a*) Steamships under way shall use a steam whistle, placed before the funnel, not less than eight feet from the deck.

(*b*) Sailing ships under way shall use a fog-horn.

(*c*) Steamships and sailing ships when not under way shall use a bell.

640....ARTICLE 11. If two sailing ships are meeting end on, or nearly end on, so as to involve risk of collision, the helms of both shall be put to port, so that each may pass on the port side of the other.

641....ARTICLE 12. When two sailing ships are crossing, so as to involve risk of collision, then, if they have the wind on different sides the ship with the wind on the port side shall keep out of the way of the ship with the wind on the starboard side, except in the case in which the ship with the wind on the port side is close-hauled, and the other ship free, in which case the latter ship shall keep out of the way. But if they have the wind on the same side, or if one of them has the wind aft, the ship which is to windward shall keep out of the way of the ship which is to leeward.

642....ARTICLE 13. If two ships under steam are meeting end on, or nearly end on, so as to involve risk of collision, the helms of both shall be put to port so that each may pass on the port side of the other.

643:...ARTICLE 14. If two ships under steam are crossing so as to involve risk of collision, the ship which has the other on her own starboard side shall keep out of the way of the other.

644....ARTICLE 15. If two ships, one of which is a sailing ship and the other a steamship, are proceeding in such directions as to involve risk of collision, the steamship shall keep out of the way of the sailing ship.

645....ARTICLE 16. Every steamship, when approaching another ship so as to involve risk of collision, shall slacken her speed, or if necessary stop and reverse; and every steamship shall, when in a fog, go at a moderate speed.

646....ARTICLE 17. Every vessel overtaking any other vessel shall keep out of the way of the said last-mentioned vessel.

648....ARTICLE 18. Where, by the above rules, one of two ships is to keep out of the way, the other shall keep her course, subject to the qualifications contained in the following article.

648....ARTICLE 19. In obeying and construing these rules due regard must be had to all dangers of navigation, and due regard must also be had to any special circumstances which may exist in any particular case, rendering a departure from the above rules necessary in order to avoid immediate danger.

649....ARTICLE 20. Nothing in these rules shall exonerate any ship, or the owner or master or crew thereof, from the consequences of any neglect to carry lights or signals, or of any neglect to keep a proper look out, or of the neglect of **any** precaution which may be required by the ordinary practice of seamen, or by the special circumstances of the case.

650....Should a collision unfortunately take place, each commanding officer is required to furnish the Department with the following information :

1st. His own report, that of the pilot, the officer of the deck, and other officers who witnessed the occurrence. These reports and statements are to be exemplified by a diagram, and must contain the courses steered, the point at which the vessel was first seen, the bearing, the time when the engine was slowed, when the vessel was stopped, whether in motion, and if so at what speed at the moment of collision, the direction of the wind, the condition of the weather and atmosphere, what lookouts were placed, what lights were exhibited by both vessels, whether either vessel deviated from the above rules and regulations, whether any blame can attach to any one, and if so to whom, and any and all other facts bearing upon the subject.

2d. Written statements and estimate of damage from officers of the vessel with which the vessel of the United States navy collided, if they can be obtained.

3d. Survey of the injury to both vessels by United States officers.

4th. If the vessel is in charge of a pilot, and the collision has occurred from his acting in violation of the above rules and regulations, the fact must be established in the report, and no pilotage paid to him.

ARTICLE X.

Preservation of the Crew.

651....As cleanliness, dryness, and pure air are essential to health, the Commanding Officer is to use his utmost endeavor to secure each in the greatest degree possible. Sea water is not to be admitted to the holds, the ship is always to be pumped dry, the pump-well frequently swabbed out and dried, and chloride of lime and whitewash used wherever it is practicable. He is to take care that there is a free passage fore and aft for water, and that those places where from the trim of the ship a lodgment may occur, be bailed and swabbed out

Preservation of the Crew.

frequently. In steam vessels, especially, he is to take care that every possible means be taken for the free circulation of air; that the bilges be frequently cleansed and whitewashed, and that all offensive matter be removed from the limbers. The man-hole plates of the coal-bunkers should be kept off during the day, whenever the state of the weather will permit.

652....He will personally inspect the vessel frequently, on which occasions he shall be accompanied by the Executive Officer, and shall satisfy himself that nothing has been neglected for the efficiency of the vessel or the health of the crew.

653....He shall cause the bedding and clothing of the crew to be inspected by the officers of divisions once a month, and the bedding and clothing aired and cleansed once a fortnight, when the weather will permit.

654....He shall not allow men to sleep about the deck in situations where they will be exposed to night dews or rains, to sleep in wet clothes or bedding, or to take them below the gun-deck, when it can be avoided.

655....He shall cause the crew to bathe or wash themselves daily, and when they are washing decks or scrubbing clothes or hammocks, he will direct that they take off their shoes and stockings and roll up their trowsers, unless the temperature of the water or air should be at or below 45° Fahrenheit.

656....He shall pay great attention to the suitable clothing of the men, obliging them to make such changes as, in the opinion of the Medical Officers and himself, will be most conducive to health, according to the changes of climate to which they may be subjected.

657....He shall take care that the boats' crews have their breakfasts before leaving the vessel, and their other meals at the usual times, except special duties shall prevent it.

658....He shall not allow the boats to be away from the ship after sunset, without his special permission.

659....He shall prevent all unnecessary exposure of those under his command.

660....He shall adopt suitable precautions to prevent the use o improper fruits or of other articles which may endanger the health of the crew.

661....Before water is received on board to be placed in the tanks or for present use, he will cause it to be tested by the senior Medical Officer, and will not permit any to be drunk which is impure.

662....Unless absolutely indispensable, the men are not to be placed on a daily allowance of water of less than one gallon.

663....When in port he may cause fresh meat and vegetables to be issued to the crew, not exceeding four days in the week, unless the Surgeon may recommend more frequent issue as necessary to their health.

664....He will require from the Surgeon a daily report of the state of the sick, and, whenever he may think proper, his opinion of the best means of preserving or restoring health.

665....When men are sent to the hospital, (which is not to be done without the sanction of the superior officer in command of the station, except in cases not admitting of delay,) they are to be accompanied by a Medical Officer, with a statement of the case, who is to see that the clothing and bedding of the men are carefully delivered to the proper officer of the hospital, with a complete list of the same.

666....Whenever sick or wounded men are sent from one vessel to another to be, on the arrival of the latter at her destined port, transferred to a naval hospital, the Commanding Officer of the former, will take especial care to make every necessary arrangement in his power for having them properly attended to while on board the vessel to which they are sent, and also for their being properly placed in the hospital on her arrival. If necessary to insure such attention, a suitable person will be sent in charge of them. Unless for urgent reasons, such sick or wounded men will be sent only in store or supply vessels, or other vessels of the Navy.

667....Men who may be sent to a hospital from a vessel in commission lying in the port where the hospital is located, are to be transferred to the receiving ship.

668....He shall give particular orders that the life-buoys are at all times ready to be dropped, and at sea, and in strong tide-ways in port, shall have men stationed by them. He shall cause them to be examined every evening by the gunner, and their condition reported to the Executive Officer. The quarter boats are to be kept in condition to be immediately lowered, with a crew for each in each watch, in charge of a petty officer.

Stores and Outfits.

669....He shall not expose the lives of the men by setting them to do unnecessary work outside the ship at sea or in strong tide-ways. When necessary to employ them outside, every precaution shall be taken to rescue them in case of falling overboard.

ARTICLE XI.

Stores and Outfits.

670....The Commander of a vessel, when she is first equipped, shall be furnished by the Commandant of the yard with inventories of all the articles belonging to the different departments; and he is thereafter to cause accurate accounts to be kept of all expenses incurred for the vessel in the different departments, and shall make quarterly returns to the Commander of the division, squadron, or fleet, embracing a complete abstract of the expenditure of stores in the Master's, Boatswain's, Gunner's, Carpenter's, and Sailmaker's departments, which the latter will investigate and forward to the Bureaus to which they belong, with his remarks thereon.

671....He shall examine all the returns of expenditures, all requisitions for supplies, all accounts rendered against the vessel, and, on being satisfied of their correctness, shall approve the same.

672....In making or approving requisitions for stores of any kind he will, unless otherwise specially authorized, only require or approve for the articles which may be necessary to complete such quantities as are or may be established as the allowance for the vessel or specially authorized, and the requisition must state that it is so made.

673....He shall use the utmost economy and care in everything which relates to the expenses of the vessel or the public service, and shall require from all those under his command a rigid compliance with the regulations for the receipt, conversion, and expenditure of stores of every description.

674....He shall not land any articles of outfit or stores with which the vessel may be supplied, unless the Commander-in-Chief of the squadron should so order, and he shall, before he leaves a foreign station, take on board any articles so landed, unless otherwise directed.

675....When a vessel is ordered to be placed in ordinary, he shall, unless otherwise directed, after a survey shall be made upon the different articles, cause all the stores to be tallied, and properly marked and safely delivered to the proper officers of the Navy Yard.

676....Should a cable be slipped or parted, the Commander of the vessel, or, if he cannot, the senior officer present, shall use every exertion possible to recover the lost part and anchor ; but, should neither have an opportunity so to do, then information of the fact must at once be forwarded to the Navy Department, or to the nearest public agent of the United States, whichever course may best lead to a prompt recovery.

677....When the ship is paid off or placed in ordinary, he shall require from the Yeoman and officers charged with stores an abstract statement of the receipts and expenditures of stores during each fiscal year, and the total quantity during the cruise ; and shall, under this abstract, enter the quantities remaining on hand, as shown by the general abstract expense book.   If the remaining stores shall be landed, or can be surveyed before he leaves the ship, the quantities actually landed, or found to be on hand by survey, shall also be stated under the quantities as shown by the abstract expense book ; and if any differences shall be found to exist, he shall have inquiry made as to the cause, and note the result upon the report and forward the same to the Navy Department.   If the Commander should be detached and the ship delivered over before the stores are landed or surveyed, he will sign and transmit to the Commanding Officer of the Navy Yard the required abstract of receipts and expenditures during the cruise and the quantities on hand, as shown by the expense books.

ARTICLE XII.

Apartments and Messes.

678....Apartments to be occupied by officers of different grades will be arranged on such decks of a vessel of such size and in such way as the Navy Department may direct ; and the officers of a vessel are to mess in the apartments provided for them for the purpose, and none are to be permitted to mess elsewhere on board, except as hereafter

Apartments and Messes.

provided for; nor shall separate messes be formed in the same apartment. Cabin officers in ships with two cabins, if they prefer it, may form one mess. A Commander-in-Chief may have the Fleet Lieutenant and Secretary, or either of them, in his mess, and a Commanding Officer may have his clerk; but in such cases, those officers shall be accommodated permanently in the cabin, and shall not occupy the apartments provided for them elsewhere on board.

679....A Commander-in-Chief, a Commander of a squadron or division, a Commodore, a Commanding Officer of the vessel, a Fleet Captain, or any Captain or Commander doing duty on board, is to be regarded as a cabin officer, and as entitled to mess therein, and also accommodated in other respects agreeably to these instructions.

680....A Lieutenant Commander, when the Executive Officer, or when a passenger on board a vessel commanded by an officer of higher grade than his own, a Lieutenant, a Master, an Ensign, a Surgeon, a Paymaster, a Chief Engineer, or an Engineer of any grade when placed on board to take charge of engines, an Assistant Surgeon, whether passed or otherwise; an Assistant Paymaster, a Marine Officer, a Secretary to a Commander-in-Chief, or to the Commander of a squadron or division, a Chaplain, or a Professor of Mathematics, is to be regarded as a ward-room officer, and as entitled to mess therein, to occupy it in common with his messmates, and to have the state-room connected therewith prescribed for his own accommodation, if any such there be.

681....An Assistant Engineer of any grade, when not placed on board, to be in charge of engines; a Midshipman, a Master's mate, when warranted, or when not warranted, if judged expedient by the Navy Department, or the Commander of a fleet or squadron, a clerk to a Commanding Officer, or a clerk to a Paymaster, is to be regarded as a Steerage Officer, and as entitled to mess and be otherwise accommodated therein. Assistant Engineers are to mess in the port steerage, and the other Steerage Officers in the starboard steerage. In a sailing vessel the Steerage Officers may, if expedient, be divided as equally as necessary into two messes, one to occupy the port and the other the starboard steerage.

682....A boatswain, a gunner, a carpenter, or a sailmaker, is to be regarded as a Forward Officer, and as entitled to mess in the place

Apartments and Messes.

allotted on the berth deck, and to occupy the apartment arranged for his accommodation.

683....Officers as passengers are to mess with those with whom they are associated above as to the occupation of apartments; but no such officer is to be entitled to the accommodation of a state-room to the exclusion of any officer regularly attached to the vessel who is entitled to such accommodation.

684....The Commander-in-Chief or Commanding Officer of a squadron or division, when embarked, shall be entitled, where there are two cabins on different decks, to select one of them as the apartment to be occupied by himself; and the other is to be occupied by the Commanding Officer of the vessel, Fleet Captain, and such passengers as are cabin officers.

685....The Commanding Officer of a vessel, where there is no Commander-in-Chief or Commanding Officer of a squadron or division embarked on board, and where there are two cabins on different decks, shall be entitled to select one of them as the apartment to be occupied by himself, and where there is but one cabin provided, he is to occupy it.

686....In case of there being but one cabin to a vessel having on board a Commander-in-Chief, or Commander of a division or squadron, the officer commanding her shall be entitled to one-third of the space allotted for the cabin apartment, divided off by a fore and aft bulkhead, provided such space is sufficient for the purpose, without interfering with efficiency and comfort.

687....When one of the two cabins on different decks of a vessel is vacant, and, in the judgment of her Commanding Officer, not required for other public purposes, he may permit its state-rooms to be occupied by the ward-room officers in accordance with their rank, that is to say, those on the starboard side by the line officers, and those on the port side by the Staff Officers, with the exception, however, of the senior Engineer, who, from the nature of his duties, is not to quit his regular state-room to occupy any other.

688....A Fleet Captain or principal aid to a Rear-Admiral appointed as a Commander-in-Chief of a fleet or squadron, serving on board a vessel provided with two cabins on different decks, is to mess with her

Apartments and Messes.

Commanding Officer, and be otherwise accommodated in the same cabin in which they are to mess. If there be two state-rooms in it, said Commanding Officer is to have the first choice, and the Fleet Captain the second choice with regard to them. And in any arrangement of cabin accommodations whereby there may be two state-rooms in the apartment assigned to the Commanding Officer of the vessel, the Fleet Captain shall be entitled to occupy one of them; but in other cases, although always entitled to mess with such Commanding Officer, he will be accommodated in the cabin assigned to the Commander-in-Chief.

689.... When no other arrangement is prescribed or feasible, the Commander-in-Chief, Commanding Officer of the vessel, and Fleet Captain are to occupy the cabin jointly, the choice of accommodations to be made in the order in which they are here mentioned.

690.... The state-rooms of ward-rooms as ordinarily arranged on board ships of our Navy are appropriated to the proper officers by paragraphs 30 and 31; but in those ships where the ward-rooms are forward of the berth deck, while the respective sides appropriated to line and staff officers remain as provided in the above referred to paragraph, the relative positions of the state-rooms of the different officers are to be reversed, so that the Executive Officer will occupy the after state-room, and the other line officers will come next to him according to rank; a similar change of position, from forward to aft, will take place in the state-rooms of Staff Officers, on the port side of the ward-room.

691.... In all vessels of the first class, and in those of the second class having a covered gun deck, the Boatswain and Gunner will each have a separate room on the starboard side, forward of the steerage, and the carpenter and sailmaker will also each have a separate room on the port side; but in vessels below the above, the Boatswain and Gunner will occupy one room jointly, fitted with two berths, on the starboard side, and the carpenter and sailmaker a similar room on the port side.

692.... State-rooms in the cock-pit, or on the orlop or berth deck of a vessel, remaining vacant, are to be assigned by the Commanding Officer to such officers entitled to the accommodation of rooms as have not been provided with them, agreeably to their rank or seniority, giving preference, in all cases, to the watch officers, in the regular order of rank.

---

693 .... In all messes of officers the senior Line Officer shall preside, and the senior Line Officer present will be held responsible for the order and decorum of the mess. In messes of engineers the senior one shall preside, and the senior one present will be held responsible for the order and decorum of the mess.

694 .... Wines, ales, and other liquors not prohibted by law on board vessels of the Navy, shall be regarded as private stores, belonging to individuals only, and shall not be brought on board without the sanction of the Commanding Officer. In no case shall they form a part of the outfit or stores of any mess, and no member thereof shall be required to pay any share towards their purchase.

695 .... Petty Officers will be messed by themselves, and shall not be required to perform the duty of mess cooks.

696 .... The boys will be distributed amongst the messes, but shall be berthed by themselves, under the charge of the schoolmaster or one of the Petty Officers.

ARTICLE XIII.

Naval Transports.

697 .... Unless otherwise specially directed by the President, officers of the Army, when ordered to take passage in vessels-of-war, shall, if of the rank of General Officers, live with the Commander of the squadron, if one is embarked in the same vessel; otherwise, such General Officers, and all Field Officers by commission, in their respective corps or regiments, shall live in the apartments of the Captain or Commanding Officer of such vessel; and all other officers of regiments, or corps, with the Lieutenants or Wardroom Officers of the Navy, or with those having the same designation, or who perform similar duties, but without interfering with the sleeping-apartments of the Navy Officers.

698 .... When officers of the Army are embarked, with troops, in a transport or troop-ship commanded and officered by Navy Officers, the Navy Officers shall occupy the same apartments which they usually occupy when employed on other service, and separate accommodations shall be provided for the special use of the officers of the Army and those under their command.

Naval Transports....Convoys.

699.... Officers of the Army ordered for passage in ships-of-war may mess separately from the officers of the Navy, in which case a mess-place will be assigned to them ; or, by mutual agreement or order of the Department, may mess with the officers with whom they are authorized to live, they paying their proportion of mess expenses.

700.... Officers of the Army embarked with troops in Navy transports, or in troop-ships, shall mess together, and separately from the Officers of the Navy, unless otherwise mutually agreed upon with the sanction of the Commanding Officer of the vessel and of the troops.

701.... When any part of the Army, volunteers or militia, of the United States shall be embarked in any vessel of the Navy for *duty* therein, they shall, until they are regularly detached therefrom, be subject to the laws for the government of the Navy, and to the regulations of police for the vessel, in the same manner and to the same extent as marines when they form a part of the complement of a vessel.

702.... Whenever any part of the Army, volunteers or militia, of the United States shall be embarked on board any vessel of the Navy for transportation only, they shall not be subject to the laws and regulations for the government of the Navy, but to the laws for the government of the Army ; but they shall, nevertheless, be subject and conform to the internal regulations of the vessel in which they may be embarked, upon pain of confinement by the Commander of such vessel while on board, and of such punishment as an army court-martial may direct, after they shall have been landed.

703.... No army courts-martial shall be held on board any vessel in the Navy when in commission, nor shall army, volunteer, or militia officers order any public punishment or confinement in irons to be inflicted on board such vessel, without the previous approval of the Commanding Officer of such vessel.

ARTICLE XIV.

Convoys.

704.... The Commanding Officer of a vessel ordered to afford convoy to merchant vessels, is to arrange with their masters such signals as

Convoys.

will enable him to regulate movements, and them to communicate wants ; and he will give them in writing, or in print, such directions for their government as may be necessary for their protection. Should it be expedient to provide them with secret instructions or signals, he will enjoin upon each master not to inform any person of the same, and not to allow an enemy, in the event of capture, to become possessed of the same.

705....He shall take a list of the names of the vessels under his convoy, specifying their rig, the places to which they belong and are bound, the date of their joining, and the names of their masters, owners, and supercargoes, a copy of which he is to transmit to the Secretary of the Navy ; and on his arrival in port he is to send another list to the Secretary of the Navy, setting forth the names, &c., of the vessels that arrived with him, and of those that did not so arrive, mentioning, with regard to the latter, the time and supposed cause of their separation.

706....Before taking under his convoy a vessel bound to a belligerent port, he shall require satisfactory proof that there are no articles of contraband on board ; and without such proof he is not to take her under his convoy, or afford her protection *en route* against a belligerent claim, unless specially directed.

707....An officer charged with a convoy must be very vigilant in guarding against attack or surprise, and if attacked he must defend it. He must never weaken the convoying force by detaching a part of it to go in chase beyond signal distance, nor must he himself separate from the convoy, unless such course would be the means of preserving it from an enemy.

708....He shall adopt all possible measures to prevent the separation of the convoy, and may direct such vessels to repeat his signals as he may deem proper.

709....He will make report to the Secretary of the Navy of the name of any vessel, and of the master, who shall disobey the instructions or signals for the convoy, or leave the convoy without permission, or otherwise misbehave, stating the particulars of his misconduct, so that insurance offices may be informed of the same.

710....Whenever the master of any vessel under convoy shall wilfully or repeatedly neglect or refuse to conform to the instructions

Convoys.

or signals of the Commanding Officer of the convoying force, the said Commanding Officer may refuse him any further protection, and be released from any further responsibility for the safety of the vessel.

711....When different convoys shall sail at the same time, or shall meet at sea, they shall sail together as long as their course shall be in the same direction ; but the different convoys shall be kept as distinct from each other as circumstances will allow.

712....While two convoys continue together, the senior Officer commands the whole ; and the vessels of the convoying forces will wear different distinguishing flags, for the information of the respective convoys.

713....The Commanding Officer is enjoined not to receive, or suffer any person under his authority to receive, under any pretence, any fee, reward, or gratuity, from any owner or master, or other person, for the protection afforded.

714....Vessels-of-war of the United States are not to take under their convoy the vessels of any power at war with another with which the United States is at peace, nor the vessels of a neutral power, unless specially ordered so to do, or some very particular circumstances should occur to render it expedient and proper, of which they are to advise the Navy Department at the earliest possible moment.

715....The Commanding Officer of a vessel of the Navy, about to sail from a foreign port during war, or when it is probable that war will soon occur, is, if the nature of the orders under which he is acting will permit, to give timely information to the merchant vessels of the United States lying therein of the day of his intended departure, and to take under his protection all such bound the same way as may be desirous and ready to accompany him ; and he is also to take under his protection any other vessels of the United States that he may fall in with on the passage, which may desire it, and conduct them in safety as far as his course and theirs are the same.

716....No lights are to be carried at night by either the public or private vessels of a convoy, except by the authority of the officer who may command it. If he directs any one or more of these vessels to carry one or more of them, they are to do so.

717....The Commanding Officer of a convoy is not to permit the vessels under his protection to be searched or detained by any belligerent or other cruiser.

ARTICLE XV.

Prizes, or Vessels Seized as Such, and Prisoners.

718....The attention of Commanding Officers of the Navy is particularly called to the laws in relation to captured vessels.

719....When a vessel shall be seized as a prize, it shall be the duty of the Commander of the vessel making the capture, to cause all the hatches and passages leading to the cargo to be secured and sealed, except such as may be indispensably necessary for the use of the persons on board and for the management of the vessel. The log-book, and all papers relating to the vessel and cargo, shall also be sealed up, and placed in charge of the prize-master, for delivery with the vessel and cargo.

720....Should it be absolutely necessary to take out of a vessel seized as a prize any property, either for its better preservation or for the use of vessels or armed forces of the United States, a correct inventory shall be made of it, and also a careful appraisement of its value, by suitable officers, qualified to judge of such value. This inventory and appraisement shall be made in duplicate, one part of which shall be transmitted to the Secretary of the Navy, and the other to the judge or United States attorney of the district to which the prize may be sent.

721....If, from unavoidable circumstances, it should become necessary to sell any portion of the captured property, a full report of the facts shall be made to the United States attorney or judge of the district into which the prize is sent, and any proceeds of sale shall be held subject to the order of the district court.

722....The prize-master will vigilantly guard the captured or seized property intrusted to his care from spoliation and theft, such offences leading to a forfeiture of the prize-money, and such other punishment as a prize court may inflict, both of the crew and the prize-master.

723....The Commanding Officer of any vessel of the Navy making a capture, shall report to the Navy Department all the material facts attending it ; and shall in this report, and also in his report to the

Prizes, or Vessels Seized as Such, and Prisoners.

United States district judge, state the names of all vessels within signal distance at the time, together with all the circumstances of their position, so far as he may be cognizant of them.

724....The Commanding Officers of all vessels claiming to share in a prize shall cause the prize list, which they are required by law to transmit to the Navy Department, to exhibit not only the name and rank, or rating, but also the rate of annual or monthly pay of each person borne on the books at the time of the capture to which the list refers. They shall also, in all cases, forward a statement of their claims, with the grounds upon which they are based, to the Department, and to the judge of the district to which the prize was sent.

725....On forwarding prize lists to the Department, they will see that a note is made against the name of any person who may come under the seventh section of the act approved February 24th, 1864, for enrolling and calling out the national forces.

726....The law requires that the master of the captured or seized vessel shall be sent in, his evidence being considered primary; and as many of the officers and crew of the captured or seized vessel as can properly be taken care of should be sent forward, in custody of the prize master, who will report, immediately on his arrival, to the United States Attorney, as well as to the Department. The mate and supercargo, next to the master, are the most important witnesses before a prize court, and should always be sent with the captured or seized vessel, or carried into the port to which she may be sent for adjudication, without delay.

727....Although in time of war the Commander of a vessel is to exercise constant vigilance to prevent supplies of arms, munitions, and contraband articles being conveyed to the enemy, yet under no circumstances is he to seize any vessel within the waters of a friendly nation.

728....A Commanding Officer in time of war is to diligently exercise the right of visitation and search on all suspected vessels, yet in no case is he authorized to chase and fire at a vessel without showing any colors and giving her the customary preliminary notice of a desire to speak and visit her; *i. e.*, first, a blank cartridge shall be fired; second, a shotted gun, aimed so as not to hit; third, a shot fired at the vessel; nor is he to chase or fire at any such vessel, or commit acts of hostility or of authority within a marine league of any foreign country with which we are at peace.

729....When such a visit shall be made, the vessel, if neutral, is not then to be seized without a search carefully made, so far as to render it reasonable to believe that she is engaged in carrying contraband of war for or to the enemy, and to his ports, directly or indirectly; or unless she is attempting to violate a blockade established by the United States. If, after visitation and search, it shall appear to the satisfaction of the commanding officer that the vessel is in good faith and without contraband actually bound and passing from one friendly or neutral point to another, and not bound or proceeding to or from a port in the possession of the enemy, then she cannot be lawfully seized. It shall be the duty of the officer making the search to indorse upon the ship's register or license the fact of the visit, the nature of the search, by what vessel made, the name of her Commander, the latitude and longitude, the time of detention, and when released.

, 730....In order to avoid difficulty and error in relation to papers found on board a neutral vessel that may have been seized, the commanding officer will take care that official seals, or fastenings of foreign authorities, are in no case, nor on any pretext, to be broken, or parcels covered by them read by any naval authorities ; but all bags or other things covering such parcels, and duly sealed or fastened by foreign authorities, will be remitted to the prize court.

731....If information should be received by a Commanding Officer that a suspicious vessel has come, or intends to come, within the limits of his prescribed cruising ground, he will not be authorized to depart from the usual practice in regard to visitation, search, or capture, but shall, in the event of falling in with her, proceed in all respects as provided for in paragraphs No. 728 and 729.

732....The officers and crew of a neutral vessel seized are by no means to be confined either in irons or otherwise, except by detention on board, unless by their own conduct they should render such restraint necessary. Their personal property is to be respected, and a full and proper allowance of provisions is to be.distributed to them. If any cruelty or unnecessary force is used towards such crew, a prize court will decree damages to the injured parties.

Prizes, or Vessels Seized as Such, and Prisoners.

733....A neutral vessel seized is to wear the flag of her own country until she is adjudged to be a lawful prize by a competent court. The flag of the United States, however, may be exhibited at the fore, when necessary, to indicate that she is, for the time, in the possession of officers of the United States.

734....The form of a letter of instructions to be given to prize masters, to be observed by Commanding Officers, will be found in the Appendix, No. 15.

735....The Navigator, or other officer, or prize master, in whose charge instruments are placed, or the prize master to whom arms are intrusted, will be held strictly accountable for their condition, and in case of loss or damage, by neglect or any other cause not satisfactorily explained, the value will be charged to his account. The officer appointing a prize master will require to give a receipt in duplicate for the instruments and arms with which he may be furnished, one of the same to be forwarded to the Commanding Officer of the station to which the prize vessel is bound, and the other to be retained by such appointing officer; and in case of any deficiency in the delivery of these instruments and arms, or of any palpable abuse, the Commanding Officer of the station will at once have the matter investigated, and report the result to the proper bureau of the Navy Department.

736....Prisoners of war are to be treated with humanity; their personal property shall be carefully protected; they shall have a proper allowance of provisions, and every comfort of air and exercise which circumstances admit of, shall be allowed them. Every precaution must be taken to prevent any hostile attempt on their part, and if necessary or expedient, they may be ironed or closely confined. If officers consent to give their parole not to attempt any hostile act on board the vessel, and to conform to such requirements as the Commanding Officer may consider necessary, they may be permitted such privileges of quarters and of the deck as he may deem proper.

737....If any vessel shall be taken acting as a vessel of war, or a privateer, without having a proper commission so to act, the officers and crew shall be considered as pirates and treated accordingly.

738....When a vessel is detailed to act in the suppression of the slave

9

---

trade, her Commanding Officer, if acting singly, will be furnished by the Department with the necessary instructions, slave trade papers, &c., but if acting otherwise, by the Commander-in Chief of the squadron.

ARTICLE XVI.

PAROLING AND FLAGS OF TRUCE.

Section 1.

Paroling.

739....Paroling must always take place by the interchange of signed duplicates of a written document, in which the names and rank of the persons paroled are correctly and distinctly stated. Any one who intentionally misstates his rank forfeits the benefit of his parole, and is liable to punishment.

740....None but Commissioned Officers can give the parole for themselves and their command, and no inferior officer can give a parole without the authority of his superior, if within reach.

741....No paroling of entire bodies of men after a battle or capture, and no dismissal of large numbers of prisoners with a general declaration that they are paroled, is permitted, or will be considered of any value.

742....An officer who shall give a parole for himself or his command without referring to his superior, when it is in his power to do so, will be considered as giving "aid and comfort to the enemy," and may be considered as a deserter, and be punished accordingly.

743....For the officer the pledging of his parole is an individual act, and no wholesale paroling by an officer for a number of inferiors in rank, in violation of paragraph No. 739, is permitted or will be considered valid.

744....No Non-commissioned or Warranted Officer, or seaman, or private marine, or other person belonging to the Navy, can give his parole except through a Commissioned Officer. Individual paroles not given through an officer are not only void, but make the individuals giving them amenable to punishment as deserters. The only admissable exception is when individuals, properly separated from their commanders, have suffered long confinement without the possibility of being paroled through an officer.

745....No prisoner of war can be forced by the hostile government to pledge his parole, and any threats or ill-treatment to force the giving of the parole is contrary to the law of war.

746....No prisoner of war can enter into engagements inconsistent with his character and duties as a citizen and a subject of his state. He can only bind himself not to bear arms against his captor for a limited period, or until he is exchanged, and this only with the stipulated or implied consent of his own government. If the engagement which he makes is not approved by his government, he is bound to return and surrender himself as a prisoner of war. His own government cannot, at the same time, disown his engagement and refuse his return as a prisoner.

747....No one can pledge his parole that he will never bear arms against the government of his captors, nor that he will not bear arms against any other enemy of his government not at the time the ally of his captors. Such agreements have reference only to the existing enemy and his existing allies, and the existing war, and not to future belligerents.

748.... While the pledging of the military parole is a voluntary act of the individual, the capturing power is not obliged to grant it.

749....Paroles not authorized by the common law of war are not valid until approved by the government of the individual so pledging his parole.

750....The pledging of any unauthorized military parole is a miliary offence, punishable under the common law of war.

SECTION 2.

Flags of Truce.

751....A flag of truce is, in its nature, of a sacred character, and is ever to be so regarded by all persons in the Navy of the United States.

752....To use it to obtain surreptitiously naval knowledge or information against the interests or wishes of an enemy, is to abuse it, and to subject the bearer of it to the punishment of a spy.

753....The senior officer present is alone authorized to despatch, or to admit communication with, a flag of truce ; but a vessel in a position to discover the approach of a flag of truce earlier than the rest, is, whenever one appears, to communicate promptly the fact by signal.

754....A flag of truce is always to be admitted with great circumspection, and should never be allowed to approach so as to be a means of acquiring useful information. The firing of a gun, with a blank charge, by the flag or senior officer's ship, is generally understood as a warning to a flag of truce not to approach any nearer.

755....Unnecessary frequency in the use of a flag of truce is to be carefully avoided.

756....A flag of truce on the water should be met at a suitable distance off, or at the point previously agreed upon, by a boat or vessel from the senior officer's ship, in charge of a commissioned and discreet officer, and having a white flag kept plainly displayed forward from the time of leaving until that of return.

757....And in despatching a flag of truce the same precaution as to a suitable officer to be placed in charge, and as to keeping the white flag displayed, is to be observed.

758....Whenever the white flag is used, the ensign is also to be exhibited.

759....No flag of truce can insist on being admitted ; and as a rare exception only should a flag of truce be admitted during an engagement. If then admitted, it is no breach of faith to retain it. Firing is not necessarily to cease at the appearance of a flag of truce in battle, and if any one connected with it be killed, no complaint can be made. If, however, the white flag be exhibited evidently as a token of submission, then, of course, firing should cease.

760....An attacking force should avoid firing on hospitals whenever they are designated by flags or other symbols distinctly understood ; but it is an act of bad faith, amounting to infamy, to hoist the hospital protective flag over any other building than a hospital, unless the attacking force should request or consent that it might be used in order to spare edifices dedicated to science or literature, or containing works of art.

ARTICLE XVII.

Quarantine.

761....Commanding Officers in going into port, whether foreign or domestic, are to comply strictly with all its regulations regarding quarantine.

762....In boarding vessels just arrived care is to be taken that it is not done in violation of the rules of the port, and, in case they are subject to quarantine, the Boarding Officer is to obtain the information he desires without going alongside of them ; and in boarding vessels at sea care is to be observed not to do so, unless absolutely indispensable, if there be any cases of an infectious disease among their crews, or if they come from places without a clean bill of health, or be otherwise liable to be subjected to quarantine. No concealment is to be countenanced with regard to anything that may have been done by a vessel of the Navy subjecting her to quarantine.

763....If a vessel of the Navy should arrive in any port with an infectious disease among her crew, or if a disease of the sort should break out among her crew while lying in port, her Commanding Officer is to have the quarantine flag hoisted, and to prevent all communication at all liable to engender the disease elsewhere, until the proper authorities of the place may extend to her the privilege of pratique. To prevent the spreading of an epidemic on board a vessel of the Navy, the Commanding Officer is authorized to arrange with the authorities of the port for the care and treatment of the invalids, either on shore or on board a hulk in the harbor.

764....If a vessel of the Navy should be at sea in company with other vessels, and an infectious disease should exist or appear on board of her, the Commanding Officer is to keep her quarantine flag exhibited until it ceases, and to do all in his power to prevent its dissemination.

765....Commanding Officers, whether liable to quarantine or not, are, on arriving in the waters of a port, to extend every facility to health-boats in making their visits, and to afford all the information they may require. If the vessel be under way she is to heave to, if necessary, on their approach.

766....Commanding Officers will direct the Medical Officer of the vessel, on leaving ports, to procure bills of health whenever they may think that such will prove of service elsewhere.

ARTICLE XVIII.

TRANSFERS, DISCHARGES, AND DESERTIONS.

SECTION 1.

Transfers.

767....No Commander of a vessel of the Navy is ever to transfer any person belonging to his vessel to any other vessel or station, unless specially authorized by competent authority. The Commanding Officer of a squadron may authorize transfers from one vessel to another under his command, when on a foreign station, and when, in his judgment, the good of the public service shall render it expedient or necessary.

768....An officer transferred from a vessel, navy yard, or station to any other vessel, navy yard, or station, or to any prize, is to be furnished with his account at the time, signed by the Commanding Officer and Paymaster of the vessel, navy yard, or station from which he goes, specifying his rank, the sums paid, and the balance due.

769....When any person other than an officer shall be transferred from one vessel, navy yard, or station to any other vessel, navy yard, or station, or to any prize or hospital, the Commanding Officer of the vessel, navy yard, or station from which he goes shall take care that he is accompanied by his account, signed by himself and the Paymaster, specifying the date of his entry, the period and term of service, the sums paid, the balance due, and the quality in which he was rated ; and also by a complete descriptive, transcript, and clothes list.

SECTION 2.

Discharges.

770....Persons enlisted for the naval service, and serving on board vessels within the United States, may be discharged by order of the Commanding Officer of a vessel acting singly, squadron, or station, for either of the following reasons, but not otherwise, except by the authority of the Department: Expiration of service, sentence of a general or summary court-martial, or unfitness for service from causes ascertained by survey to have existed prior to enlistment.

771.... Enlisted persons found by survey unfit for the naval service from causes originating subsequent to their enlistments may, at their own request, if judged expedient, be discharged in the United States by the authority of the Department, but not otherwise.

772.... As a prerequisite for granting a discharge to any enlisted person in the naval service, under any circumstances, before the expiration of his time, a favorable recommendation from the Commanding Officer of the vessel or station to which the person belongs is indispensable, else no application to the Department on the subject will be entertained.

773.... Persons claiming to be legally entitled to their discharge, on the score of being minors or aliens, must apply to the courts having cognizance of such cases.

774.... No person enlisted for the naval service shall be discharged whilst absent from the United States, except by order of the Secretary of the Navy, or by the sentence of a general court-martial: *Provided,* however, that upon the expiration of the term of his enlistment, any person whose detention on board may not "be very essential to the public interests" may be discharged upon his own request in writing, by order of the Commander-in-Chief or of the senior officer present ; and the fact that the request was so made shall be stated on the face of the discharge. Whenever a discharge shall be given for any of the reasons above mentioned, a report of all the circumstances shall be made to the Navy Department, and information shall be given to the nearest Consul of the United States, that he may regulate his conduct towards the person so discharged, with a full knowledge of the facts.

775.... Every discharge paper, whether honorable or otherwise, issued to a person of the Navy must contain upon its face or back (see forms 22 and 23) a full and complete descriptive list of the individual to whom it is given.

776.... Petty officers *appointed* by the Commanding Officer, or with his approval, shall not be discharged before the expiration of the term for which they agreed to serve, except by sentence of a court-martial, by order of superior authority, or for good and sufficient reasons, of which the Commanding Officer will be the judge.   The latter will never authorize such discharges for the purpose of avoiding a court-martial, nor unless he is satisfied that the public interests will not be injured thereby.   Hospital and Paymasters' Stewards and Nurses are never to be discharged without the consent of the officers appointing them or their successors, except by sentence of a court-martial.

777.... A Yeoman shall in no case be discharged during the continuance of the cruise for which he engaged to serve, until his accounts shall have been examined and the stores under his charge found correct.

778.... A Yeoman is not to be discharged at the expiration of a cruise until his accounts have been audited and approved by the Commandant of the yard, as required by the Ordnance and other instructions.   If found correct, the Commandant of the yard will then give him a discharge; but if not so found, that officer is at once to make to the Bureau of Equipment and Recruiting, or to the Bureau of Ordnance, as the case may require, a statement of deficiencies, covering their amounts, and of any circumstances which may have come to his knowledge attending them, for the decision of the Department.

Section 3.

Honorable Discharges.

779.... Commanding Officers, upon returning from a cruise, when directed to discharge the whole or any part of the crew, will furnish to those petty officers and others of inferior rating, who enlisted for three years, and who, in their judgment, are, on being discharged, entitled to it as a testimonial of fidelity and obedience, an honorable discharge, and forward immediately to the Secretary of the Navy returns of the names and descriptions of those to whom it has been given.

780.... Blanks for the honorable discharges, and the returns in relation to them, will be furnished by the Department, and great care is hereby enjoined as to the filling up of both completely and accurately.

781.... When any petty officer or person of inferior rating, who, having received an honorable discharge, shall within three months from the date thereof present said discharge at any naval rendezvous, or account for its loss in a satisfactory manner, answer the description it contains, and be found physically fit for the service, he may be re-enlisted for three years; and upon his transfer to a receiving vessel, he will be entitled to three months' gratuitous pay, equal in amount to what he would have been entitled to receive if he had remained employed in actual service for three months, with the rate specified on the face of the honorable discharge.

782....If the honorable discharge should have been lost, reference can be made to the files of the Department for corroboration that the person presenting himself did receive an honorable discharge, and for a descriptive list of his person.

783....The three months' pay, to which a petty officer or person of inferior rating is entitled who shall enlist for three years within three months after his honorable discharge, shall be considered "honorable discharge money," and so denominated. It will not, however, be paid in one sum at the time of re-enlistment, but shall be reserved for payment during the term of his re-enlistment, at such times, and in such sums, as the Commanding Officer may direct.

784....No person discharged at his own request, or for his own convenience, before the expiration of his term of enlistment, shall be given an honorable discharge.

785....Every petty officer or person of inferior rating who shall receive an "honorable discharge" will wear upon the left sleeve of the jacket or frock, above the elbow, a foul anchor, two and a half inches in length, to be white if worn on blue, or blue if worn on white, to be called "the honorable discharge badge;" and for every additional honorable discharge a star half an inch in diameter will be added to the badge.

786....When invalids are sent to the United States from a foreign station, the Commanding Officer of the vessel to which they belonged will transmit a list of their names to the Department, stating the general character of each, and designating such as, in his opinion, are entitled to the honorable discharge, in order that the Commandant of the station at which they may arrive in the United States may be directed to grant the said discharge to those deserving it. A duplicate of the list is to be sent also to the Commandant of the station where they are to arrive.

Section IV.

Desertions.

787....Desertion being an offence of the gravest character, every possible endeavor must be made by the officers of the Navy to check it, as well as absence without leave, or straggling, and to apprehend promptly all persons who may desert or so absent themselves. In each case descriptive lists, signed by the commanding officer, showing on their face the amount of reward offered, are to be distributed among the police of the place, but not without the permission of the local authorities. (Form No. 4)

788.....A reward not exceeding twenty dollars may be offered for the recovery of a deserter, and a reward not exceeding ten dollars may be offered for the recovery of a straggler, but in neither case is it to be paid until the delinquent is actually delivered on board the vessel, or at the place on shore where he belongs, and from which he deserted or went without authority. If, however, the vessel should have departed from the port at which the offence occurred, then the delivery of the delinquent to the Commanding naval officer thereat is to be regarded as equivalent to his delivery on board of her. Any reward which may be paid for the apprehension and delivery of a deserter or straggler is at once to be charged to his account.

789....In addition to the reward above authorized to be paid for the apprehension and delivery of deserters and stragglers, there may be paid a reasonable amount to cover such expenses attending their lodgment, subsistence, and travelling as may appear to have been fairly incurred ; and this amount, entered separately, is also to be charged against them. No claim, however, for loss of time, or for subsistence, that may be made by any person apprehending and delivering a deserter or straggler, is to be entertained.

790....A reward for the apprehension of an officer is not to be offered unless specially authorized by the Navy Department, or, on a foreign station, by the Commander-in-Chief of a squadron.

791....Absence without leave, and with a manifest intention not to return, is always to be regarded as desertion. Absence without leave, coupled with a probability that the party does not intend to remain permanently away, is, at first, to be regarded as straggling, and, at the expiration of ten days, if the party still remains absent, as desertion. In either case the Commanding Officer, on informing himself of the facts attending it, is, primarily, to decide the point of intention, and to cause the party to be entered on the log and marked on the books of the Paymaster as above indicated.

792....The wages due a deserter are to be regarded as forfeited to the United States; or, if in debt to the government, the proceeds of his effects left on board are to be applied to liquidate it, and the balance, if any, is to be accounted for to the Fourth Auditor of the Treasury by the Paymaster. If not so in debt, the whole of said proceeds are to be so accounted for.

793....The letter R, marked against a person's name on the books of the Paymaster, is to signify desertion, and no application to the Department for its removal will be entertained unless the Department is furnished with sufficient evidence, either direct or circumstantial, that, in reality, there was no intention to desert.

794....If the account of any person returning or delivered on board with an R already appearing against his name has not actually been transmitted to the Fourth Auditor, the Commander of a squadron, or of a vessel acting singly, may have it removed if he is satisfied upon explanation that it ought not in justice to remain, in which case the party is to be re-credited with the wages that were due him when the R was placed against his name, and credited with the proceeds that may have resulted from the sale of his effects left on board, or, if he was in debt, with any balance of them that may appear in his favor; but under no circumstances is any allowance of wages to be made to him for the time of his unauthorized absence.

795....Should desertions occur from a vessel in a port of the United States, her commanding officer, before sailing, is to transmit to the Bureau of Equipment and Recruiting a list and description of the deserters, and a duplicate of the same, with a statement of the reward offered in each case, to the Commanding Officer of the station, if there be one at the place, and if not, to the commanding officer of the station nearest to it, in order that he may receive such deserters if apprehended and have the reward offered for them paid.

796....If a deserter from any vessel of the navy shall take refuge on board of a foreign vessel-of-war, the senior officer present in command shall make a formal request for his delivery ; but if this be refused, he is not to resort to force for his recovery, yet he is, however, to report the case and circumstances immediately to the Navy Department.

797....In case of shipwreck, or any other circumstance except capture by an enemy, whereby any person belonging to a vessel of the Navy shall become unavoidably separated from the command, it shall be his duty to proceed at once to the nearest ship, squadron, or station, and report himself to the officer in command.   In the event of failure to do this, he will be regarded as a deserter, and no claim for wages will be allowed unless he shall prove, to the satisfaction of the Department, that he was prevented by circumstances beyond his control.

ARTICLE XIX.

Medals of Honor.

798....By an act of Congress, approved December 21, 1861, the Secretary of the Navy is authorized to cause two hundred " *Medals of Honor* " to be prepared, with suitable emblematic devices, to be bestowed upon such petty officers, others of inferior rating, and marines, as shall most distinguish themselves by their gallantry in action and other commendable qualities during the present war.   Medals have accordingly been prepared, and each consists of a star of five rays, in bronze, with a device emblematic of the Union crushing the monster Rebellion—the star itself sustained, as a means of wearing it as intended, by the flukes of an anchor.   The following rules are to be observed concerning it :

> 1. It is to be worn suspended from the left breast by a ribbon of the same pattern as that which will be found attached on its presentation, showing all blue at top for half an inch downwards, and thirteen vertical stripes, alternately red and white, for eight-tenths of an inch, or the rest of its length to the ring of the anchor.

Medals of Honor.

2. The name of the recipient is to be engraved on the back of the medal.

3. The names of all those upon whom the Navy Department may be pleased to confer the medal shall be publicly made known, and a registry thereof kept in the Department.

4. The medal shall only be awarded to those petty officers, and others indicated, who shall have evinced in battle some signal act of valor or devotion to their country ; and nothing save such conduct, coupled with good general qualities in the service, shall be held to establish a sufficient claim to it.

5. In order to enable the Department to discriminate fairly and properly in the premises, Commanding Officers, in recommending parties for the medal, are to state minutely the grounds of their recommendation—precisely what the deeds of valor or devotion were, and the circumstances attending them ; and they are also to state the impressions made by the parties as to their general public worth.

6 Every person selected for the medal shall receive it publicly, from the hands of the senior officer present in command, before the crew to which he belongs, and at the instance of a general order from the Navy Department stating the cause of his special distinction.

7. Any one who, after having received the medal, shall again perform an act which, if he had not received the distinction, would have entitled him to it, shall have the authority conferred upon him by the Department to wear a bar attached to the ribbon by which the medal is suspended ; and for every additional act of the kind an additional bar shall be added.

8. To preserve pure this "*Medal of Honor,*" it is to be distinctly understood that if any person on whom it shall have been conferred be subsequently convicted of treason, cowardice, felony, or any infamous crime, or if he be accused of any such offence, and do not, after a reasonable time, surrender himself to be tried therefor, his name shall forthwith be erased from the registry above mentioned by a general order from the Secretary of the Navy, who alone is to be the judge of the circumstances demanding the expulsion.

9. An act of Congress, approved July 16, 1862, further directs that seamen distinguishing themselves in battle, or by extraordinary heroism in the line of their profession, may be promoted to forward warrant officers, or acting master's mates, as they may be best qualified, upon the recommendation of their Commanding Officer, approved by the Flag Officer and the Department; and that, upon such promotion, they shall receive a gratuity of one hundred dollars, and a " *Medal of Honor.*"

10. In all cases of selections as above authorized, Commanding Officers are to communicate the names of the individuals without delay, in order that the Department may take prompt action with regard to them ; and if the selection involve promotion, as contemplated by the act of Congress just mentioned, those officers are to be particular in stating whether it should be that of a forward warrant officer, or to that of an acting master's mate, together with their reasons therefor. Special attention to clauses 5 and 9 of these instructions is enjoined upon all Commanding Officers.

ARTICLE XX.

Allotments.

799.....An allotment must not exceed one-half the pay of the person granting it, except by the special permission of the Secretary of the Navy. It must be confined to making provision for the support of the family or other relatives of the grantor, for such time as he may be absent from them on public duty. It must not be made payable on any other than the last day of the month. After having been signed, it must have the approval of the Secretary of the Navy, or of the Commander of the vessel or station to which the person making it is attached, and will be registered by the Paymaster of such vessel or station, who will be responsible for its deduction from the grantor's pay ; or, in special cases, it will be registered at the Fourth Auditor's Office. It will be executed in duplicate, and in the case of commis-

Allotments.

sioned or warrant officers, one part will be transmitted by the Paymaster who has registered it, to the Fourth Auditor's Office, and, in the case of any other person, both parts will be so transmitted. The Paymaster will send, with the allotments registered by him, a general abstract for the use of the Fourth Auditor's Office, and a particular abstract for each of the pay agents by whom they are payable. The death, discharge, forfeiture of pay by sentence of a court-martial, or desertion of a person who has an allotment running, will be communicated, by the Paymaster of the vessel·or station to which he was attached, to the Fourth Auditor's Office, and to the pay agent by whom it is payable, by the first opportunity that may occur ; in default of which, the Paymaster will be held liable for the amount paid by the pay agent in consequence of such neglect. In case of a discharge abroad, he will charge the allotment for as many months in advance as will probably be required for information of the discharge to reach the Fourth Auditor's Office. Immediately upon the return of a vessel to the United States, at the expiration of her cruise, the Paymaster will send to the Fourth Auditor's Office, and to the several pay agents by whom they are payable, a list of the allotments to be stopped. When an allotment is to be discontinued by request of the person granting the same, the reason must be assigned for its discontinuance. One letter should be addressed to the Fourth Auditor's Office, and one to the pay agent by whom it is payable.

800.... All persons enlisting for the Navy, on being transferred to a sea-going vessel, will be allowed to allot only a sum not exceeding one-half the wages corresponding with the rate they received on enlisting. Any subsequent rating conferred on board such vessel is not to govern in determining the amount that may be allotted.

801.... Allotment tickets shall be made out by the Paymaster for all those persons on board who may wish to leave them for the benefit of their families or relatives, at the earliest moment after the' ship is put in commission, and shall be promptly forwarded by him as required, in order to insure payment when due. In cases of capture of officers or men who have granted allotments which may expire after their capture, the monthly payments of the same are to be continued by pay agents until otherwise ordered.

ARTICLE XXI.

STATIONS AND NAVY YARDS.

SECTION 1.

Commanding Officer of a Station.

802.... Whenever an officer shall be appointed to the command of a station in the United States, and not at the same time to the imme. diate command of a particular navy yard, the geographical limits of his command will be defined by the Secretary of the Navy.

803 .... All vessels of the United States in commission which shall arrive or be stationed within the limits of his command shall make their reports and submit all requisitions to him for examination and approval, and shall obey his orders, unless they shall be commanded by superior officers, or shall be under the orders and in the presence of his superior officer.

804.... The Commanding Officer of a station will conform to all the regulations prescribed for Commanders-in-Chief of fleets or squadrons respecting the procuring and disbursement of stores and the discipline of the service, unless otherwise specially directed.

805.... The Commanding Officer of a station, appointed as above, shall exercise no authority or control over the Commanding Officer of a navy yard, or other shore establishment not placed expressly under his command, or over the vessels and persons put in charge or under the authority of such officer of a yard or other establishment, unless expressly directed so to do by the Secretary of the Navy, or in cases of great emergency, where time will not permit to refer to the Department for orders, and in all such cases he will make immediate report of the facts and of the reasons which governed him to the Department.

806.... The rendezvous for recruits, receiving vessels, and naval hospitals, at a place or places within the limits of the Commanding Officer of a station, will be under his command.

807 .... He shall cause all vessels which may be fitted for, or return from sea, at the port where he may be, which are not commanded by

Commanding Officer of a Station.

his superior or senior officer, to be inspected by a board, to be composed of three Line Officers, (including an inspector of ordnance where one is available,) who shall report the state of their preparation for battle, discipline, and general condition and efficiency for service, in such form as may be prescribed by the Navy Department.

808.... He shall also cause an inspection to be made at the same time, by an engineer, a surgeon, and a paymaster, of the machinery, medical, and pay departments, respectively, who will report to him their condition.

809.... Whenever the vessel to be inspected shall be under the orders and in the presence of a superior or senior officer, such superior or senior officer shall direct the above inspection to be made.

810.... The inspecting officers shall, when vessels have just returned from sea, ascertain and report if any alterations have been made in the vessel, her armament, equipment, or arrangement during the cruise; and if so, the extent, and by whose orders, or by what authority.

811.... The senior officer in command of the station will give the necessary instructions to the purchasing agent to procure proper transportation for such men as he may be directed to send to any other place when he has no public vessel at his disposal for that purpose, and will send proper officers to take charge of them, informing the Secretary of the Navy of every draft so sent, and their number, the rate and amount of passage money, and the names of the officers under whose charge they were placed.

812.... The Commanding Officer of a station is not to suffer any vessel of the Navy, commanded by an officer junior to himself, and not under the authority of one senior to himself present, to remain in port longer than shall be absolutely necessary after her Commanding Officer has received orders to depart; but he is to send her off in the execution of her instructions the moment she shall be in a condition to proceed to sea, if the state of the weather will permit.

813.... When the officer appointed or ordered to command a station is temporarily away—absent either on leave or duty—or unable to perform his duties by illness or otherwise, the Line Officer on shore duty, or on board a receiving vessel, within the limits of his command, next to him in rank or seniority, is to act in his stead.

10

SECTION 2.

Commanding Officer of a Navy Yard who is also the Commanding Officer of the Station about it.

814....When the Commanding Officer of a navy yard is also the Commanding Officer of the station about it, he is to govern himself, in discharging the duties of the latter office, by the above instructions for the Commanding Officer of a station as far as they can be made appli_ cable to him.

SECTION 3.

Commanding Officer of a Navy Yard.

815.... The Commanding Officer shall, under the direction of the Secretary of the Navy and heads of bureaus, exercise entire control over every department in the navy yard, and will be considered respon- sible for the due preservation of all buildings and stores contained therein, and of all vessels in ordinary or repairing, and for the judicious application of all labor.

816....In the event of his being temporarily away—absent either on leave or duty—or unable to perform his duties by illness or other- wise, the Line Officer belonging to his command, next to him in rank or seniority, is to act in his stead, but he shall not alter any of the regulations established for the yard.

817....He will cause the mechanics and others employed in the yard to be mustered conformably to the instructions which have been or may be given on the subject. He will be particularly careful that none but effective men are employed, and no more than are requisite, and that they are obtained on the most favorable terms to the United States consistent with the instructions he may receive from the Navy Department.

818....The hours of labor and the rate of wages of the employés in the navy yards shall conform, as nearly as is consistent with the public interest, with those of private establishments in the immediate vicinity of the respective yards, to be determined by the commandants of the navy yards, subject to the approval and revision of the Secretary of the Navy.

819....He is to approve all pay-rolls for labor, and bills for supplies furnished, upon being satisfied of their correctness and with the prices charged.

820....He shall see that all officers and other persons employed in the yard perform their duties in a proper manner, and that all reports and returns are made within the time and in the manner which may be directed by the Navy Department, and not allow any materials of any kind to be used except for public purposes, nor any mechanic, laborer, or other person, or horses or cattle, to work for any officer or others, directly or indirectly, during working hours.

821....He will cause all lights and fires on board vessels under his control to be extinguished as early in the evening as is directed to be done on board vessels in commission, and he will establish proper regulations to guard against accident from fire in the vessels under his charge, and in the dwellings and other buildings within the yard.

822....He will see that the fire-engines are at all times in good order, and will organize a fire department in the yard, and appoint proper fire companies, including hook-and-ladder, from the navy officers and the master and other workmen, excepting those who belong to or are members of fire companies without and in the vicinity of the yard; and once in every month, before the time of breaking off work in the afternoon, the fire companies shall exercise one hour, or until the time to break off work arrives.

823....The refusal of any master or other workman in the yard to perform duty in the fire companies of the yard shall, unless he belongs to a fire company without and in the immediate vicinity of the yard, be considered good cause for his immediate dismissal from the Government employ; or when, on any alarm of fire in the yard, any such person does not appear at his post, unless he can give satisfactory reason for his absence, he shall be considered equally liable to dismissal. All absentees at the exercise of the fire companies are to be reported to the Commandant.

824....The executive officer will be appointed to direct the fire department, and he will frequently examine the engines and all apparatus for subduing fires, and report at once any deficiencies, and once a month at least, in writing, their actual condition. The chief engineer of the yard, or other proper person, will take charge of and keep in order the engines, hose, and fire-buckets, and will report to the officer in command of the fire department any deficiencies, that they may be immediately remedied.

825....An alarm of fire in the yard will be given by the ringing of the yard and ships' bells, and the firing of a gun if it can be readily done, and the same alarm may be given for fires adjacent to or near the yard which may expose it to danger.

826....When he shall deem it prudent and advisable, he will direct the fire-engines and other apparatus to be sent to extinguish fires near to the yard, but they are to be kept under the control of their own officers, and must return to the yard immediately if so directed by the Commanding Officer.

827....He is not to authorize or allow any alterations in the prescribed arrangements or plans of the yard, nor the purchase of any surplus stores, nor the sale of any articles, unless specially directed or authorized by the Navy Department.

828....All vessels intended for in-shore service during the war must be provided with a substantial wire boarding netting, amply secured against all attempts to cut it away.

829....The password for the night, and the countersign, when he shall deem proper, may be issued by the Commanding Officer of the yard to such persons only as he may direct to be intrusted with them.

830....He shall draw up regulations for the police of the yard and transmit them to the Bureau of Yards and Docks for alteration or approval.

831....A regular journal shall be kept by the line officer second in rank after the executive officer, under the direction of the Commanding Officer, in which shall be entered the time when all officers report for duty at or shall be detached from the yard, when any vessel is received for repairs or put in commission, the number of mechanics and others employed, the arrival and departure of all vessels-of-war and of vessels with stores of any kind for the yard, the time when any vessel is taken into or removed from the dock, the state of the wind and weather, as

Commanding Officer of a Navy Yard.

well as the barometer and thermometer, and the other principal transactions of the yard.

832....He shall exercise no authority over, nor in any manner interfere with, vessels in commission when they are not placed under hi direction, unless in cases of urgent necessity, and should such cases occur, he shall give immediate information to the Secretary of the Navy.

833....When a vessel is directed to be placed in ordinary, or given into his charge for repair, he will cause her to be properly moored or otherwise secured, in which he is to be assisted by the officers and crew of the vessel, unless otherwise directed by the Department or the senior officer in command upon the station.

834....Although the control of the commander of a vessel is to cease when the vessel is placed in charge of the Commanding Officer. of a yard for repairs or equipment, it is hereby made the duty of such commander to point out to the Commandant of the yard any defects or deficiencies which he may have discovered.

835....Whenever the Commander or other officers belonging to a vessel fitting out or undergoing repairs at a navy yard shall be directed to report to the Commanding Officer of the yard, such officers and any other persons belonging to the vessel may be employed in stowing or equipping her, or in preparing her equipments, whenever it can be done to advantage.

836....When a vessel in commission shall be placed in a proper situation to receive any repairs that may have been ordered, her officers and crew may, if he deems necessary, be removed to some other vessel or quarters until her repairs shall be completed, and strict care must be taken that such vessel or quarters, and all articles belonging to them are at all times kept perfectly clean and in good order by the persons using them for the time being.

837....He will not permit any vessel in commission to be repaired at the yard under his command without the sanction of the Bureau of Construction, except in cases of emergency, and in all such urgent cases surveying officers shall be duly appointed, and a copy of their report shall be forwarded to said bureau without delay.

838....He shall report to the Bureau of Construction the time when he receives a vessel for repair, when the repairs are commenced, and the time when she is returned into the charge of the Commander, or when her repairs are completed.

839....When a vessel in ordinary is to be equipped for service the equipments shall be made under the direction of the Commanding Officer of the yard, conformably to general regulations, or to such orders as he may receive from the proper bureau or the Secretary of the Navy. The decks of all vessels below the gun-deck are to be covered with shellac, to avoid holy-stoning.

840....When a vessel shall be stowed and equipped under his direction, he shall take care that the officer who is appointed to take command shall be furnished with the drawings and plans referred to in paragraph 330, and with lists of all the stores and provisions which may have been put on board of her in the respective departments, and their cost, with the draught of water when the vessel is light and at other times.

841....When he shall be directed to build, equip, or repair any vessel, or to construct any building, or to make any improvement in the navy yard, he will direct an account to be opened against such vessel, building or improvement, debiting it with the number of days' work, and the cost of labor performed by each class of mechanics and laborers, and the quantity and cost of the different material used, detailed reports of which are to be forwarded to the proper bureau when the objects are completed.

842....When requisitions duly approved are made upon the storekeeper for articles which are not in store, he will direct the storekeeper to make requisitions for such as he may deem necessary, upon the purchasing agent, in the case of open purchases, or upon the contractor when the required article is deliverable under contract, and will approve and forward them, that the articles may be promptly furnished.

843....He will keep a bill-book, in which shall be copied all bills for articles which may be delivered for any special object in the yard, and be approved by him, keeping each appropriation and object distinct from every other. He shall keep marginal duplicates of all requisitions upon the storekeeper which he may approve. He shall cause his clerks to examine the entries in the Storekeeper's returns, and compare them with the bill-books and marginal duplicate requisitions, and certify

Commanding Officer at a Navy Yard.

that they are correctly entered, before he approves the storekeeper's returns of receipts and expenditures.

844....The officers of the Navy employed in navy yards are to have the charge of masting, rigging, stowing, arming, equipping, dismasting, and mooring all vessels at the yard ; and all persons employed for those purposes are to be under their general superintendence and direction, as may be ordered by the Commandant of the yard.

845....He will direct the constructor to furnish the clerk of the yard daily with lists of the distribution of the workmen employed under his superintendence ; the chief steam and civil Engineers, the same in reference to those employed under their direction ; and the master workmen not under the Constructor, Chief, or Civil Engineer, will report in the same manner as to those employed under them.

846....He will cause prudent scrutiny to be exercised over all articles and packages passing in or out of the yard ; and when articles or packages shall be suspected as improper to be passed, they are to be stopped and examined, and if found to be of improper character to be passed in or out of the yard, are to be detained and reported to the Commanding Officer.

847....He will impress upon mechanics and all others that it is one condition of their employment that they conform to the established regulations of the yard.

848....He will not allow smoking in the yard, except in the officers' quarters and their enclosures, and the quarters of the ordinary men.

849....He will cause the entering gates of the yard to be closed at sunset, and no visitors will be allowed after that time, unless to the officers attached to the yard, or persons on board the vessels alongside the yard.

850....No alterations must be made in the arrangements of the hull, the dimensions or arrangements of the masts, spars, boats, or other equipments of any vessel which may be ordered for repair or equipment, without the previous sanction of the Department ; but if, in the opinion of the Commanding Officer of the yard, any changes can be made to improve the qualities of a vessel, or increase the accommodation of her crew, he will make timely reports of the same to the proper bureau, with the reasons for recommending the alterations, and an estimate of the probable increase of expense which such alterations would occasion. The hatches over the engine-room and passages to it are not to be kept bright nor scrubbed, and ash wood must not be used in the coamings, but all such are to be painted.

851....When a vessel is transferred to the Commandant of a yard at the expiration of a cruise, he will take care that all the stores and outfits in the several departments are duly surveyed and delivered into the charge of the proper officers ; he will use every precaution to prevent losses in the transfer from the ship to the storehouses, and will require all officers in charge of stores to superintend the removal.

852....When the Commandant, Executive Officer, and two Lieutenants reside within a navy yard, he will not permit the yard to be left without the presence of two of said officers.

853....If there are fewer than four of said officers, and not less than two of them reside in the yard, he will not permit the yard to be left without the presence of one of them.

Section 4.

Executive Officer of a Navy Yard.

854....The Line Officer attached to a navy yard to perform general duties therein, who is next in rank or seniority to the officer appointed to its command, shall be the Executive Officer of the establishment; and he is to perform such duties as may be assigned to him by the Commanding Officer.

855....He shall, under the direction of his Commanding Officer, regulate the police of the yard, correct all abuses, and report to him such as are important.

856....In the absence of the Executive Officer, the Line Officer next in rank or seniority is to attend to his duties.

Section 5.

Lieutenants, Masters, and Ensigns of a Navy Yard.

857....The Line Officer next in rank or seniority to the Executive Officer is, under his direction, to observe a general superintendence over the yard ; and he will correct, as far as may be in his power, all irregularities that may come under his notice, and report such as may require further notice to the Executive Officer.

, 858....When the number of officers attached to a yard will permit, a Lieutenant, Master, or Ensign is to be present at the muster of the mechanics and laborers, to see that they answer properly to their names, and repair, without noise or delay, to their respective places of employment.

859....In the absence of the Line Officer next in rank to the Executive Officer, the Line Officer next in rank or seniority to him will attend to his duties ; and so, too, with regard to the absence of any other Line Officer, below the Executive Officer ; the one next in rank is to attend to his duties.

SECTION 6.

Ordnance Officer at a Navy Yard.

860....He is to take charge of all ordnance and ordnance stores, and see that they are properly stowed and cared for, making weekly, monthly, and quarterly returns of the same, agreeably to the forms prescribed, and to keep the Ordnance Bureau informed of their condition.

861....He is to examine carefully all ordnance articles received from contractors, manufacturers, or others, and only to give receipts for them when satisfied that the terms of contract or agreement have been fully complied with.

862....He is to supervise the work done in the Ordnance Department of the yard, and to keep the bureau informed of its progress.

863....He is to supply all vessels, when fitting for sea, with such armaments and ordnance stores as may be directed by the Bureau of Ordnance, taking receipts therefor and transmitting them to the bureau.

864....He will be careful to make his requisitions upon the bureau in ample time for all articles with which he is concerned, in order to answer promptly the demands that will probably be made upon him.

SECTION 7.

Navigation Officer at a Navy Yard.

865....He will have charge of all instruments, charts, nautical books, signal books, log books, and books for ships' libraries, and of all other apparatus and supplies coming under the supervision of the Bureau of Navigation.

866....He will see to the proper care of these various articles, and make the returns prescribed for him by the Bureau of Navigation.

867....He will examine carefully all articles coming under his cognizance received from contractors, manufacturers, or dealers, and only give receipts for them when he is satisfied that the terms of contract or agreement have been fully complied with.

868....He will supervise any work done in the yard for the Navigation Office.

869....He will supply all vessels fitting for sea with the articles to be issued from the Navigation Office, taking receipts for the same and transmitting them to the bureau.

870....He will examine the construction of every vessel in the vicinity of the steering apparatus, and ascertain by personal inspection that there are no iron bars, rods, stanchions, axles, or other iron fastenings in or about the pilot-house, or sufficiently near the binnacle, to affect the compasses, but that, on the contrary, all metallic fastenings or mountings are made of copper or other suitable composition. He will also specially examine into the condition of the compasses of the vessel after they shall have been put on board and in the places selected for them. The result of both of these examinations, for which he will be held responsible, he will report to the bureau.

871....He will be careful to make timely requisitions upon the bureau for all articles which he is expected to have in charge, in order to answer promptly the demands that may be made upon him.

SECTION 8.

Chief Engineer of a Navy Yard.

872....When a Chief Engineer of the Navy shall be attached to a navy yard he shall, under the direction of the Commandant and of the Bureau of Steam Engineering, have the superintendence of the construction and repairs of the steam and other machinery.

873....He shall have the supervision, under the Commandant, of the master workmen and other men employed in the machine and boiler shops and foundries, and of all the material used in those departments, and be responsible for its preservation and proper use.

874....He will state, in writing, to the Commandant, the number of persons required, and suggest names in the various departments under his charge, and, when the services of any are no longer necessary, he will inform the Commandant of the persons that may be dispensed with.

875....He will make such suggestions to the Commandant of the yard, in the line of his profession or duty, as he may consider to the interest of the service.

876....The inspection, weighing, and measuring of all materials and of all work under his charge will be under his supervision and control.

877....All requisitions for materials or articles in his department are to be made by the master workmen employed under his direction, and when countersigned by him are to be submitted for the approval of the Commandant of the yard, who will allow such as he may deem necessary. No articles or materials are to be purchased without previous requisitions, nor are any to be used till they are duly inspected, approved, and received. He will have proper requisitions made to cover the expenditure of all articles or materials which may have been used or condemned during the preceding half month by the master workmen.

878....He will examine and certify to the correctness of all bills for materials and supplies for work under his charge ; will examine as to the correctness of the pay-roll for labor ; will have made out and sign the semi-monthly and other reports in his department that are required to be made by the Commandant of the yard to the Bureau of Steam Engineering, the Commandant causing him to be furnished with the costs and expenditures necessary for this purpose.

879....Master workmen under him will report at the middle and end of each month the expenditure of materials and labor upon the several objects under their immediate superintendence.

880....He will have an exact account kept of all materials and labor expended on each and every object, and report to the Commandant semi-monthly the operations on the same, distinguishing the number and classes of men employed, and the kind and quantities of materials used in each.

881....He will, at the end of each fiscal year, submit to the Commandant a report of the engines and boilers that have been made or repaired, showing the original estimate and the actual expenditure.

882....He will carefully examine, at least once a month, the engines and boilers of all vessels which may be in ordinary, to see that they are as effectually guarded against injury as circumstances will permit, and make a written report to the Commandant of the yard.

SECTION 9.

Surgeon of a Navy Yard.

883....The Surgeon of a navy yard will, in addition to the duties required in the " Instructions for the Government of Medical Officers," have charge of all medicines, medical stores, instruments, and other articles provided by the Bureau of Medicine and Surgery for use at the yard for vessels fitting out or received from vessels arriving there.

884....He will give his professional attention, when necessary, to all officers and other persons belonging to the Navy and Marine corps who are attached to the yard for duty. Naval officers are only entitled to the attendance of naval surgeons when they are attached to shore stations where a surgeon is employed, to vessels in commission, or are in a naval hospital.

885....In case of wounds or injuries received by mechanics or laborers while at work in the yard, he is required to apply a first dressing, and will expend whatever may be necessary for the purpose from public stores in his charge.

886....He will report daily to the Commandant the names of all persons attached to the navy yard who are excused from duty on account of sickness, and to the officer in command of marines the names of all marines who may be unfit for duty.

Surgeon, Passed and other Assistant Surgeons of a Navy Yard or Hospital.

887....He will inspect the persons of all recruits who may offer to enlist in the Marine corps at the navy yard, and of all candidates for any appointment in the navy who may present themselves under proper authority. The report in each case must be made according to Form No. 24, Appendix.

Section 10.

Surgeon of a Naval Hospital.

888....In addition to the "Instructions for the Government of Medical Officers," the Surgeon of a hospital will conform to the following :

889....Whenever patients are left in a hospital after the sailing of the vessel from which they were sent, he must, whenever any of them are in a situation to justify their removal, send them to the receiving vessel, or report to the Commandant of the station, that they may be sent to some other vessel or discharged.

890....Whenever any enlisted person shall not have so far recovered as to justify his removal from the hospital when his term of service shall have expired, or if the injuries or disease of any person sent to the hospital will, in the opinion of the Surgeon, prove incurable, or produce long continued inability to perform duty, the Surgeon must immediately report such cases to the Commander of the station, making a particular statement of all the facts and circumstances connected with each case within his knowledge, that they may be transmitted to the Secretary of the Navy for his decision.

891....If any clothing or other articles be furnished to men while in a hospital, a statement of them with their cost is to be made upon the back of the clothes lists which accompanied them to the hospital, and this is to be duly certified by the proper officer of the hospital, in order that the articles may be charged against the pay of those who received them.

Section 11.

Passed and other Assistant Surgeons of a Navy Yard or Hospital.

892....They will be guided by the regulations prescribed for medical officers of the same grade attached to vessels for sea service.

Section 12.

Paymaster of a Navy Yard.

893....The Paymaster of a navy yard shall pay all officers and enlisted persons belonging to the navy attached to the yard and to vessels in ordinary at the yard, and, if so ordered, of those belonging to receiving vessels, and of such officers as may have their accounts transferred to him.

894....He shall pay all mechanics and laborers who may be employed under the direction of the Commandant, upon pay-rolls, (which shall have been properly made out, certified, and approved,) after he shall have satisfied himself of the correctness of the calculation.

895....As it is important that no more of the working day be absorbed in paying the men than can be avoided, they are therefore to be divided into convenient gangs, not exceeding one hundred each, and be conducted to the pay-office by the master-workmen or quartermen in the order of their names on the rolls.   The names of absentees will be called a second time after the gang to which they belong has been paid, and all those who do not answer the second call, except in cases of sickness, shall not be paid until the next pay day.   The master-workmen or quartermen will be responsible for the quiet and proper deportment of the men.

896....He will make all payments in specie, or in funds which he may receive from the government for public use.

897....He shall make requisitions semi-monthly, under the direction and with the approval of the Commanding Officer, for such amount of money as may be deemed necessary for the public service in his department.

898....He shall keep distinct accounts of moneys received and expended under the different appropriations, and never apply them to any other objects than those for which they were drawn, except by special written authority from the Secretary of the Navy.

899....He will forward to the Department, on the first of every month, or as soon thereafter as practicable, a summary statement, showing his receipts and expenditures during the previous month, with the balances then on hand under each head of appropriation ; also an estimate of the amount required under each head for the succeeding month.

SECTION 13.

Inspectors in Charge of Paymasters' Stores.

900....Inspecting officers at navy yards, connected with the Bureau of Provisions and Clothing, in addition to the duties prescribed in the "Instructions for the Government of Inspectors in charge of stores, Naval Storekeepers, Paymasters, and Assistant Paymasters," are charged with the following : To receive and inspect all stores offered, by authority, for delivery under contract, and to prepare for issue all such as strictly conform to the conditions of the contract and to the samples where they have been provided ; to receive stores from ships returned from sea, and to keep and issue these under the direction of the bureau.

901....The term " stores," as applicable to articles belonging to the Bureau of Provisions and Clothing, is to be understood as meaning provisions, clothing, small stores, candles, Paymaster's stationery and blanks, and Steward's stores.

902....Inspectors in charge are hereby required to exercise a constant supervision over the stores in their custody, and to protect them against deterioration by every means in their power.

SECTION 14.

Naval Constructors.

903....The Naval Constructor will act under the direction of the Commandant of the yard, and the Chief of the Bureau of Construction and Repairs.

904....He will have the general superintendence and charge of the construction and repairs of all vessels depending upon the Bureau of Construction and Repairs, and also the immediate superintendence and direction of all master-workmen, mechanics, and laborers employed on the work confided to him, and give them their instructions accordingly.

905....He will conform strictly to the instructions he may receive for the building, repair, and equipment of ships, being furnished with copies of orders and contracts relating thereto ; if, in the course of the repairs of any vessel, defects should be discovered which were not previously known, and which will be likely to increase the expense or delay the work, he will make immediate report of the same to the Commandant for further instructions, suggesting such modifications as will be likely to diminish the expense or increase the utility of the work. He will prepare bills of materials and schedules for advertisements, and also the accounts of cost of building and repairing ships, for transmission, when duly approved, to the Bureau of Construction and Repairs.

906....He will, at the end of each fiscal year, submit to the Commandant a report of the vessels that have been built, repaired, and for which work has been done, giving the original estimate and the actual expenditure.

907....He will make such suggestions to the Commandant of the yard, in the line of his profession or duty, as he may consider to be to the interest of the service.

908....He will inform the Commandant in writing of the number of persons required, and suggest names in the various departments under his control, and will recommend their respective wages ; when the services of any are no longer required, he will report to the Commandant the persons that may be dispensed with ; and he will report any irregularity, incompetence, neglect, or misconduct of persons under his direction.

909.....The inspection and measurement of all materials used on work under his charge, and the storage and preservation of timber and wood materials for the same, will be under his supervision and control. He will adopt measures to prevent the use or conversion of any timber or other wood material or metals until such account is taken of them as will secure a correct expenditure ; and he will cause daily returns to be made to the inspector of timber of the wood materials which may have been used or converted, and to what object applied, that he may be able to furnish the information necessary, in order that requisitions may be made to cover the expenditure. He will have

Naval Constructors.

such records and registers of timber kept as may be prescribed, that the particular species and quantities remaining on hand may at all times be known. All *condemned timber* shall be expended as such, and shall be included in the semi-monthly requisitions accordingly, as if expended in any other manner.

910....He will examine and certify to the correctness of all bills for materials and supplies for work under his charge ; will examine as to the correctness of the pay-roll for labor ; will have made and sign the semi-monthly and other reports in his department that are required to be made by the Commandant of the yard to the Bureau of Construction and Repairs, the Commandant causing him to be furnished with the costs and expenditures necessary for this purpose.

911....All requisitions for materials or articles in his department are to be made by the master workmen employed under his direction, and when countersigned by him are to be submitted for the approval of the Commandant of the yard, who will allow such as he may deem necessary. No articles or materials are to be purchased without previous requisitions, nor are any to be used till they are duly inspected, approved, and received. He will have proper requisitions made to cover the expenditure of all the timber and wood materials which may have been used or condemned during the preceding half month by the master workmen.

912....Master workmen under him will report at the middle and end of each month the expenditure of materials and labor upon the several objects under their immediate superintendence.

913....He will be responsible for all waste and improper use of materials by those under his general superintendence.

914....He will have an exact account kept of all materials and labor expended on each and every object, and report to the Commandant semi-monthly the operations on the same, distinguishing the number and classes of the men employed, and the kind and quantities of materials used on each.

915....He will carefully examine, at least once a month, all the vessels which may be on the stocks or in ordinary, to see that they are as effectually guarded against change of form or decay as circumstances will permit, and make a written report to the Commandant of the yard.

11

Naval Constructors.....Civil Engineers.

916....In docking or undocking a vessel he will make all the
needful preparations for taking her in and out properly; and, when
docked, the moving, placing, and securing her will be done under his
superintendence.

917....When there is no Civil Engineer attached to a navy yard,
his duties will devolve upon the Naval Constructor, until some other
person shall be appointed by the Navy Department to perform them.

SECTION 15.

Civil Engineers.

918....When there shall be a Civil Engineer or Architect employed
at any navy yard, he will act under the direction of the Commandant,
and Chief of the Bureau of Yards and Docks.

919....He will have the superintendence and charge of the erection
and repairs of all buildings in the yards, and of all docks and wharves.
He will have the immediate superintendence and direction of the
Architect, when one is employed at the same yard with himself, and
of all master and other workmen employed on said works, and will
recommend their respective wages, and be responsible for the proper
distribution and employment of all materials for said work.

920....He will conform strictly to the instructions he may receive
for executing the work, and will prepare plans and estimates of cost,
with bills of materials and schedules for advertisements which may be
necessary for such works as may be directed. These plans and estimates
of cost must be prepared in duplicate for transmission to the Bureau
of Yards and Docks, one of which, when duly approved, will be returned to the Commander of the yard for the guidance of the Commandant and Engineer, and the other retained in the Bureau.

921....He will, at the end of each fiscal year, submit to the Commandant a report, giving a clear and distinct statement of the condition
of the several works of improvement confided to his charge, the original
estimate to complete, the amount appropriated for each object, progress
made upon each, and the total amount expended during the year, the
amount of appropriations unexpended for each, and the additional

amount, if any, required to complete such work ; and if more is required than was originally estimated, the reasons must be fully stated.

922.... He will make such suggestions to the Commandant of the yard, in the line of his profession or duty, as he may consider advantageous to the interest of the service.

923.... He will inform the Commandant, in writing, of the number of persons required, and suggest names, in the various departments under his control, and when the services of any are no longer required, he will report to the Commandant the persons that may be dispensed with.

924.... The inspection and measurement of all materials, and of all works under his charge, will be under his supervision and control.

925.... He will examine and certify to the correctness of all bills for materials and supplies for works under his charge ; will examine as to the correctness of the pay-roll for labor, and sign monthly and semi-monthly reports, in his department, that are required to be made by the Commandant of the yard to the Bureau of Yards and Docks.

926.... All requisitions for materials or articles in his department are to be made by the master workmen employed under his direction, countersigned by him, and sent for approval to the Commandant of the yard, who will allow such as he may deem necessary. No articles or materials are to be purchased without previous requisition, nor are any to be used till they are duly inspected, approved, and receipted for.

927.... Master workmen under him will report, at the middle and end of each month, the expenditure of materials and labor upon the several objects under their immediate superintendence.

928.... He will be responsible for all waste or improper use of materials by those under his general superintendence.

929.... He will keep an exact account of all materials and labor expended upon each object, and report to the Commandant, semi-monthly, the operations on the same, distinguishing the number and classes of the men employed, and the kind and quantities of materials used on each.

930.... He will be careful that the sums expended, and the liabilities incurred, shall not exceed the appropriation for any work ; to which end he will be furnished by the Commandant with copies of appropriations and contracts made, and of orders issued in relation to any of the works under his control ; and he will be held responsible for the execution of the works confided to him according to the plans approved by the bureau, and within the time and amount estimated by him. On failing to do so, he will be required to account satisfactorily therefor.

Section 16.

Master Workmen.

931....A board will inquire into the qualifications of those selected by the Navy Department for appointment as master workmen, and report upon their fitness to the Bureau of Yards and Docks. The board will consist of the Executive Officer, the Chief Engineer, the Naval Constructor, or the Civil Engineer of the yard, as the case may demand. In the absence of the Constructor or Engineer his assistant shall act in his place.

932....The master workmen shall, either alone or with others who may be employed in the navy yard, when they may be directed, inspect stores that may be received into the yard in their respective departments, and certify as to the quality, and reasonableness of price.

933....They shall be in the yard at the times of commencing work, and keep, in due form, an account of the labor performed by each individual in their respective departments, upon different objects, and hand copies of the same, daily, to the clerk of the Commanding Officer, and also to the Chief Engineer, Naval Constructor, or Civil Engineer, if under the direction of either, and if not, to the clerk of the yard.

934....They shall have the immediate control of, and be vigilant to insure constant diligence from, all those who may be employed under their special direction.

935....They shall attend all surveys and conversions of materials in their respective departments, and, if necessary, they may suggest measures for their better preservation.

936....In the selection of workmen they may suggest the names of persons to be employed, but their employment shall be made with the approval of their superiors in office. Whenever men shall be required, and new ones taken into the yard who may not be known to the Chiefs of the respective departments as good workmen in their several branches, they shall be examined by the chief of the department, whether it be the Chief Engineer, Naval Constructor, or Civil Engineer, and are not to be received unless they are found to be competent and correct men. When a reduction is required, they may suggest the names of the persons, but the selection for discharge shall be approved by the head of the department, under the direction of the Commandant, and embrace those whose services can best be dispensed with consistently with the interest of the government and justice to individuals.

937....They will hand to the clerk of the Chief Engineer, Naval Constructor, or Civil Engineer, daily, an account of all the timber and other materials which may have been taken for use the preceding day by them, or by their direction.

938....No article whatever is to be taken or used without the knowledge of the proper master workman.

939....The master workmen must give their regular personal attendance, and are only to be paid, like all other persons who receive daily pay, for the time they actually attend to their duty in the yard, except when special exemptions shall be granted with the approbation of the Navy Department.

940....No master workman shall leave the yard during working hours without the knowledge and consent of the head of the department in which he is employed, who shall report his absence to the Commandant. No person employed under him shall leave the yard during working hours without the permission of the Commandant or Executive Officer.

941....If any mechanic or other person employed in a navy yard shall be dismissed for misconduct, by proper authority, such person shall not again be employed in any navy yard, except by direction of the Secretary of the Navy.

SECTION 17.

Naval Storekeepers.

942....The Naval Storekeeper shall take charge of such stores and materials, excepting such as come under the cognizance of the Bureaus of Ordnance, Navigation, Medicine and Surgery, and Provisions and Clothing, as may be received into the yard for the public service, and confided to him, and be held responsible for the expenditure of the same, conformably to the general instructions of the service, or to the special orders of the Navy Department.

943....He will, under the direction of the Commanding Officer of the yard, have charge of the keys of all storehouses and buildings containing articles for which he is responsible. They must never be taken out of the yard, and when not in use must be kept hung up in some safe and accessible place.

944....Whenever he may be directed by the Commanding Officer, he shall make requisitions upon the purchasing agents for open purchases, or upon contractors, when the required articles are deliverable under contract, for all articles which may be wanted, and present the same to him for his approval. Such requisitions must always specify the appropriation and class, and, when practicable, the particular object for which the articles are required ; and separate requisitions must be made under each appropriation for which articles may be wanted. Requisitions for articles purchased at the expense of contractors must be made in the form given in section 20 of this article.

945....He shall not give a receipt for any articles delivered in the yard, whether purchased by purchasing agents or delivered by contractors, until he shall have been furnished with an invoice or bill stating the particular articles, their cost, and the object or appropriation for which they were purchased, nor until they shall have been certified to be of proper quality by the inspecting officers, unless directed by written order of the Commanding Officer.

946....All articles which may be received into the yard for public service, or which may be placed in the Storekeeper's charge by the orders of the Commanding Officer, shall be immediately entered by the Storekeeper in his books under the respective appropriations to which they belong.

947....He shall not deliver articles for any other object or appropriation than that for which they were originally received, except by a written order of, or upon a requisition approved by, the Commanding

Officer of the yard, which order or requisition he must produce as the authority for such transfer or loan.

948....He will issue no articles (timber, timber materials, and coal excepted) but by the previous written order of, or upon requisitions duly approved by, the Commanding Officer of the yard. These requisitions or orders must specify the appropriation, and the object for which the articles are wanted; and when they are to be drawn from an appropriation different from that for which they are wanted, it must be distinctly stated on the face of the requisition. Requisitions for timber, timber materials, and coal can be made semi-monthly to cover the quantities which may have been used, condemned, or transferred during the preceding half month.

949....He will deliver articles to vessels in commission upon requisitions when signed by the Commanding Officer of the vessel, approved by the senior officer present in command of such vessels and by the Commanding Officer of the yard, taking receipts, as directed in the next following paragraph.

950....He will take receipts for all articles delivered upon the requisitions themselves, and preserve them as vouchers for his expenditures, and also upon invoices prepared in triplicate, one of which he will leave for the use and government of the officer receipting for the same. He shall give credit to the proper objects, and charge himself on the books with all surplus stores that may have been required for any object and returned to him again as not having been wanted.

951....He shall examine all accounts rendered for supplies furnished which shall have been duly certified to have passed inspection, and, on being satisfied of their accuracy and the reasonableness of the prices charged, shall receipt the same and send them immediately to the Commanding Officer for approval; but if he shall believe any article to be overcharged, or shall discover any defect or deficiency, he shall call the attention of the Commanding Officer to such charge, defect, or deficiency before receipting for the same.

952....After survey shall have been held upon stores returned from a ship, he shall receive them on store account, excepting such as shall have been condemned. When articles recommended for repairs are repaired, he will credit the vessel with their original value, less the

cost of repairs. The articles so received may be issued to other vessels, by order of the Commandant of the yard, when it can be advan-
tageously done ; and these second handed articles must be entered and
expended on separate lines from other articles

953....He will notify the Commanding Officer whenever any article
of stores may be so nearly expended as to require replenishing, and
when any additional measures may be necessary for the proper preservation of articles in his charge.

954....When there are any articles in store which may be used
without impairing efficiency, though not of the precise dimensions,
form, or quality named in a requisition upon the Naval Storekeeper,
they are to be supplied in place of those required, to prevent the necessity of open purchases, unless otherwise specially directed by the
Commandant of the yard.

955....He shall be responsible for the shipment of all stores under
his charge from the yard at which he is stationed to other places by
such conveyances as may be furnished by the purchasing agent or other
duly authorized person, and conformably to such orders as he may receive upon the subject. Particular attention must be paid by him to
have all the articles thus to be transported delivered by the bills of
lading at the *precise place* to which they may have been ordered, and
that they are in good shipping order. The price, rate, or amount of
freight to be paid must be specifically inserted in all bills of lading,
and not left to the phrase, "according to usage."

956....All articles forwarded from the navy yard must be accompanied by a bill or invoice stating the particular contents of each
package, the cost of the separate articles, and the appropriation to
which they belong.

957....He shall keep his books and make his returns in such manner and at such times as may be prescribed by the Navy Department.

958....Whenever articles contracted for are, in consequence of the
failure of the contractor to furnish them, purchased in open market,
he will receipt for them accordingly, keeping a record of the same, and
make a quarterly return to the proper bureau of the excess of cost over
that of the contract price.

SECTION 18.

Clerk of the Yard.

959....The Clerk of the yard is responsible for the proper mustering of the men, and for making correct returns of their time and the pay allowed them.

960....He is to get his orders from the Commanding Officer with regard to the times and manner of mustering the workmen, and he must be present, duly prepared, precisely at the times prescribed, and then commence the musters. He is to make out, semi-monthly, the pay-rolls by which the workmen are to be paid the wages they have earned, and these, containing the names of the workmen, the number of days' work each has performed, the class to which each belongs, the rate of pay established by the Commandant for each class, the amount due to each individual, the whole amount chargeable to each appropriation, and marginal notes of all extra work performed, are to be certified by him as correct in every particular. He is also to make out monthly a copy or transcript of the last two semi-monthly pay-rolls, which is to be signed by himself, and then approved and forwarded by the Commandant to the Chief of the Bureau of Yards and Docks.

SECTION 19.

Mustering Workmen and Check Officers.

961....It is of the utmost importance to the public interest that no more of the working day should be absorbed in conducting the necessary musters than can be avoided, and therefore, whenever practicable, the mechanics and laborers employed at a navy yard are to be divided as equally as needs be into mustering gangs, no one of which to exceed six hundred in number, and each to be designated by a letter of the alphabet, so as to repair, for the purpose of being mustered at the prescribed times, to the mustering office or station exhibiting a corresponding letter. As fast as the men are mustered they are to go promptly and quietly to the work assigned them.

962....A Check Officer, who is to be either a lieutenant, master, or ensign, whenever arrangements will permit, is to be present at each mustering office or station whenever a muster takes place, and, with a verified copy of the roll used thereat, furnished under the responsibility of the clerk of the yard by the mustering clerk, he is to note, as the roll is called, the presence or absence of each individual, and to enter the name of any new man, not already on the roll, presenting himself to be received by due authority. Immediately after the muster has ended he is to compare his roll with that of the mustering clerk, and if any disagreement should be found an investigation must take place without delay, to ascertain the cause of the discrepancy and correct the error. The rolls kept by Check Officers, when filled, are to be returned by them to the Commandant's office, and there filed for reference. In case of a deficiency of officers to serve as just mentioned, the Commandant is to direct as many of the clerks or writers already employed in the yard as may be necessary to act in their stead, and they are to do so in addition to the ordinary duties exacted of them. The clerk of the yard is to select, with the approval of the Commandant, suitable persons to perform the duties of mustering clerks, and to be allowed one to an average of every six hundred workmen employed, he himself mustering, &c., one of the gangs, and being regarded, therefore, so far, as one of those clerks. The mustering clerks are to assist the clerk of the yard in computing and preparing the rolls for the inspection and government of the disbursing officer in paying the men off, and by this arrangement it is expected that the clerk of the yard will never fail to make his rolls and returns as promptly as required.

Section 20.

Purchasing Agents at Shore Stations.

963....All requisitions for stores will be approved by the Commandant of the navy yard ; and those for articles not under contract will be made upon the Purchasing Agent, who will procure them and be responsible that they are forthcoming, at the lowest market price, and of the best quality, subject to the usual inspection at the navy yard before being received.   If articles are to be *selected*, the person to select them will call upon the Purchasing Agent for such instructions as he may have to give, and when the articles are obtained the Commandant will satisfy himself of the correctness of the bills in all respects before approving them.   This order will not apply to articles specially ordered by the Department or Bureaus.   All requisitions for stores contracted for will be made on the contractor directly.

964.... Whenever it becomes necessary to purchase articles contracted for in open market, in consequence of the failure of the contractor to furnish them, the requisition will be made on the Purchasing Agent, and will state upon its face: "There is required to be purchased in open market for immediate use, to supply deficiencies under the contract of," (here state the contractor's name,) "dated ———, the following articles, which must conform in quality as near to the contract as practicable."   The bills must be certified by the Purchasing Agent, thus : " The above-named articles were purchased at the lowest market prices, in open market, for immediate use, to supply deficiencies under the contract of ———, dated ———."   The Purchasing Agent will keep a record of these purchases, showing the aggregate amount thereof, to be returned to the respective bureaus quarterly.

965.... He will procure all freight or transportation of articles not specially provided for by the bureaus, on the requisitions of the Commandant of the yard, and will be responsible for the efficient means as well as the proper rate of freight or terms of transportation.   When it becomes necessary to send drafts of men from one naval station to another, he will, upon the requisition of the Commandant, or senior officer present, furnish the necessary means of transportation.

966.... He will certify on all bills for purchases in open market, and for freight and transportation made or procured by him, that the prices are the lowest market rates.

967.... If he shall send articles from one place to another for the navy, particular attention must be paid to make them deliverable by the charter-party, bill of lading, or other agreement, at the precise place where they may be specially required, and a particular rate of freight be inserted, and not left " according to usage."   The number of lay days, and the amount of daily demurrage after they shall have expired, must be explicitly stated in the charter-party and bill of lading.

968.... Disbursing Agents and Paymasters at shore stations will keep their deposits with the nearest Assistant Treasurers, except those stationed at Washington, who will keep their deposits with the Treasurer of the United States.

969.... He shall have no private interest, directly or indirectly, in the supply of any article which it may be his duty to procure for the navy. The practice, by inexperienced officers, of giving certificates to persons with whom they have had trading dealings, or to inventors whose works they may have superficially examined, being deemed prejudicial to the true interests of the service, it is directed that hereafter no such certificates or recommendations be given by any person attached to the Navy Department within the United States, unless sanctioned by the Secretary of the Navy, and, if abroad, by the written approval and indorsement of the senior officer present.

970.... He is to make no sale of articles belonging to the United States, nor any purchases, nor incur any public expense, without the sanction of the senior officer upon the station, the Commanding Officer of the navy yard, the Navy Department, or one of the Bureaus thereof.

971.... He shall pay no bills for articles furnished, or services rendered to navy yards, or vessels under the control of the Commanding Officer of the yard, without the previous approval of that officer; nor any bills for articles furnished, or services rendered, directly to vessels in commission, without the certificate of the Commander of the vessel, and the approval of the senior officer in command of the station, unless sanctioned by the Navy Department.

972.... He will not pay bills under one appropriation from any money belonging to another appropriation, without the express sanction of the Secretary of the Navy; and whenever money shall be so transferred, he shall note it particularly in his next return.

973.... His requisitions upon the Department and Bureaus for money must be made under the specific heads of appropriation, and those upon the Bureaus must be accompanied by triplicates of the bills for the payment of which they are intended.

974.... He must make monthly returns to the Navy Department of all moneys received, expended, and remaining on hand, under each appropriation, in such form as may be prescribed. These returns must be made out and forwarded within ten days after the expiration of each month, unless otherwise directed by the Secretary of the Treasury under the Act approved July 17, 1862.

975 .... Whenever he shall be authorized by the Secretary of the Navy to make advances of pay to officers bound on a cruise, it shall be the duty of the Paymaster of the vessel to furnish him, as his guide, a correct list, signed by himself and approved by the Commanding Officer, of all the officers entitled to an advance of pay, which list must exhibit their names, rank, and monthly pay.

ARTICLE XXII.

MARINES.

SECTION 1.

When Embarked.

976 .... Whenever instructions are given to the Commandant of the marine corps to prepare a guard for a vessel going into commission, he will immediately cause the proper number of officers and men to be detailed and kept in readiness for embarcation.

977 .... When a vessel is ready for the reception of the marines, the Commanding Officer of the station will notify the Commanding Marine Officer, whose duty it shall be to have sent to the designated place of embarcation the detachment which may have been previously ordered for such vessel.

978 .... When marines are received on board a vessel they are to be entered separately on her books as part of the complement, or as supernumeraries, as the case may require, and are to be, in all respects, upon the same footing as the seamen with regard to provisions and short allowances.

979 .... The senior marine officer shall report daily in writing to the Commander of the vessel the state of the guard.

980 .... They are not to be diverted from their appropriate duties,

Marines— When Embarked.

or called upon to coal ship, or work as mechanics, except in case of emergency.

981....They may be furnished by the Paymaster with clothing and small stores when the Commanding Marine Officer shall certify that they require them, and the Commander of the vessel approves the issue.

982....The Commanding Marine Officer is to have charge of, and will be accountable for, the arms, accoutrements, and clothing belonging to the marines, and he will be careful to have the whole preserved in the best possible manner. He will report any injury that may result to them from the neglect or misconduct of any person, that the amount may be recovered from him.

983....A detachment of marines, on joining a vessel-of-war for sea service, will always be accompanied by the officers who are attached to it.

984....They will be exercised in the manual of arms, and duties of the soldier, by their officers, at such times and places as the Commander may appoint.

985....As occasions may arise when it may become necessary to employ marines at the great guns, they shall be instructed as full gun's crews by their own officers, and also may be assigned as parts of ordinary gun's crews under other officers of divisions. But the Commanding Officer will be careful not so to assign marines except in cases of necessity.

986....When not on guard, or on duty as sentinels, they are to be subject to the orders of the sea officers in the same manner as the seamen.

987....All general orders to sentinels shall pass through the Marine Officer. The sentinels on the spar deck may receive special orders from the Officer of the Deck when an emergency may require it ; should they be of an important character, the latter shall inform the Senior Marine Officer and the Commander of the vessel.

988....Any misbehavior of the marines on guard duty, or on duty as sentinels, is to be reported to the Officer of the Deck, and by him made known to the Senior Marine Officer on board, who will report the same to the Executive Officer, who, if requisite, will refer the case to the Commanding Officer.

989....No officer of the navy of inferior relative rank shall give orders to a marine officer, unless such navy officer be at the time in command of the vessel, or be the Executive Officer, or Officer of the Deck.

990....The Commanding Marine Officer will be particularly attentive to the comfort and cleanliness of his men, as well as their soldier-like appearance and efficiency. He will inspect the clothing at least once a month, and report to the Commanding Officer of the vessel in case of any loss or abuse.

991....If repairs of the arms and accoutrements become necessary, the Marine Officer will apply to the Executive Officer for such assistance as can be afforded.

992....The Marine Officer, with the approval of the Commander of the vessel, may reduce non-commissioned officers for misconduct or incompetency, and make promotions to supply vacancies; should no Marine Officer be attached to the vessel, the Commanding Officer may order such reductions and promotions.

993....The clothing accounts, muster-rolls, and such other accounts as may be directed by the Commandant of the marine corps, will be kept by the officer or non-commissioned officer in charge of the guard of any vessel, who will forward them, through the prescribed channel, to the Senior Marine Officer of the fleet.

994.... When there shall be more than one marine officer attached to a vessel, one shall at all times be on board for duty, unless upon very particular occasions, to be judged of by the Commanding Officer of the vessel.

995.... When a vessel is to be put out of commission, the marine officer, with the guard, shall remain on board until all the officers and crew are detached, and the ship regularly turned over to the officers of the navy yard or station where they may arrive.

SECTION 2.

Enlistments.

996....The regulations for the recruiting service of the Army of the United States will be applied to the recruiting service of the marine corps as far as practicable.

SECTION 3.

When at the Navy Yards.

997....The marine detachment serving within a navy yard is to be subject to the orders of the Commandant of the yard ; but no part of the detachment shall be relieved or withdrawn therefrom except by order of the Commandant of the marine corps, approved by the Secretary of the Navy. All such orders shall pass through the Commandant of the yard.

998....When a marine officer is ordered to relieve another officer commanding the marines within a navy yard, he shall, on his arrival, report himself to the Commandant of the yard. Marine officers joining a navy yard will report to the Commandant and Commanding Marine Officer.

999....The Commanding Marine Officer within a navy yard will cause to be posted such sentinels for the protection of the yard and vessels in ordinary as may be directed by the Commandant of the yard. He will make to the Commandant of the yard a daily report of the amount and disposition of the force under his command, specifying by name officers who may have joined in the previous twenty-four hours.

1000....He will, unless the Commandant shall think proper to issue it himself, transmit every morning, in writing and under seal, to the Commandant of the yard, and to such other officers and such only as he may designate, the countersign for the ensuing night.

1001....The police and internal government of marines, when in barracks within or without a navy yard, and their instruction shall be under the direction of the Commanding Marine Officer, but must not conflict with the general police regulations of the Commandant of the yard.

1002....Non-commissioned officers serving within a navy yard or garrison may be reduced by the Commanding Marine Officer, he reporting the particulars of the case to the Commandant of the corps ; and he may promote to fill vacancies, with the sanction of the Commandant of the corps.

1003.... Marine officers belonging to a navy yard desiring leave of absence will conform to the general rules of the Navy on that subject The customary liberty to non-commissioned officers, musicians, and privates may be granted at the discretion of the commanding marine officer.

1004.... All official communications to and from officers and enlisted men of the marine corps serving at navy yards shall be forwarded through the Commanding Officer of the yard.

1005.... Deficiencies in the complements of marines in vessels on the eve of sailing may, by order of the Commandant of the yard, be supplied by the Commanding marine officer, and the circumstances of the case reported, without delay, to the Commandant of the corps by the Commanding officer of the marines, and by the Commandant of the navy yard to the Navy Department.

1006.... All offences or neglects which may be committed by marines as sentinels, or in violation of orders given by the Commandant of the yard, must be reported to him. Other offences which may be committed by marines, either in barrack enclosures or elsewhere, may be punished by the Commanding marine officer as by law allowed, or be reported to the Commandant of the marine corps.

1007.... Marines, when stationed at or employed within a navy yard, are to conform to all regulations which may be issued by the Commandant thereof for its government and security.

1008.... The exercises and formation of marines at parades, reviews, inspections, escorts, guard mountings and funerals, challenges of persons, police and regulations for camp and garrison duties, and salutes, will be the same as those established, or which may be hereafter established, for the army.

1009.... When marines are transferred from one station to another it shall be the duty of the officer transferring them to forward their returns forthwith to the officer to whom they are transferred.

1010.... It is the duty of officers serving with detachments to assist their Commander in making out rolls, reports, and returns ; keeping the books of the detachment, attending to issues, and to everything

12

connected with the welfare of the command.   The Commander will see that their assistance is rendered.

1011....The officer of the day will inspect the provisions daily issued to the troops, and if not of good quality, will report the same to the Commanding Officer.   He will also inspect the different meals, to see that the rations are properly cooked and served.

1012....Officers and soldiers in garrison will wear the prescribed uniform of the corps.

1013....When a deserter is apprehended, or surrenders himself, the officer in whose charge he is will immediately report the same to the headquarters of the corps, and to the Commanding Officer of the station or detachment from whence he deserted.

ARTICLE XXIII

RECRUITING AND RECEIVING VESSELS.

Section 1.

Recruiting.

1014....As the appointment of officers to attend to the recruiting service is intended not only to hasten the collection of recruits for the Navy, but to guard against the enlistment of improper, unsound, or incompetent persons, strict and constant attention to the duties of the rendezvous is to be given, the hours of which are to be from 9 a. m. to 3 p. m., and later when emergencies require it.

1015....The junior officers who may be ordered upon this duty are intended as assistants to the Commanding Officer, and not to act as his substitutes, except in cases where he is unable to attend by reason of sickness, or when absent on leave with the sanction of the Department; under all other circumstances he will be expected to attend daily at the rendezvous, and to personally question the persons offering to enlist, examine into their qualifications, and determine whether they may enter or not, and in what capacity or rating.

Recruiting.

1016....Boys shall not be enlisted under thirteen years of age, nor under four feet eight inches in height, unless as apprentices No person whatever shall be received under the age of eighteen without the con-sent of his parent or guardian, if any such can be found. If the evi-dence of the parent or guardian cannot be obtained, the doubt is to be noted on the descriptive lists, and no advance money will be paid; the required clothing and bedding being supplied on board the receiv-ing vessel. No person shall be entered as landsman over the age of thirty-three unless he possesses some mechanical trade, nor shall he be entered after thirty-eight, even though possessing a trade, without special authority of the Department. No person shall be entered as ordinary seaman unless he shall have been two years at sea, nor as sea-man unless he shall have been four years at sea and passed a satis-factory examination. The recruit may be required to declare on oath, in presence of the Commanding Officer of the rendezvous, that he makes a true statement of age, to the best of his knowledge and belief, unless he proves his age in some other manner.

1017....Except by special authority from the Navy Department, no person shall be enlisted for the naval service unless the Commanding Officer of the rendezvous or vessel, and the Medical Officer required to examine him physically, shall both pronounce favorably as to his fitness.

1018....Every one enlisting at a naval rendezvous is, before signing the shipping articles, to take the oath of allegiance prescribed by an act of Congress approved August 6, 1861, and to sign it.

1019....Every one enlisting at a naval rendezvous who has already been in the service of the United States should produce his discharge therefrom, in order to guard against shipping a person who was dis-charged dishonorably. Should it have been lost, and time will permit, the Department can be applied to for information as to the nature of the discharge with which the party was furnished. In all cases of doubt or suspicion as to the kind of discharge given to the individual, the Department must be consulted, and the communication be addressed to the Bureau of Equipment and Recruiting.

1020....The shipping articles are to be read to every one about to enlist by a commissioned officer of the rendezvous, in order that such person may fully understand the nature and extent of the obligation he is about to assume.

1021....No person in a state of intoxication shall be submitted to examination, nor shall any person known to have been convicted of an infamous crime be received into the naval service.

1022....No person on enlisting is to be rated as a petty officer, or higher than a seaman, unless he be a fireman.

1023....No firemen or coal-heavers shall be shipped as such until they have passed a satisfactory examination by one or more medical officers of the navy in respect to their health and vigor, nor shall firemen be so shipped until they have passed a satisfactory examination by one or more engineer officers of the navy upon their ability to manage fires properly with different kinds of fuel, and to use skilfully smith's tools in the repair and preservation of steam machinery and boilers.

1024....If persons should be enlisted to perform particular duties with complaints or injuries which, in the opinion of the Medical Officer and the Commander of the station, will not interfere with the proper discharge of these duties, their condition must be fully described and carefully noted on all the descriptive lists containing their names, in order that no improper claims for pensions may be afterwards allowed.

1025....The Commanding Officer of a rendezvous, on enlisting a person for the service, should request the surety for the recruit, or the recruit himself, if he has not received any money, to repair without delay on board the receiving ship, where good naval clothing, appropriate to the season, will be furnished him by the Paymaster, and deducted from his advance, or bounty money, to be then paid to the recruit. Clothing sufficient only for cleanliness and proper appearance should be furnished the recruit. Thus his whole advance will not be appropriated for clothing, and a quantity of unnecessary articles stowed in his bag, to be stolen or lost. When finally transferred to a sea-going ship, his wardrobe can be amply supplied there, and his clothing properly and cheaply altered or made by shipmates, if unable to do so himself.

1026....Each enlisted person delivered on board a receiving or

Recruiting.

other vessel intended to receive recruits must be accompanied by both a transcript list and a descriptive list, (Forms Nos. 11 and 12.)

1027....The transcript list must set forth in full the name of the recruit; the year, month, and day of his enlistment; the term or period for which he enlisted; whether he enlisted for general or special service or for coast survey; the date of the honorable discharge under which he may have re-enlisted, together with the name of the vessel from which such discharge was received, and the rating he held on board of her when discharged; his rating under present enlistment; his wages per month under the same; the wages advanced or bounty paid to him, if any, at the rendezvous, and the name of his surety, if any was exacted or given.

1028....The descriptive list must set forth in full the name of the recruit, his previous naval service, and the capacity in which he last served; his place of birth, age, and trade or occupation; the color of his eyes, hair, and complexion; his height, and the permanent marks or scars about his person.

1029....The transcript and descriptive lists are both to be prepared at the rendezvous, under the direction of its Commanding Officer, to be signed by him or by the officer serving in his stead, and to be addressed to the Commanding Officer of the vessel to which the recruit is sent; and a copy of each is to be duly and carefully recorded and retained at the rendezvous.

1030....The Commanding Officer will see that a note is made upon all accounts, transfers, and descriptive lists, and on all shipping articles and enlistment returns, against the name of every person who may come under the seventh section of the act approved February 24, 1864, for enrolling and calling out the national forces.

1031....Should a person holding an honorable discharge prove physically disqualified, it will be so written by the Recruiting Officer on the face of the discharge, and such discharge shall not entitle the holder to be received under it.

1032....The Recruiting Officer will write on the face of the honorable discharge, over his official signature, the date of re-enlistment. After the reception on board the receiving ship of the person re-enlisted, the Commanding Officer, also, will write on the face of the honorable

Recruiting.

discharge, over his official signature, that the three months' pay has been credited or paid him, with the date of such credit or payment and the amount thereof.

1033....Should it become necessary or expedient to provide a Recruiting Officer with money in order to secure men for the service, he is not to hold in his possession, at any one time, more than one thousand dollars, and therefore, in making his requisitions upon the pay agent, he is to govern himself accordingly, and the Commanding Officer of the station, before approving them, is to satisfy himself as to their propriety. A Recruiting Officer intrusted with public money is to report weekly to the Chief of the Bureau of Equipment and Recruiting, and to the Commanding Officer of the station, whatever balance he may have on hand.

1034....Recruiting Officers shall make no advance of pay, nor give any bounty, except by express orders from the Secretary of the Navy, or of the officer under whose orders they may be placed; and in all cases of making advances, the amount advanced to petty officers, if any such enlistment should be authorized, shall not exceed the amount authorized for seamen, and good security is to be taken for all advances until the persons receiving it shall have been duly received and mustered on board the receiving vessel, or some other vessel of the United States.

1035....Recruiting Officers shall not pay over any advance or bounty money except to the person duly entitled to receive it; and they must produce his receipt for the same, together with a certificate from the Commanding Officer of the receiving or other vessel to which the person may be sent, that he was actually received on board, before any credit can be allowed them for such advance or bounty money so paid.

1036....Recruiting Officers, when authorized to make advances of any sort with their own hands, are to do all in their power to induce recruits to repair on board the vessels to which they are to be sent, and there receive the amounts in clothing and other necessaries.

1037....When recruits are willing to repair on board the receiving vessels, and there receive the requisite clothing and other necessaries,

Recruiting.

the recruiting officers are to notify the Commanding Officers of the vessels of the fact, and securities may be dispensed with.

1038....Every Commanding Officer of a rendezvous must report, every Saturday evening, to the Chief of the Bureau of Equipment and Recruiting, the number of recruits he has enlisted during the week ending at the close of the rendezvous on that day, specifying particularly their names; the dates and periods of their enlistment; their ratings; whether they were enlisted for general service or coast survey; the dates of the honorable discharges under which they may have re-enlisted, together with the names of the vessels from which said discharges were received, and the ratings they held on board of them when discharged; their previous naval services, and the capacities respectively in which they last served; their places of birth, ages, and trades or occupations; the color of their eyes, hair, and complexions; their height, and the permanent marks or scars about their persons, according to Form No. 13; and every such Commanding Officer must also report on the same day of each week, and up to the same time, to the Commanding Officer of the station, the number of each rating of persons he has enlisted in the course of it, together with the number of colored ones among them, according to Form No. 21.

1039....Each vessel of the navy shall be furnished, by the Commanding Officer of the station from which she departs on a cruise, with one printed copy of the prescribed shipping articles, and with seventy-five printed forms of the descriptive list for every two hundred men composing her crew; and each Commanding Officer of a vessel on foreign service, or in the United States where there is no established naval rendezvous, may enlist seamen, firemen, coal-heavers, and persons of inferior rating to fill vacancies which may exist in her complement, provided the rules concerning enlistments at rendezvous be adhered to, so far as they can be made applicable, and that the advance money is not to exceed one month's pay. The term for persons so enlisted may be for a less period than three years, and so as to correspond with the time, as nearly as practicable, at which the rest of the crew generally will probably be discharged.

SECTION 2.

Receiving Vessels.

1040.... The Commander of a vessel receiving recruits shall take charge of, and receipt for daily, to the officer sending them, all such as may be duly forwarded; and if, after an examination severally by himself and his Medical Officer, they shall be found fit for the service, he shall cause them to be regularly entered upon her books, and paid, under the restrictions provided in paragraph 1025 of the preceding section, the advance money allowed. He is also to receipt to the recruiting officer for the descriptive lists directed to accompany the recruits, and to direct the Paymaster of his vessel to receipt to that officer for the transcript lists he is ordered to furnish, and to certify to him that the amounts of money against the recruits, as exhibited by his accounts, have been duly charged to them respectively. The recruit will be carefully inspected to see that he conforms to the descriptive list accompanying him, in order that no person may be delivered on board the receiving vessel who had not previously passed examination at the rendezvous.

1041.... No person is to be considered as finally shipped in the naval service until he shall have passed medical inspection on board the receiving ship where he is to be delivered. If this examination should develop any cause why the recruit should not be accepted, the Commander of the receiving vessel will report the case to the Commandant of the station, who will forthwith order a survey by two or three medical officers, and, as far as practicable, senior to the Medical Officer of the rendezvous where the primary examination was held; and if the recruit is found unfit for service, the objections are to be fully stated by the board of survey, whereupon the recruit shall not be received. The order for survey and medical report shall in all cases be transmitted to the Bureau of Equipment and Recruiting.

1042.... The descriptive lists accompanying recruits are to be carefully verified, under the direction of the Commanding Officer of the vessel to which they are sent ; and should discrepancies be detected, he is to notify the Commanding Officer of the rendezvous of all the facts attending them without delay.

1043....The descriptive lists are to be kept by the Executive Officer, who is to have a copy of them recorded in a book for the purpose, to be retained on board for reference when necessary.

1044....Descriptive and other lists must always accompany recruits whenever they are transferred from one vessel to another, and the name of the vessel to which they are transferred, preceded by the words, "transferred to," must be noted on the descriptive lists, as well as a statement of their probable qualifications ; and all such transfers must be duly noted on the muster-book of the vessel making them.

1045.....The transcript lists are to be kept by the Paymaster, who is to have a copy of them recorded in a book for the purpose, to be retained on board for reference when necessary.

1046....Accounts, specifying the sums paid and balance due, and transcript lists, both signed by the Commanding Officer and Paymaster, must always accompany recruits whenever they are transferred from one vessel to another.

1047....The Commander will have the clothing and bedding of all recruits carefully examined and marked, and lists of the same taken when they are first received on board, and take all measures for their preservation and safe-keeping. No recruit will be allowed to bring on board any other outside clothing than that prescribed by the uniform regulations.

1048....Neither clothing nor small stores are to be issued to recruits on board a receiving vessel, without the written order of the Commanding Officer ; and this must be preserved by the Paymaster as a voucher, in case a person to whom an issue of them was made should die or desert while in debt to the United States.

1049....The Commander of the receiving vessel is to adopt proper precautions to prevent desertions, and is not to allow any recruit to go on shore on liberty without the consent of the Commanding Officer of the station.

1050....Receiving vessels shall be sufficiently equipped to furnish the means for exercising the recruits who may be on board. The

Commanding Officer will, under the direction of the Commanding Officer of the station, have them exercised at the guns, small arms, &c., sails, pulling in boats, and exercise of the boats' howitzers ; and he will report to the Department at the end of each month the exercises had during the month. Particular attention will be paid to the instruction of landsmen and boys.

1051....The recruits on board a receiving vessel are not to be employed upon duties unconnected with that vessel, except by the order or sanction of the Commander of the station ; and when employed in aid of the force in navy yards for rigging or equipping vessels, or for any other service, he will see that they are placed under the direction of proper navy officers. Unless for some special service, he will not authorize the employment of the recruits in a navy yard upon other duties than such as are immediately connected with the equipment of vessels, or the preparation of their outfits and stores.

1052....No recruit intended for general service is to be rated a petty officer whilst on board a receiving vessel, as that authority is to be exercised by the Commanding Officer of the sea-going vessel to which he may be transferred.

1053....When the Commanding Officer of a receiving vessel is directed to transfer men to a sea-going vessel, if there be more than a sufficient number of any class on board to comply with the order, he is to make an impartial selection, preferring those who have been longest shipped, and sending a fair proportion of such as may be supposed qualified for petty officers, of useful mechanics, and persons of foreign birth and colored persons.

1054....When men are to be drafted from the receiving vessel to a sea-going vessel, the selection shall be made by the Commander of the receiving vessel ; and no officer, whatever may be his rank, shall be permitted to visit the receiving vessel and make selections for the vessel which he is to command.

1055....In case of complaint or dissatisfaction as to the character or condition of the draft on the part of the Commander of the vessel to which men are transferred from a receiving vessel, it shall be the duty of the Commander of the station to order a survey, on which he will decide the case ; but no men are to be returned and exchanged

Receiving Vessels.

except for good causes, and by his written order, in which the reasons for the same will be expressed.

1056....Should authority be given to enlist men for a particular vessel, such men shall not be detailed for any other vessel except by order of the Department.

1057....When persons who have entered at the rendezvous are brought on board the receiving vessel, care shall be taken that they are in a proper condition to be received; and if any person, when brought on board, shall be so much intoxicated as to require restraint, he shall not be received until he becomes sober.

1058....If, between the time of a person being entered at the rendezvous and his appearance on board the receiving or other ship, he shall receive an injury which, in the opinion of the inspecting and medical officer of the receiving ship, unfits him for the service, he shall not be received.

1059....The Commander and other officers attached to the vessel designated to receive recruits are to conform to the general regulations for other vessels in commission, as far as they are applicable, and are to live on board, unless specially exempted by the Secretary of the Navy, in the same manner as though under orders for sea service.

1060....A return for each week, ending on Saturday, signed by the Commanding Officer of the receiving vessel and the Paymaster attached to her, showing all the changes with regard to recruits that have taken place in the course of it, whether resulting from deaths, desertions, discharges, apprehensions, surrenders, or transfers, is to be made to the Chief of the Bureau of Equipment and Recruiting, agreeably to Form No. 14, through the Commanding Officer of the station.

1061....The Commanding Officers of receiving vessels will see that a note is made upon all accounts, transfer and descriptive lists, and on all shipping articles and enlistment returns, against the name of every person who may come under the seventh section of the act approved February 24, 1864, for enrolling and calling out the national forces.

ARTICLE XXIV.

Surveys.

1062.... Whenever articles are received under a contract or purchase at a navy yard, or station on shore, concerning which there is no regular inspector thereat, or received on board ship directly from a contractor or furnisher, a proper officer with the master workman under whose direction they are to be used, or the officer to whose department they may pertain, are to inspect them carefully in order to guard the government against imposition or loss, and his report, in ordinary cases, may be deemed sufficient ; but if they be in doubt, or their decision be questioned, the Commanding Officer is then to have the inspection or survey made by at least three competent persons, of whom the master workman or department officer aforesaid is, if practicable, to be one, and their decision, when approved by the Commanding Officer, is to be regarded as conclusive.

1063.... All applications for surveys upon articles supposed to be defective or unfit for use, or to be unequal to sample, or deficient in quality, must be made in writing, according to the prescribed form, » (No. 19, Appendix,) by the person having charge of the same, to his immediate Commanding Officer, and if he deems such survey necessary he will, if acting independently, order it at once, or if not so acting, but serving in a fleet, he will transmit the same to the Commanding Officer of the division or squadron to which he belongs, who, unless otherwise directed by the Commander-in-Chief, will order such survey. When not in company with the Commander of a division or squadron, Commanders of vessels are to transmit the applications in view, when approved by themselves, to the senior officer present.

1064.... Officers who may order surveys upon articles reported as defective, or requiring repairs, will, when practicable, select at least two commissioned officers for that duty, of a rank proportioned to the importance of the survey to be held, so that the United States may not be exposed to loss from the inexperience of the surveying officers, and, when it can be done, the officers shall be selected from other vessels than those to which the articles may belong.

Surveys.

1065.....Surveying officers may call upon the person having charge of the articles to be surveyed, or upon any other person, for information which may assist them in making correct statements upon the subject they may have been directed to investigate ; and if any person shall endeavor to deceive the surveying officers by knowingly giving false statements, or if the surveying officers shall discover, or find reason to suspect, any fraud, they shall notice it particularly in their report.

1066.....The report of officers directed to survey articles represented to be unfit for service must specify by whose order the survey was held, each particular article surveyed, the state in which found, and the most proper disposition to be made of it ; and if the articles are found to be damaged, or of improper quality, their report must further state, if possible, by whom they were furnished, and whether the damage or injury was or was not owing to the misconduct or neglect of any particular person or persons. Contractor's and inspector's marks must be noted.

1067.....When officers are ordered to ascertain the quantity of articles, they are not to take the account of them from the officer who has charge of them, unless it shall be impracticable to make a personal examination, or they shall be directed to take the account from him by the person ordering the examination, and when the quantity of articles shall be so taken, it must be particularly noted in their report, with the reasons why it was so taken, and they shall state what, if any, articles are found to be defective.

1068.....Reports of all surveys, except such as are hereafter provided for in this section, shall be made in triplicate, one part of which shall be written on the back of the order, or attached to it, and be furnished to the officer who requested the survey, another to the Commander of the vessel, and a third shall be transmitted to the proper bureau of the Navy Department, by the officer ordering the survey.

1069.....Discrepancies between the marks and contents of packages as to quantity or kind are to be determined and reported upon by a board of survey. It must embrace the marks of the parties who furnished and inspected them.

1070.....No stores, provisions, or clothing, are to be thrown overboard, unless they are entirely useless, and except the surveying officers shall, in their report, represent them as being, in their opinion, prejudicial to the health of the ship's company, in which case the Commander of the vessel shall cause them to be thrown overboard as soon as the report of the survey is duly approved or confirmed, and the certificate of one of the surveying officers that they were so disposed of is to be attached to the report, but all other articles are to be converted to some other use, or turned into store.

1071.... If any officer of the Navy having charge of money, provisions, or other stores belonging to the United States, shall die, be suspended, removed, or otherwise separated from his vessel or station, so as to render it necessay to appoint another person to perform his duties, it shall be immediately reported by his Commander to the Senior Officer present in command, who shall order, in writing, a survey to be held by proper officers, and, when practicable, in presence of the officer who is to succeed to the charge of the articles aforesaid, and the surveying officers shall make out a statement, in writing, of the amount, quantity, or number, state and condition of such articles, in quadruplicate, and sign the same, and transmit them in a report to the officer ordering the survey, one copy to be retained by him, and three sent to the officer appointed to take charge of the money and stores, two of which he will receipt and hand over to the officer relieved, or to the representative of the officer if deceased, one to be retained by him, and the other to be forwarded to the Navy Department.

1072....All officers ordered upon surveys are strictly required to perform that duty with the utmost attention and fidelity, and to make their reports with the strictest impartiality, so that, should they be called upon, they may be able conscientiously to make oath of their correctness.

1073....In all reports of surveys involving quantities, they must be expressed in writing, and never exclusively in figures.

1074....In all cases of survey, the officer superior or senior in rank is to prepare the report.

1075....Whenever any important accident or derangement shall occur to the machinery of a steamer, there shall be held upon it a strict and careful survey by a board, composed of one Line Officer and at least

Surveys.

two Engineer Officers, who shall report, in writing, the nature and extent of the accident or derangement, the cause thereof, the probable time of repair, and to whom, if to any one, blame in connexion therewith is to be attributed. The report is to embrace every detail necessary to a complete understanding of the case. The order of the survey shall accompany the report, which is to be made in duplicate, and forwarded to the Department by the first opportunity.

1076.... Whenever, in the opinion of the Commanding Officer of a vessel, any person attached to her is unfit for service, he shall, if on separate or detached service, order a survey to be held upon such person by the Medical Officers of the vessel, and such others as may be convenient, not exceeding three, though two will suffice where the full number cannot be procured. In extreme cases the survey may be conducted by the Medical Officer of the ship, but if serving in squadron the Commanding Officer of the vessel shall report all such cases to the officer in command of the squadron or Senior Officer present, who shall order the survey to be held. The board shall examine and report upon such person, in accordance with the form prescribed by the regulations of the Bureau of Medicine and Surgery. When the person is found unfit for duty, the report shall state the general character of the disease or injury, its probable duration as far as can be predicted, and in every case all the facts and circumstances connecting the disease or injury with the performance of duty or exposure incident thereto. Medical Officers are strictly forbidden to give unofficial certificates of ill health or inability to perform duty, and all such private or unofficial statements will be disregarded by the Department when officers present themselves for the purpose of seeking an extension of leave or change of duty. Whenever such person may be reported unfit for duty, and the survey is approved by the officer ordering it, he shall be disposed of as promptly as possible, in the manner recommended by the board, and in case of discharge from service, without reference to the state of his account.

1077.... In case the person reported unfit for duty shall be found to have received his disability in the performance of duty, and is thereby entitled to a pension, the forms of the Pension Office, and the "Instructions of the Bureau of Medicine and Surgery," shall be strictly observed in preparing the reports and certificates. All reports of surveys, whether on account of temporary disability or for pension, shall be made out in duplicate, and be forwarded through the prescribed channels to the Bureau of Medicine and Surgery.

1078.... Besides the surveys above directed, the Commander of a vessel, when practicable, shall appoint, at the commencement of each regular quarter, to serve to the end of it, three suitable officers, to whom, as a continued board of survey, the Paymaster, or any other officer responsible for stores, shall refer, through the senior of the three, either verbally or in writing, all such articles in his department as he may judge to be unfit for use, or not to correspond with their marks in quantity or kind, provided they do not exceed in quantity, on any one occasion, the bulk of a package of clothing, or, in the case of provisions, two barrels ; and this board shall survey and pronounce upon said articles, which, with the consent of the Commanding Officer, are to be disposed of accordingly.

1079.... At the end of the quarter, or earlier if ordered, the board is to report in form, and in triplicate, to the Commanding Officer for his action and signature, separately for each department, and separately, also, in the case of clothing or small stores, upon all the articles it has condemned in the course of it, and the disposition which has been made of them, in order that these reports may answer as authenticated vouchers.

1080.... Should any of the board die, or be detached, during the quarter, the above report is to be made up to the time of the occurrence, signed by the survivors in one case, who are to append a note as to the cause of the absence of more signatures, and by all the members in the other. In either event, another report is to be made at the end of the quarter, if surveys have been held in the mean time.

ARTICLE XXV.

LEAVES OF ABSENCE AND FURLOUGHS.

Section 1.

Leaves of Absence.

1081.... Permission to leave the United States can only be granted by the Secretary of the Navy, and no officer is ever to leave the United

States under any leave of absence unless such leave shall expressly authorize it.

1082....Within the United States leave of absence for a longer time than one week will only be granted by the Secretary of the Navy, except in cases of great emergency, which must be immediately reported to him.

1083....Commanding Officers, acting under the immediate orders of the Secretary of the Navy, may, within the United States, grant leave of absence to persons under their command for not exceeding one week, provided it can be done without delaying the equipment of the vessel to which they may belong, or producing other injury to the public service, and that no leave is granted to any officer belonging to a vessel under sailing orders.

1084....Commanders-in-Chief of squadrons, and Commanders of navy yards or stations in the United States, shall not leave the limits of their command for a longer period than one week in any successive two months without the permission of the Secretary of the Navy.

1085....Permission will not hereafter be granted by Commanding Officers of squadrons or vessels in commission to any officer or man under their command to leave his station for any causes connected with health till a board of medical survey shall have pronounced such a measure essential to early recovery, or have reported the officer or man unfitted for further duty on his station ; and Commanding Officers of squadrons abroad will not hereafter grant leaves of absence, unless authorized by the Navy Department, to officers to return to the United States, except upon the recommendation of a medical board of survey. This order is not intended to supersede the instructions of October 3, 1861, authorizing the Commanding Officer of a vessel detached from a squadron, or on separate service, to transfer sick or invalids upon the report of the medical officer of the vessel. Officers on leave, in consequence of medical survey or sick ticket, will report their state of health to the Department every fifteen days.

1086....Officers of the navy applying for a leave of absence, or an extension thereof, on the score of ill health, must forward at the same time to the Department the certificate of a surgeon in the navy, if

13

Leaves of Absence.

there be one in their vicinity, or, if there be no naval surgeon, of some respectable surgeon or physician, of their inability to perform duty. Such certificates must state the nature of the disease and the probable duration thereof, as far as can be judged.

1087....Unless otherwise directed by competent authority, temporary leave to officers may be granted by their Commanding Officers ; but no such leave is to exceed twenty-four hours, unless sanctioned by the Commander-in-Chief or senior officer present.

1088....The petty officers and men belonging to vessels in the navy will be permitted to visit the shore on suitable occasions, when it can be done without injury to the public service. In foreign ports such permission will not be granted if objected to by the proper authorities thereof. The senior officer present must always be consulted before such leave in foreign ports is granted.   Leaves of absence, or permission to go on liberty, will not be granted to any enlisted man by any person other than the Commanding Officer of the vessel to which he is attached ; and should the Commanding Officer be absent on service, or on temporary leave, the officer left in command shall have no power to grant leave to any enlisted man unless specially authorized by the Commanding Officer.   The names of those to whom leave is to be granted must be specified in writing, and signed by the Commanding Officer previous to his absenting himself from the vessel.

1089....Leave is not to be granted to men of a crew in debt to the Government unless they deposit as security the full amount of their indebtedness, and in no case unless, in the judgment of the Commanding Officer, there is no probability of desertion.   Hereafter all funds deposited by enlisted men, as security for their return from absence on leave, and forfeited by their desertion, and any bounty money or advanced pay refunded by minors or others discharged from the service, will be deposited by the Paymaster with the nearest United States Assistant Treasurer ; the advance pay to the credit of ''pay of the navy,'' and the bounty and other money to the appropriation for naval bounties. The certificate of deposit, in the case of advanced pay, is to be transmitted to the Navy Department, and in other cases to the Bureau of Equipment and Recruiting, to be sent to the Fourth Auditor of the Treasury.

SECTION 2.

Furloughs.

1090....Officers can only be placed on furlough by the Secretary of the Navy or by sentence of a court-martial.

1091....Officers on furlough are not to wear their uniforms, except on occasions of special ceremonies.

ARTICLE XXVI.

Correspondence.

1092....Officers of the navy and marine corps, and all other persons connected with the naval service, will observe the following rules in their correspondence with the Secretary of the Navy and the bureaus of the Department:

- 1093....All communications are to be written in a clear and legible hand, in concise terms, without erasures or interlineations, and on one side only of each half sheet.

1094....If the subject-matter can be completed on one page, and no communications or papers are enclosed with the letter, a half sheet only shall be used; but if communications or papers are enclosed with the letter, a whole sheet shall be used, and such communications or papers shall be placed between the leaves.

1095....Enclosures are to be separately numbered, and referred to accordingly.

1096....The paper used is to be white foolscap, $13\frac{1}{2}$ by $16\frac{1}{2}$ inches, weighing sixteen pounds to the ream, and made of linen stock; to be stop-ruled, with twenty-four blue lines on the first and third pages only, leaving one inch margin back and front, top and bottom.

1097....Separate letters are to be written on separate subjects.

1098....Letters are to be folded twice, parallel with the ruling, indorsed with the name and rank of the writer, place or vessel, date, and brief statement of the contents.

Correspondence.

1099....Signatures are to be distinctly legible, and the writer is to annex his rank or rate. This rule is also to be observed on all occasions of officers signing their names to official documents.

1100....Commanders of squadrons and stations, and all other officers having a regular correspondence with the Department, are to number their letters. A new series is to commence on the 1st of January of each year.

1101....When letters or documents are dated at sea, the latitude and longitude are to be stated.

1102....In all communications dated on board ship, the rate of the vessel shall be stated after her name.

1103....In order to facilitate the public business and prevent errors, the dates of all circulars, orders, telegrams, or letters, to which reference is made in corresponding with the Department or any of its bureaus, *shall be distinctly quoted.* And the same rule is to be observed in forwarding triplicate bills, bills of lading, and invoices, the date of the order or orders being written across the face in red ink.

1104....All letters and documents transmitted in a foreign language are, when possible, to be accompanied by translations.

1105....Commanders-in-Chief and other officers abroad are to forward, by different conveyances, duplicates, and, if necessary, triplicates, of all important letters they may write, either to the Secretary of the Navy or to any of the bureaus, and on these occasions they are to state at the top of each letter, in red ink, when and by what conveyance the original was sent.

1106....Every person in the navy making a report, application, requisition, or communication of any kind whatever to the Secretary of the Navy, a bureau, the Commander-in-Chief, or to any authority other than his Commanding Officer, will send the same unsealed to such Commanding Officer, to be by him remarked upon and forwarded to its address.

1107....All officers through whom communications from inferiors are to be forwarded to the Department, one of the bureaus, or any authority higher than themselves, must forward the same, if couched in respectful language, as soon after being received as practicable ; and they will invariably state their opinions in writing, by indorsement or otherwise, in relation to every subject presented for decision. The term " forwarded " is only to be indorsed upon such papers as require no action from the Department or other authority.

1108....The general routine to be observed in forwarding communications, or in submitting requisitions or reports, is as follows : Commanders of vessels to transmit them to the Commander of the division to which they belong ; Commanders of divisions to the Commander of the squadron to which they belong ; Commanders of squadrons to the Commander-in-Chief; Commander-in-Chief to the Navy Department. Each of said officers, in forwarding papers from others, to append his approval, or such remarks as he may judge necessary and proper. Fleet officers shall forward all communications through the chief of the staff. The senior marine officer of the fleet, squadron, or division will forward all reports or returns from the several vessels through the chief of the staff. Should he be in command of the guard of the vessel in which he is serving, all reports or returns relating to that vessel will be forwarded through the Commanding Officer.

1109....If there be no Commanders of divisions, Commanders of vessels will transmit them to the Commander of the squadron ; and if there be no Commander-in-Chief other than the Commander of the squadron, he will refer such as may be necessary to the Navy Department.

1110....In case vessels of a squadron should be separated from the Commander-in-Chief, then, in the absence of their divisional Commander, the senior officer present is to be regarded in the light of a Commander of a division.

1111....In case of a vessel acting singly, and being alone, her Commanding Officer is, of his own authority, to dispose of requisitions and reports, and to be the medium of reference to the Navy Department ; but if not alone, the senior officer present, whoever he may be, is to discharge those functions.

1112....Should the same communication be made to the Secretary of the Navy and any bureau, the person forwarding such duplicates shall state the same in his communication.

1113....When officers are separated from the Commander-in-Chief, and important or useful information is likely to be delayed by trans-

---

Correspondence.

---

mission through the latter, reports will be sent directly to the Department and copies to the Commander-in-Chief.

1114....The receipt of all communications, except acknowledgments, or other communications clearly requiring neither action nor reply, from the Secretary of the Navy, or from any bureau of the Department, is to be immediately acknowledged, taking care to refer to the subject to which they respectively allude.

1115....There are established in the Navy Department the following bureaus :

1. Bureau of Yards and Docks.
2. Bureau of Equipment and Recruiting.
3. Bureau of Navigation.
4. Bureau of Ordnance.
5. Bureau of Construction and Repair.
6. Bureau of Steam Engineering.
7. Bureau of Provisions and Clothing.
8. Bureau of Medicine and Surgery.

All orders, circulars, and instructions, issued by a Chief of Bureau, and relating solely to subjects with which his bureau is specially charged, are to be considered as emanating from the Secretary of the Navy, and shall have full force and effect as such. Official letters relating solely to subjects with which a bureau is intrusted, are to be addressed to the Chief of a Bureau. All other correspondence must be with the Secretary of the Navy.

1116....All persons in the Navy are forbidden to publish, or cause or permit to be published, directly or indirectly, any official instructions, reports, or letters, or to furnish copies of the same to any person, without the permission of the Secretary of the Navy.

1117....Officers are prohibited from commenting, in their private correspondence, upon the operations or condition of the vessel or squadron to which they may be attached, or from giving any information of their destination or intended operations, lest such communications may be published to the injury of the public service.

1118....Officers must enter, in proper books, copies of all the official letters they may write, and carefully file and preserve all official documents. The date of the receipts and of the acknowledgments of all such documents shall be written on their face.

1119....Letter-books, containing copies of all orders given, or official letters written, and the originals of all letters received on public service, at the different navy yards and at other shore stations, by the Commanding Officer thereof, must be left at those yards and stations, and carefully preserved as records. The Commanding Officers may, if they think proper, take copies for their own use of all orders or letters which they may receive or write.

1120....All reports from the Executive Officer, officers of divisions, Engineer, Surgeon, Paymaster, or any other person, made to the Commander of a vessel after battle, or any important service, shall be forwarded to the Navy Department, but such Commander will retain copies of them for future reference.

1121....Copies of all general orders and instructions issued by a Commander-in-Chief, of all official correspondence of public interest, and of all internal rules that may be issued by Commanders of vessels, shall be sent to the Navy Department.

1122....Commanding Officers will observe great care in forwarding reports to the Department in relation to the official conduct of those under their command, and shall in all cases, when it will not be clearly injurious to the public service, inform the officer complained of, or reported, of the nature of the representations in relation to him.

1123....No application for a revocation or modification of orders from any officer of the Navy ordered to report for duty at any place or station will be considered or replied to by the Department until such officer, if able to travel, has reported in obedience to such order.

ARTICLE XXVII.

Approval of Requisitions, Accounts, and Muster Books, Purchases and Articles Delivered.

1124....The approval of a requisition for money, or other articles, is to be considered as a certificate, on the part of the approving officer, that, in his opinion, the articles named in the requisition are necessary for the public service, and are conformable to such allowances as may be established ; and the approval of such requisition by the officer whose approval will authorize the procurement or delivery of such articles, according to these regulations, or instructions from the Navy Department, is to have the force and responsibility of an order. In the procurement and expenditure of stores, Commanding and all other officers concerned are peremptorily enjoined to be governed by the allowances established by the Navy Department, and by the exercise of the most scrupulous economy, to make them last for the full time they are intended, and as much longer as practicable. Unless in a case of absolute necessity, arising from some unavoidable accident, or from a formal condemnation by survey—to be plainly set forth on the face of the requisition—or the article be of a character the quantity of which for a given time cannot possibly be well regulated—that is, tar of any kind, oil for burning, oil or other grease for lubricating, waste for wiping, emery, rivets, files, boiler-iron for patching, material for making or repairing joints about steam works, slacked lime, a disinfectant, a medicinal, or stationery for the Commander-in-Chief—no departure from said allowances will be tolerated, either by the procurement, at the public expense, of anything which they do not embrace, or of anything which they do, in advance of the expiration of the time for which it is furnished to last. Commanding Officers will be held to a strict account for any requisitions they may approve in violation of these instructions ; and for any want of proper care or interest on their part to secure the utmost practicable economy in the use of the public property with which they are intrusted, or over which they are required and expected to exercise control, they will be held to a rigid responsibility ; and to this end they will forward copies of all bills of purchases to the proper bureau of the Navy Department, accompanying them with a statement of the quantity of the respective articles put on board when the vessel was fitted out, and the date of their final expenditure.

1125....The approval or signature of a Commanding Officer of a vessel to a muster-book or muster-roll is to be considered as his certificate of the correctness of all the entries made therein in relation to the date of enlistment, ratings, terms, and expiration of service ; and

Approval of Requisitions, Accounts and Muster Books, Purchases, &c.

he will be particularly careful to examine all such books or rolls, that full confidence may be placed in such as are thus signed or approved.

. 1126 .... The approval of a Commanding Officer to a quarterly muster and pay-roll, or to a transfer-roll, or account, given to or sent with men transferred, is to be considered as his certificate of the correctness of those parts which are a transcript from the general muster-book, relating to the dates of enlistment, ratings, terms, and expiration of service, but not to the correctness of those parts relating to their accounts, which are upon the responsibility of the Paymaster, and to be certified by his signature to the said transfer-rolls or accounts.

1127 .... The approval of an officer to a bill for articles purchased, or services rendered, is to be received as a certificate that the purchase or service was duly authorized; that the articles have been received by a responsible officer of the government, or that the service has been performed; that they conform to the contract, or are otherwise satisfactory as regards the performance of the duty, and the quality and price of the articles, but not for the correctness of the calculations determining the amounts charged. The person receipting such bills of articles is to examine and report any errors, but the person paying them is to be finally responsible for their correctness.

1128 .... The approval of an officer, whose approval, by the instructions of the Treasury or Navy Department, will authorize the payment of money, is to have the force and to be given under the responsibility of an order for such payment, and is always to be accompanied by the rank of the officer and the date of the approval.

1129 .... All accounts must bear the date of approval, and the sum for which the account is approved must be written in words at length.

1130 .... On a change of command on a foreign station, the officer who relinquishes the command will take care that all bills for articles, the requisitions for which have been approved by him, are settled before he relinquishes the command; but if from any circumstances this cannot be done, the officer who approved the requisitions will be responsible for the correctness of the purchases, though the bills may be authorized to be paid by his successor.

1131 .... The Commander of a fleet or a single ship, when acting alone, shall, before leaving a port at which he may have received supplies, notify the persons who may have furnished the same to attend at some specified time and place with their accounts, so that none may be left without receiving his inspection and approval, should they be correct.

1132.... Purchases made for the Navy by any agent of the Navy Department, upon requisitions or orders addressed to him, are to be made, after due inquiry and comparison, by such agent on the most favorable terms for the government, and upon prices agreed upon before the purchase is made, and he shall certify the same upon the bills rendered for the articles.

1133.... Where articles are delivered by or under the direction of an agent who purchased the same, the officer who is to take charge of and receipt for them shall examine the bills rendered, and if, in his opinion, any of the articles are charged above the fair market price, he shall report the same to the officer under whose approval they were required before receipting for them, that such approving officer may institute inquiries and take such other measures as the case may require.

1134.... Where inspections are required to determine the quality of articles, or their conformity with contracts or agreements, no receipts are to be given for them until the inspecting officers shall have certified their satisfaction with the articles delivered.

ARTICLE XXVIII.

General Muster Book.

1135.... Every person on board any United States vessel-of-war, who receives either wages or provisions, must be entered in the general muster-book ; but, as they will not all be in the same class or situation, it will be necessary to have several lists, separated from each other on the book by convenient spaces, and a separate series of numbers for the several entries in each list. The lists required to keep the necessary distinctions are the following :

1. A list of the commissioned and warranted Navy Officers, including secretaries and clerks.

2. A list of petty officers, seamen, ordinary seamen, lands-men, boys, firemen, coal-heavers, and others borne for pay and provisions.

3. A list of officers, non-commissioned officers, musicians, and privates of marines.

4. A list of supernumeraries for pay and provisions only.

5. A list of all other supernumeraries.

6. A list of prisoners of war.

1136.....The letter "D" is to be placed against the name of every person who has been detached; the letter "T" against the name of every person who has been transferred; the letters "Dis" against the name of every person who has been discharged alive; the letters "D D" against the name of every person who may have died, and therefore discharged dead; the letter "S" against the name of every person pronounced a straggler; and the letter "R" against the name of every person pronounced a deserter.

1137....The entry in each list of the muster-book must be distinguished by a number in the first column, to be exclusively appropriated to it, and which must never be applied to any other entry in the same list, but to each new entry a new number must be given.

1138....The muster-book shall be kept in such form as the Navy Department shall prescribe.

ARTICLE XXIX.

Books.

1139....The receipt to the officer delivering the books allowed a vessel is to be given by her Navigating Officer.

1140....On board flag vessels they are to be kept in the apartment occupied by the Commander of a fleet, squadron, or division, under the immediate charge of his secretary, who is to receipt for them to the Navigating Officer. On board all other vessels they are to be kept in the apartment occupied by the Commanding Officer, under the immediate charge of his clerk, who is to receipt for them to the Navigating Officer. On board all vessels the Navigating Officer is to ascer.

tain quarterly, or oftener if necessary, if any of them are missing, and to report such as may be to the officer in whose apartment they were kept.   This will relieve him from the responsibility of losses, and place it upon the secretary or clerk, as the case may be.   At the end of the cruise the Navigating Officer is to see that the books are properly returned into store,

ARTICLE XXX.

Travelling and other Allowances—Rules Concerning the Commencement and End of Rates of Pay.

1141....No officer or other person can be paid mileage except for travel actually performed free of government transportation or expense, and in obedience to orders.   To entitle an officer of the Navy, including a secretary or clerk, to travelling expenses, he must furnish the pay agent, or Paymaster of his vessel, with a certified copy of his orders and indorsements thereon, after having reported for duty.   Officers and others ordered from one station to another, as members of courts-martial, courts of inquiry, boards of examination, inspection, &c., or as witnesses, will be allowed travelling expenses, from the place whence ordered and back again, (unless other orders are given,) upon presentation to the pay agent of a certified copy of their order to that service and discharge therefrom.   When enlisted men are *honorably* discharged, within the United States, from vessels returning from sea, they shall be entitled to three cents per mile as travelling expenses from the place of discharge to the place of enlistment if within the United States; and this allowance will be paid by the Paymaster of the vessel, with the final account of the person entitled thereto.

1142....The allowance for the travelling expenses of officers of the Navy within the United States is fixed by law at ten cents per mile. For travelling out of the United States the actual expenses only are allowed.   Detention at any place on the route for more than one day is not considered as part of the travelling, unless certified by the officer to have been necessarily incurred in awaiting the next conveyance. The expenses must be shown by vouchers in the usual form, unless the officer certify that it was not practicable to obtain them, in which case his own certificate to a detailed statement of the actual and necessary expenses will be received as sufficient evidence. The travelling expenses of officers within the United States will be paid by the pay agent at the place to which they shall have been ordered, or by the Paymaster of the vessel to which their orders attach them. When a doubt exists as to the distance travelled, the certificate of the officer, stating the route by which he travelled, with the distance thereon, and that it was the shortest route usually travelled, will be received as evidence, where the Post Office records do not determine, and he should certify that a public conveyance was not furnished.

1143....The actual and necessary travelling expenses of officers proceeding from the United States, under orders for foreign service, will be paid upon the production of bills and receipts, or if they shall certify that it was not practicable to obtain receipts, then upon a statement of the actual and necessary expenses, made with as much particularity as may be in their power, and certified to be correct. The travelling expenses of officers returning to the United States from foreign service under orders, or under permission granted in consequence of sickness or medical survey, will be paid upon the same evidence as is required by the last rule in the case of officers going abroad.

1144....Paymasters are not entitled to travelling expenses in coming to Washington to settle their accounts, unless they do so under orders from the Department.

1145....Stewards to Paymasters and Surgeons are not allowed travelling expenses, unless by special direction of the Department.

1146....When an officer shall be ordered to proceed with recruits from one station to another, his passage shall be agreed for and paid by the pay agent.

1147....The act of March 3, 1835, prohibits any allowance to officers of the Navy beyond their pay, except for travelling expenses. No allowance can be made, therefore, to any such officer for expenses which he may have incurred by reason of sickness, whether for medical attendance or otherwise.

1148....Any fireman, coal-heaver, seaman, ordinary seaman, landsman, or boy, who re-enlists for the term of three years within three months after an honorable discharge, pursuant to the act entitled "An act to provide a more efficient discipline of the Navy," approved March 2, 1855, and to the act approved June 7, 1864, is entitled to three months' pay according to the rating borne upon his discharge, although the re-enlistment may take place immediately after such discharge. This gratuity is conferred only on *enlisted* men; stewards and other persons who are *appointed* are not entitled, though possessing such a discharge.

1149....Paymasters will be allowed the unavoidable loss sustained on clothing and small stores committed to their charge, not exceeding on the former one-and-a-half per cent., or on the latter two per cent., upon their presenting their own certificate of the amount of the loss, and of its having been unavoidably incurred, and a certificate of the Commander of the vessel of his belief that the Paymaster, in the preservation and issuing of the articles intrusted to him, used all the care and diligence which a prudent man would use in respect to his own property.

1150....To entitle any person to the one-fourth additional pay granted by the act of July 17, 1862, he must either have re-enlisted to serve until the return of the vessel in which he is serving, and his discharge therefrom in the United States, or he must have been detained by the Commanding Officer under the seventeenth section of the said act. In order to sustain a charge for such additional payment, therefore, it will be necessary for the Paymaster by whom it shall have been made, to produce, upon the settlement of his account, a certificate of the Commanding Officer that the persons to whom such additional compensation shall have been allowed (mentioning their names) did actually re-enlist as aforesaid, or were detained by him under the said section of the act referred to. This additional pay, under the seventeenth section of the act of July 17, 1862, is to be allowed to all enlisted men detained after the expiration of their terms of enlistment, whether serving on foreign stations or home squadrons.

1151....For the subsistence of prisoners on board of public vessels, who may mess in either the cabin or ward-room, one dollar per day shall be credited to the mess, and paid by the Paymaster for each person. For their subsistence in any other offi-cers' mess, there shall be so credited and paid seventy-five cents per day for each person; and for their subsistence in any other mess on board than an officers', or by themselves, one ration will be allowed. It is strictly required, in every case, that the caterer of the mess claiming such credit from the Paymaster shall furnish to him his certificate, approved by the Commanding Officer of the vessel, that the actual cost is equal to the amount charged; if less, then to what-ever lesser sum such subsistence may cost the mess. No other charge shall be made, nor shall any such person conveyed on board such ves-sels, be required to pay to the mess in which he may live, any compen-sation for subsistence or passage.

1152.....When officers of the Navy are ordered to take passage in any vessel of the United States Navy, no allowance will be made to any mess for the subsistence of such officers.

1153....For the subsistence of pilots, who may mess in the ward-room, one dollar per day shall be credited to the mess, and paid by the Paymaster for each person. For their subsistence in any other officers' mess there shall be so credited and paid seventy-five cents per day for each person; and for their subsistence in any other mess on board than an officers', or by themselves, one ration will be allowed.

1154....Although it is usual for our ministers to be conveyed in ships-of-war, no allowance is made for the expenses of their mainte-nance whilst on board. In every such case provision is to be made and the expense to be defrayed by the minister himself, just as it would be if he took passage in a private vessel.

1155....The five cents per day allowed by law to each person in the Navy in lieu of the spirit ration is in addition to pay. Pay offi-cers will credit this allowance on their rolls, under the separate head of "undrawn spirits," to each person on board ship entitled to a ration, and at the end of each quarter will pay the amount due to such of the crew and marines as may elect to receive it. If any per-son shall decline to receive such payment, it must remain to his credit on the books of the ship, and be accounted for in the same manner as other pay. The commutation price of the Navy ration will continue to be twenty-five cents, without reference to the five cents allowed as above mentioned.

1156....The *necessary* and proper funeral expenses of all persons who shall die while in actual service of the United States will be paid, when sanctioned by the Navy Department, or by the Commander-in-Chief of the squadron, when on foreign service.

1157....A marine officer commanding a guard of a man-of-war, the complement of the guard of which is forty men or upwards, will hereafter be entitled to an allowance of ten dollars per month for responsibility of clothing, arms, and accoutrements.

1158....Double rations are not to be allowed to marine officers commanding guards on board receiving vessels, nor to the marine officer in command of the guard at the navy yard gate in the city of Washington, D. C.

1159....No officer in any branch of the public service, or any other person whose salary, pay, or emolument is fixed by laws or regulations, shall receive any additional pay, extra allowance, or compensation, in any form whatever, for the disbursement of public money, or any other service or duty whatsoever, unless the same shall be authorized by law, and the appropriation therefor explicitly set forth that it is for such additional pay, extra allowance, or compensation.

1160....No charge will be allowed in the accounts of Paymasters for a commission paid to any person for making purchases for the vessels-of-war of the United States on foreign stations. Such purchases shall be made by the paymasters themselves, or by the resident Naval Storekeeper, if there be one.

1161....Upon an original appointment of an officer (if he be not a bonded officer) his pay will commence at the date of acceptance. This rule applies to secretaries and clerks, but they are not to be appointed until the officers authorized to confer the appointments have left their domiciles to enter upon the service on which they may be ordered. The "*leave*" pay of an appointed disbursing officer begins on the date of his first order for duty; his "*other duty*" and "*sea*" pay commence, respectively, as above stated respecting other appointed officers.

1162....The pay of all promoted officers commences from the date of the signature of an appointment to perform the duty, should one be given before the issue of a warrant or commission; or from the date of the signature of a warrant or commission, should no appointment have been previously given.

1163.... When ordered on sea-service, officers are entitled only to "shore" or "other duty" pay from the day they leave their domiciles, in obedience thereof, to the date of their report for such service, at the place where the vessel to which they are attached is preparing for sea, or, if the vessel is already at sea, to the Commander of the fleet or squadron to which it is attached, or to the Commander of the vessel, from which date their sea pay, with rations, commences. The duty pay of an engineer officer is the same whether employed on shore or at sea, and commences when he leaves his domicile in obedience to orders for duty, though only entitled to rations when on sea-service.

1164.... An officer returning to the United States from duty under orders not granted at his own request, or for his own convenience or accommodation, will be considered as on "other duty," and paid accordingly.

1165.... When an officer who is attached to a vessel for sea-service enters a hospital for treatment, he shall continue to receive sea pay for three months, unless sooner detached; but at the expiration of that period, if he should still remain in the hospital, he will be allowed only leave of absence pay until he rejoins the vessel or enters upon other duty.

1166.... A clerk's pay is only allowable while the vessel to which he may be attached remains in commission, except as provided for in paragraph 1178.

1167.... Chaplains are to be paid the same pay as that specified for lieutenants in the act of 16th July, 1862. (Attorney General's Opinion of 4th September, 1862.)

1168.... The provision of the seventeenth section of the act of 16th July, 1862, viz: "In calculating the graduated pay of boatswains, gunners, carpenters, and sail-makers in the Navy, as established by law, the sea-service shall be computed from the dates of their appointments or entry into the service in their respective grades in lieu of the dates of their warrants," is regarded as effective only from the passage of that act.

14

1169....An officer attached to a vessel for sea-service, who receives from the Department a leave of absence *on account of ill health*, will be considered as entitled to sea pay, as in the case of an officer similarly attached who enters a hospital for treatment, and then to "other duty" pay until he reports for duty on shipboard ; that is, he is entitled to sea pay for three months, and to "other duty" pay until he reports or be detached.

1170....Officers of the Navy attached to vessels employed under the orders of the Department in active service in rivers are entitled to sea pay as well as to rations.

1171....An acting appointment by order of a Commanding Officer, and subsequently confirmed by the Secretary of the Navy, is deemed valid. A copy of the order, certified as such by the Commander of the vessel, may be substituted for the original. It must, however, also be shown that it was issued to supply a deficiency in the established complement of the vessel.

1172....Firemen and coal-heavers, when unable to perform their duties from other causes than sickness, or injury received in line of duty, or when they neglect them, shall receive only a reduced pay ; that is, firemen of the first class shall only receive the pay of firemen of the second ; those of the second the pay of coal-beavers, and coal-heavers the pay of ordinary seamen, so long as they neglect their duties or are unable to perform them, or until duly discharged from the service.

1173.....No person enlisted for the naval service is entitled to pay whilst at a naval hospital after the expiration of his term of enlistment, but he may be retained for hospital treatment.

1174....Officers are entitled to receive the pay due them up to the date of sailing, without reference to the advance received from the pay agent.

1175....A temporary leave of absence is not to be understood as *detaching* an officer from duty to which he has been ordered by authority of the Department, or as *affecting his rate of pay.*

1176....The accounts of officers who are paid through the Fourth Auditor's office will be settled only at the end of each quarter of the calendar year, or at the period of their transfer to some disbursing officer.

1177....The petty officers and enlisted persons serving on monitors attached to the Atlantic Blockading Squadrons, or employed in the Gulf of Mexico, will be allowed an addition of one-fourth of the rate of pay prescribed by the order of the Navy Department, dated May 16, 1864.

1178....Pay Officers will be allowed "other duty" pay for themselves and their clerks for the time employed in the settlement of their accounts, not exceeding the periods specified in paragraph 1199. And neither clerks nor stewards of the pay department shall be required to perform clerical services for any other than the pay officer of the vessel, except in cases of emergency, to be approved by the Commanding Officer.

ARTICLE XXXI.

Accounts.

1179....Disbursing Officers of the United States are required to keep their accounts with the United States separate and distinct under every bond given by them, respectively, and to state, in the caption of each quarterly account, *the date of the bond* under which it is rendered.

1180....Any Paymaster of the Navy, resident within the United States, who shall transmit to the Fourth Auditor, within ten days after the end of every month, a summary statement showing his balance at the commencement of the month, his receipts and disbursements, under each head of appropriation, during such month, and the balance at the end of the same, such statement being certified to be correct by the officer required to approve the accounts of such Paymaster, shall be authorized to render his accounts for settlement quarterly instead of monthly, provided that such accounts be duly transmitted within one month after the end of the quarter to which they refer.

1181....Paymasters of the Navy on foreign stations, or serving on board vessels actually performing blockading duty, must transmit the monthly summary statements required in the preceding paragraph, unless they furnish the Fourth Auditor with satisfactory evidence that the nature and exigencies of the service in which they were engaged

Accounts.

at that time prevented the transmission of such statements. In such cases they will be authorized to transmit their accounts quarterly, agreeably to the provisions of the act of January 31, 1823. When a Paymaster renders his account he must transmit to the Fourth Auditor :

1. A general pay-roll, embracing the individual accounts of the officers, men, and marines, with the columns added and the amount stated in ink, and a recapitulation of the several pages ; and it must be signed, in the receipt column, by officers, men, and marines, and each signature of the men and marines witnessed by an officer.

2. A muster-roll, showing the dates of entry and detachment of officers, and the entry, discharge, transfer, and desertion of the men and marines, and the expiration of the term of enlistment of the men ; and showing, also, the vessel or station to which the officers, men, and marines may have been transferred. The rolls must be approved by the Commanding Officer of the vessel.

3. Vouchers for all open purchases and other contingent bills, properly approved by the Commanding Officer and receipted.

4. A complete statement of the small-store and clothing account, with the receipts of the Storekeepers and other disbursing officers ; also, a full statement of all moneys received for provisions.

5. An account of the sales of bills of exchange, with the certificate of at least two merchants as to the rate of exchange at the time of negotiating every bill.

6. All transfer accounts and rolls of officers or men, whether to or from the vessel. Transfer accounts of officers will be made out in triplicate, one part to be sent to the Fourth Auditor, and the other two parts to the Paymaster to whom the transfer is made, one of which is to be receipted by him and returned to the Paymaster by whom the transfer is made, to accompany his final account. The accounts of the men must not be transferred to the Fourth Auditor for payment at the end of a cruise unless specially requested by the Secretary of the Navy

or Fourth Auditor. The discharge should not be given unless the man is present and receives the pay due him.

7. All original letters, or copies thereof, from pay agents, Fourth Auditor's office, and the Department, and other official papers relating to his accounts ; copies of officers' orders to join the vessel, certified by themselves, also with their certificates as to the time of accepting their orders.

8. An account current, showing all his receipts and expenditures, and the date of his bond.

1182....Paymasters on board receiving ships, or at shore stations, will be guided by these instructions in the rendering of their accounts, so far as they are applicable.

1183.....In the rendition of the accounts, Paymasters of all grades are required to forward to the Fourth Auditor's office, besides the papers above specified, all their original books from which such accounts are compiled, such as ledgers, journals, receipt books, &c.

1184....All Disbursing Officers *must prepay* the expense of transportation of their accounts to the Fourth Auditor's office for settlement if they be sent by any other conveyance than the United States mail.

1185....A general witness to signatures on the pay-roll is not sufficient. The signature of the officer witnessing the receipt must be given in each case.

1186....Paymasters will make an immediate return to the Fourth Auditor's office of the accounts of deceased officers, seamen, or marines, and transmit their wills if they shall have left any. The balances which may have been due to them at the time of their death will be paid only after a statement of their accounts at the Fourth Auditor's office.

1187....Payment of balances due deceased seamen and marines will be made to administrators who are heirs, or appointed with the consent of a majority of the heirs.

1188....When the balance due does not exceed the sum of one hundred dollars, letters of administration will be dispensed with, and the prescribed affidavits substituted. The widow, if she be the applicant, should render a certified copy of her marriage certificate.

Accounts.

1189.... Heirship may be established by the fact being inserted in the letters of administration, and additionally proven by the affidavits of two disinterested persons, taken before an officer duly empowered to administer oaths.

1190.... If the heirs be minors, guardians should be appointed. Payment of arrearages, claimed under a will, will only be made after satisfactory proof of the will is adduced to the Accounting Officers.

1191.... Wills of persons in actual service must in all cases, when possible, be in writing, and attested by an officer. A nuncupative will must be reduced to writing immediately, and be attested by at least two officers. The executor will be required to produce the original will, or a copy duly authenticated. No payment will be made to a creditor until the balance due to the deceased person shall have remained in the treasury, uncalled for by an administrator as aforesaid, for six months after information of the death of such person shall have been received at the Department; and where the balance exceeds the sum of twenty dollars, no claim of a creditor will be paid until an advertisement shall have been inserted, for three successive days, in the newspapers employed to publish the laws in the city of Washington, and also in three successive numbers of a paper nearest where the deceased resided, calling upon other claimants to present their claims at the office of the Fourth Auditor within four months; at the end of which term, if the balance shall not have been demanded by an administrator appointed as aforesaid, the claims which shall have been presented and proved before the Accounting Officers will be paid in equal proportion, the expense of the advertisement having been first defrayed out of the sum due to the deceased person at the time of his death.

1192.... In accordance with the spirit and letter of the laws of the United States, the Accounting Officers have determined that the arrears found to be due shall be paid, in all cases, to the proper parties interested in preference to attorneys.

1193.... Where supplies for the Navy are obtained without advertisement, the account must be accompanied by a certificate of the Commandant of the yard or station who has approved the requisition for the articles that the public exigencies required the immediate delivery of the articles mentioned in the bill, and that, there not being time to advertise for proposals, the articles were properly obtained by open purchase, and that the purchase is approved for the sum they cost. Where the purchase is made under contract growing out of an advertisement for proposals, the fact must be certified in like manner upon the voucher.

1194....All transfers of the accounts of officers of the Navy from one Paymaster to another will be made *directly*, and not through the office of the Fourth Auditor. The Paymaster by whom the transfer is made will give notice of it, and transmit a copy of the account to the Fourth Auditor's office. When an officer is granted leave of absence, placed on furlough, or directed to await orders, his account will be transferred to the Fourth Auditor's office, or to the Paymaster of the station nearest his intended residence, as he may prefer. When the officer desiring the transfer has allotted any portion of his pay, the Paymaster, upon transferring his account, will make a note thereon of the monthly sum allotted, and of the place of payment and date of expiration of the allotment.

1195....Before a Paymaster can receive credit at the Fourth Auditor's office for a payment made to an officer for any service, or for any amount of money checked on his books as having been advanced by a pay agent, he must produce the order under which the service has been performed, or the advance made, or a copy thereof, with all indorsements, certified by the officer to be such, together with a certificate, by the officer, of the time at which he left his domicile or station to enter upon such service. The Paymaster will always inspect the original order, and satisfy himself that all indorsements are embraced on the certified copy.

1196....Overpayments other than such as are produced by authorized advances will be invariably disallowed, whether made in money, clothing, or stores, excepting payments for the commutation of rations, or of the spirit part thereof, and excepting also such advances in clothing as may have been made by the previous order of the Commander of the vessel, upon the ground that they were necessary to the health and comfort of the men, which order, if in writing, must be produced; and if verbal, there must be a certificate of the Commander that

---

Accounts.

---

gave it.   A general approval of the roll in which the advances are
charged will not be considered sufficient.

1197....When the crew of a vessel shall have been paid off at the
end of a cruise, the Paymaster will transmit to the Paymaster of the
marine corps a pay-roll of all the marines who have been attached to
the vessel during any portion of the cruise, approved by the Commander of the vessel and the Commanding Officer of the guard.   As
the utmost despatch is required in paying off crews, Paymasters are
directed to forward to the Department, in the most expeditious manner, their requisitions for funds for that purpose.

1198....The second section of the "Joint resolution for the relief of Paymasters," &c., approved March 3, 1849, does not authorize
an advance of public money by the Paymaster to the Commanding
Officer, or to any other person, on *his* order.   But the disbursement
must be for some service rendered or article furnished.   (See Circular
of Second Comptroller of March 20, 1855.)

1199....Pay officers of the Navy will render their final accounts and
returns to the Fourth Auditor of the Treasury, and the Chief of the
Bureau of Provisions and Clothing, as soon as practicable after the
expiration of their cruise, but not exceeding the following time after
the crew shall have been paid off or transferred :

> For vessels of the first rate.............sixty days.
> For vessels of the second rate ....fifty days.
> For vessels of the third rate ....forty days.
> For vessels of all other rates............thirty days.

Final accounts in all cases will be accompanied by the necessary
vouchers for a complete settlement of such accounts.

Commanding Officers.

1200....An officer in command of a United States vessel may require the Line Officers of any grade under his command to make daily
or frequent observations and calculations for determining the latitude
and longitude, and the variation of the compass, and report the results
to him ; he will be held responsible for the safe conducting and steering of his ship, and also whenever an accident shall occur to her from
the want of due care or precaution.

Arrests and Charges.

1201....Commanding Officers are specially required to see that the Paymaster duly credits each person under their command with the amount of prize money due him, in accordance with the statement received from the Fourth Auditor of the Treasury.

ARTICLE XXXII.

ARRESTS, CHARGES, AND COURTS-MARTIAL BOARDS.

SECTION 1.

Arrests and Charges.

1202....No Commander of a vessel of the Navy is to continue the suspension from duty, arrest, or confinement, of a commissioned or warrant officer, for a longer period than ten days, unless a longer one be necessary to bring the offender to a court-martial ; and if, after the case of an offender to be tried by a court-martial has been brought to the notice of an authority empowered to convene such court, the offender, owing to imperative reasons, cannot be brought to trial within thirty days after that time, he shall, unless the Secretary of the Navy or the Commander-in-Chief otherwise direct, be released from arrest and returned to duty by his Commanding Officer, and so remain until a court-martial can be convened to try him, when he shall be again arrested on the day before this court is ordered to convene, so as to undergo his trial before it.

1203....As the law requires that the person accused shall be furnished with a true copy of the charges, with the specifications, at the time he is put under arrest, and as the officer empowered to convene a court-martial is to exercise his discretion either to dismiss a complaint against a party or have it investigated by such court, and to direct what portions of the complaint, in the event of a trial, shall be embodied or omitted in the charges and specifications preferred by a complainant, the general rule should be to leave the authority of *arresting* an officer to be exercised by the superior who may order a trial to take place.

1204....An officer placed under arrest by the orders of a Commander-in-Chief is to be brought to trial before a court-martial at the earliest moment the nature of the case itself and the exigencies of the public service will permit, unless from subsequent information or explanations the Commander-in-Chief should deem it proper and expedient to withdraw the charges entirely, release the officer fully from arrest, and restore him to duty.

1205....An offence, committed at any one time, for which a person in the Navy shall have been placed under arrest, suspension, or confinement, and subsequently entirely discharged therefrom by competent authority, or for which he shall have been otherwise fully punished, is to be regarded as expiated, and no further martial proceedings against him, for the offence itself, are ever afterwards to take place. If fully discharged from arrest or suspension by competent authority, at the instance of the party himself and by an arrangement in which he concurs, such discharge is to close forever further proceedings in the case so far as any naval authority may be exercised in relation to them.

1206....If any emergency of the service, or other sufficient cause, should render it requisite, in the opinion of the Commanding Officer or other superior authority, that an officer under suspension or arrest should be temporarily released therefrom, and, in the latter case, without the charge or charges against him being withdrawn, he may give orders to that effect, and the officer shall return to his duty accordingly ; but such release shall work no prejudice to any subsequent investigation of the case by a court of inquiry or court-martial that the authority vested with the power to institute either may think proper to order, nor to a subsequent investigation of any complaint that the party may prefer relative to his suspension or arrest.

1207....No officer placed under suspension or arrest shall be confined to his room, nor restrained from the proper use of any part of the vessel to which, before his suspension or arrest, he had a right, except the quarter-deck and poop, unless such confinement or restraint shall be necessary for the safety of the ship, or the preservation of good order and discipline; and even then, neither the confinement nor the additional restraint shall be imposed for any longer time than absolutely necessary.

Arrests and Charges.

1208.... Every officer shall, when *arrested*, deliver up his sword when required by the authority of his Commanding Officer, and shall confine himself to the limits assigned him either at the time of his arrest or afterwards, under pain of being dismissed from the service by the sentence of a court-martial, or by the President of the United States.

1209.... Officers making complaints or explanations are to confine their statements to the facts connected with the case, and they are not to express their opinions of the conduct or motives of the parties, or to use any abusive epithet or improper language in their communications.

1210.... When an officer is suspended from duty and reported to a superior, the latter will call upon him for such explanations as he may choose to afford in relation to the affair, and for a list of persons whom he may wish to have questioned in support of them, and the superior may institute general inquiry into the facts and circumstances to regulate his further proceedings.

1211.... If, after the investigation has been made by himself, or by others under his orders, the superior shall deem the offence to be of a character not sufficiently serious to require the action of a court of inquiry or court-martial, the officer against whom the complaint has been made shall be restored to duty by the orders of the superior if ten days have already elapsed from the time he was first put under suspension ; or, if this period has not so elapsed, the officer may be so restored at any time before, that the said superior may think proper.

1212.... If, on the contrary, after an investigation, the superior should deem the offence to be such as to require scrutiny by a court-martial, the case is to be referred without avoidable delay to the Secretary of the Navy, or to the Commander of a fleet or squadron authorized to convene such court, as it may require, for his decision as to whether or not a trial shall take place, and the party against whom the complaint has been made may be continued under suspension to await it. If the decision be that no trial by a court-martial is to take place, the party is to be released from suspension and restored to duty by his Commanding Officer. In so referring a case for such decision, special care is to be taken to transmit at the same time to the authority

Arrests and Charges.

to whom the appeal is made a particular statement of the offences charged, embracing dates, places, and all other facts necessary to a conclusion as to the propriety or expediency of ordering a court martial, and to frame charges and specifications in case one should be ordered. Explanations of the party accused, briefs of information given by all who may have afforded any in relation to the case, and a list of the witnesses proposed, mentioning where they are to be found, should invariably accompany the statement.

1213....On the decision of a competent officer to have a party tried by a court-martial, he will cause such charges and specifications against him to be prepared as he may consider proper, and will transmit a true copy of them, with an order for the arrest of the accused, to the proper officer, who, on exhibiting such order to the accused and carrying it into effect by receiving his sword, will at that time deliver to him said copy of the charges and specifications.

1214....In preparing charges, offences of different character should not be embraced in the same charge, but a separate charge must be made for each offence.

1215....Offences shall not be allowed to accumulate in order that collectively sufficient matter may thus be obtained for a prosecution without giving due notice to the offender, and no offence for which an offender has already been formally reprimanded is to be revived and subsequently investigated, except when it may be indispensable to prove a particular habit charged.

1216....Any letter which may be written to the president or judge advocate of the court by an officer in transmitting the charges and specifications under which a party is to be tried, or a properly authenticated copy of the same, is in all cases to be filed with the charges as a part of the record of the court.

1217....An officer whose conduct is to be investigated by a *court of inquiry* need not necessarily be put or kept under suspension for the purpose. He may, however, if expedient, be, at his own request, *excused* from attending to the particular duties of his position during such investigation.

General Courts-Martial.

Section 2.

General Courts-Martial.

1218....When a general court-martial shall be assembled in conformity to order, the person to be brought before it for trial shall be introduced. The precept for convening the court and the appointment or warrant of the Judge Advocate shall then be read by the Judge Advocate in the presence of the accused. The accused shall then be asked by the Judge Advocate if he objects to any member of the court, or to the court proceeding to his trial, and if he answers in the negative, the oaths prescribed by law will then be administered in the presence of the accused; if, however, the accused shall make any objection, such objection shall be considered, decided upon, and recorded before the court is sworn.

1219....The court having been duly sworn, and that fact noted on the minutes, the charges and specifications against the accused shall be read by the Judge Advocate, and the accused shall then be asked by him if he pleads guilty or not guilty to the charges. If he pleads guilty, the court shall warn him of the consequences, and he may then withdraw his plea; but if he repeats his plea of guilty, it shall be recorded, and the court may proceed to investigate, or at once to deliberate and determine upon the sentence. If he pleads not guilty, or stands mute, the court shall proceed to examine the testimony in the case. The record of the court must state distinctly that these questions were put, and the answers, if any, which may be given.

1220....If it shall be necessary to swear the president of a court-martial or of a court of inquiry as a witness, the prescribed oath shall be administered by the member next in rank.

1221....The president of a general court-martial, or of a court of inquiry, or the senior member of a summary court-martial, shall be empowered to preserve order, to decide upon matters relating to the routine of business, and to adjourn the court, from day to day, at and to such hours as, in his judgment, will be most convenient and proper for the transaction of the business before it; but should an adjournment be announced by the president, to which a member has some reason for objecting, he may ask leave to present such objection, which, thereupon, must be submitted for decision to the court.

1222....It shall be the duty of the Judge Advocate to lay before the court, as far as practicable, a list of the witnesses which it may be intended to produce, with a general statement of the facts expected to be proved by each. He shall then, under the direction and control of the court, proceed to examine the witnesses who have been summoned on the part of the United States to support the charge or charges.

1223....The examination of a witness having been closed on the part of the United States, he may be cross-examined by the accused ; and when the cross-examination shall be closed, the court will then ask or allow any further questions which it may deem necessary. When the examination of a witness shall be closed, the whole of his testimony shall be read over to him, that he may then correct errors, if any have been made.

1224....When the witnesses on the part of the United States shall have been examined, the witnesses on the part of the accused shall then be examined by the accused, or in his behalf, and afterwards cross-examined and examined by the court in the same manner as those who had been called on the part of the United States. Further examination of witnesses may then be continued, if the court, or the accused, with the assent of the court, shall desire it.

1225....Questions to be propounded to a witness shall be reduced to writing ; and should any objection be made to any proposed question, or to the reception of any testimony, the court shall proceed at once to determine upon the same ; and if they shall decide that such question shall not be put, or against the reception of such testimony, the question or matter rejected, shall be described, or recorded in full, in the minutes of the proceedings, as the court may decide.

1226....If a member of a court-martial shall, from any legal cause, fail to attend after the commencement of a case, and witnesses shall be examined during his absence, the court must, when he is ready to resume his seat, cause every person who may have been examined in his absence to be called into court, and the recorded testimony of each witness must be read over to him, and such witness must acknowledge the same to be correct, and be subject to such further examination as the said member may require ; and without a compliance with this rule, and an entry of it upon the record, a member who shall have been absent during the examination of a witness shall not be allowed to sit again in that particular case.

1227....The examination of the witnesses being closed, the accused shall be at liberty to make his defence, in writing, against the charges and specifications, which defence he shall submit to the court for their inspection before it is publicly read ; and if, in the opinion of the court, it shall contain anything disrespectful, they may prevent that part from being read ; but it shall be filed with the proceedings, if the accused desire it, and he will be held responsible for the same.

1228....After the defence shall have been read, the court shall be cleared, and the members shall proceed to consider the testimony (the whole of which shall be read over aloud by the Judge Advocate) and the defence of the accused. When they shall have sufficiently examined and considered the same, the question shall be put upon each specification of each charge by the Judge Advocate, beginning with the first, whether it is "proved" or "not proved," or "proved in part," the junior member voting first, and the rest in the inverse order of their rank, each member writing "proved," "not proved," or "proved in part," and if in part, what part, over his signature ; and each shall hand his vote to the Judge Advocate, who shall, when he has received all, read them aloud ; and the court shall deliberate and consider until a majority shall agree on a finding, which shall then be recorded.

1229....When the members shall have thus voted upon all the specifications of any charge, the question shall then be put upon the charge, to each member, "Is the accused guilty of this charge?" "guilty in a less degree than charged?" or "not guilty?" And then the members, in the order as above stated, shall write "guilty," "not gui ty," or "guilty in a less degree than charged," and in what degree, over their signatures, and hand them to the Judge Advocate, who shall, after receiving all the votes, read them aloud, and record the general result. When the decision on one charge shall be completed, the court will then proceed to the next charge and specifications, until votes shall have been taken and recorded, as above directed, upon all the charges and specifications.

1230....When the court shall have voted upon all the charges, if the accused shall have been found guilty, or guilty in a less degree than charged, upon any one of them, by the number of members which the law may require in the particular case, they shall next proceed to vote upon the punishment to be inflicted. In this case each member shall, in the order before directed, write down and subscribe the measure of punishment which he may think the accused ought to receive and hand it to the Judge Advocate, who shall, after receiving all the votes, read them aloud.

1231.... If the requisite majority shall not have agreed on the nature and degree of the punishment to be inflicted, the Judge Advocate shall proceed in the following manner to ascertain which of the different votes will obtain the assent of the requisite number of the members: He shall begin with the mildest punishment which shall have been proposed, and, after reading it aloud, shall ask the members, in the order hereinbefore prescribed, "Shall this be the sentence of the court?" and every member shall vote, and the Judge Advocate shall note the votes. In case the proper number shall not vote in favor of the punishment proposed on the first vote, he shall then take the next lowest proposed punishment, and proceed to take a vote as before directed, and shall thus proceed until a proper majority shall be obtained for some sentence, either proposed at first or subsequently.

1232....Sentences to suspension must state distinctly whether from rank or from duty only ; and if the pay is to be suspended, whether wholly or in part, and for what length of time.

1233....The law has never intended to vest in courts-martial the power to pardon offences, or to award a nominal punishment equivalent to a pardon. The power to pardon, remit, or mitigate, is expressly vested in the President of the United States, or the officer authorized to convene the court. The exercise of this power by a naval general court-martial will subject the individual members thereof to the charge of violating the law.

1234....The sentence having been recorded, the proceedings in each separate trial shall be signed under the sentence by all the members

General Courts-Martial.

who may have been present when the judgment was pronounced, and also by the Judge Advocate.

1235.... Any member may, after the sentence has been pronounced, move for a recommendation of the accused to the clemency of the revising power, which recommendation, with the reason therefor, is to be recorded immediately after the signatures of the court and Judge Advocate to the sentence, and must be signed by the members concurring in it.

1236.... When a general court-martial, court of inquiry, or summary court-martial has tried all the cases actually referred to it, and submitted, severally, the proceedings of each to the officer ordering the court, the president or senior officer thereof may adjourn it; but he and all the members of the court must still remain at the place they are, in readiness to reassemble, if the action of the officer ordering the court should require such a course to be pursued, and until he orders the court to be *dissolved*.

1237.... The court may allow counsel to the accused for the purpose of aiding in his defence, but always under the restriction that all motions or communications shall be made in writing, and in the name of the accused.

1238.... If from any cause, after a court shall have been sworn, the number of members required by law to form a court shall not assemble on the day to which the court was adjourned, and the court, by that fact, should be dissolved, the proceedings up to the period of dissolution, and the fact of the dissolution itself, must, nevertheless, be authenticated by the signatures of the members present, and by that of the Judge Advocate, and transmitted by the senior member on hand to the officer who ordered the court, that such further measures may be directed as circumstances shall require.

1239.... The sentences of all courts-martial which shall be approved on a foreign station will be communicated in a general order to the Commander of each vessel in the squadron, that they may be made public; and when approved in the United States, they shall, in the same manner and for the same purpose, be communicated to the Commander of each vessel or station in the United States.

15

1240....Should the proceedings of a court-martial be disapproved for any informality or irregularity of the court, the particular irregularity or informality will be made known in general orders, so as to prevent, if possible, a recurrence of similar irregularities.

1241....No person in the Navy shall be liable to be, tried and punished by a court-martial for any offence which shall appear to have been committed more than three years before the issuing of the order for such trial, unless the person by reason of having absented himself, or some other manifest impediment, shall not have been amenable to justice within that time.

1242....The president of a general court martial may order an officer of the Navy, not above the grade of Lieutenant, or an officer of the marine corps, not above the grade of Captain, to act as its provost marshal, whose duty it shall be to hold in charge the person on trial; to be accountable to the court for the due appearance of such person whenever the court is assembled; to serve notices to witnesses, and to act otherwise as the police officer of the court.

1243....In the case of a trial of a petty officer, or person of inferior rating of the Navy, or of a non-commissioned officer, musician, or private of marines, the person to act as provost marshal may, if the president of the court thinks proper, be either a petty officer of the Navy, or a non-commissioned officer of marines.

1244....At the request of the president of a court of inquiry, or of the senior officer of a summary court-martial, the Commander of a vessel or station on board or at which it is held is to direct an orderly to be detailed to attend its meetings and execute orders.

1245....The defence made before a court-martial or a court of inquiry being a part of the official record, and the trial not being complete until the proceedings have been passed upon by the revising authority, it is strictly forbidden to any person who shall be tried by either court to publish, or cause or permit to be published, his defence, in whole or in part, until final action has been had in the case, on pain of such punishment as a court-martial may impose for disobedience of orders.

1246....In detailing officers for a court-martial or court of inquiry before which a medical, pay, marine, or engineer officer is to appear, it is proper, if the exigencies and interests of the public service will permit, that one commissioned officer, or more, of the same department or corps as the person to be tried, should be placed upon it; and in detailing officers for a summary court-martial, it is equally proper, under like circumstances, if a non-commissioned officer, musician, or private of the marine corps is to be brought before it, that one or more marine officers should be of the number.

SECTION 3.

Summary Courts-Martial.

1247....In conformity with the ninth section of the "Act to provide a more efficient discipline for the Navy," the following rules and forms, approved by the President of the United States, are to be observed by summary courts-martial convened under the authority of said act :

1. Summary courts-martial will adopt the same forms of proceedings and rules of evidence as naval general courts-martial, so far as they shall be applicable and not inconsistent with the conciseness and precision enjoined by the law, nor with the provisions of this general order.

2. The form of convening a summary court-martial will be by a brief written order addressed by the Commander of the vessel to the senior member of the court, stating the names and rank of the members of the court, and of the recorder, and of the time and place of meeting, and by written or verbal orders to the other members of the court and the recorder. The written order to the senior member will be appended to the record of the proceedings.

3. The record will state that the oath prescribed by the law was duly administered to each member and to the recorder in the presence of the accused.

4. If objection is made by the accused to any member of the court, it will be so stated in the record of proceedings, and made known, if the court think fit, to the Commander of the

Summary Courts-Martial.   --

vessel, who will, at his discretion, order another member of the court, or continue the member objected to.

5. The accused shall be furnished, before trial, with a written specification of the offence, or offences, for which he is to be tried. The specifications shall be as brief as practicable, without unnecessary repetition, or circumlocution, or accumulation of epithets, but explicit; and all offences or misconduct committed at any one time by the same individual, and intended to be charged against him, shall be comprised in the same specification, which shall be approved, before trial, by the officer ordering the court, and a duplicate of it be annexed to the record.

6. The accused shall not be required to plead guilty or not guilty to the specification ; but if a plea of guilty be made, the court may, at its discretion, admit testimony as to the character of the offender, or in extenuation of the offence. And, in any case, the court may find the accused guilty of the whole or any part of the misconduct charged, according to the evidence, and adjudge punishment for so much as shall be found proved.

7. Witnesses shall be summoned by the recorder through the Executive Officer of the vessel, and the summons shall be obeyed, unless disapproved by the Commanding Officer for some reason to be stated in the record.

8. The court, if requested by the accused, may allow a commissioned, warrant, or petty officer to appear as counsel, and cross-examine witnesses in his behalf ; but no written defence or argument, nor any protracted oral defence or argument, shall be admitted. Nor shall any testimony not clearly relevant be admitted, nor any documentary evidence be read to the court or appended to the record.

9. If more than one case be tried by the same court, the record of each case shall be separate ; the order for convening the court shall be appended to the record of the first case, and be referred to in each subsequent record, so as to show that the proceedings of the court are continuous. And in each case the prescribed oath shall be administered anew to the members and the recorder of the court.

Boards.

Section 4.

Boards.

1248....Officers on boards are to take their seats in the same order, of rank or seniority as on courts-martial.

1249....The senior or presiding member is to preserve order, to decide upon matters relating to the routine of business, to decide upon a recess, and to adjourn the board from day to day, at and to such hours as, in his judgment, will be most convenient and proper for the transaction of the business before it. Should, however, an objection be made by another member of the board to an adjournment announced by the senior officer, a vote is to be taken with regard to it, and the decision of the majority is to govern.

1250....No board is to transact any other business than an adjournment unless at least two-thirds of the members be present.

1251....No member of a board, unless prevented by illness or some insuperable difficulty, ordered away by competent authority, or excused by the officer ordering it, is to fail in his attendance at the appointed times; and in case of such failure, the senior officer present of the board is to inform the officer ordering it of the fact, and also of the reasons of the failure, if known to him, in order that the vacancy may be supplied if necessary.

1252....A member absent when the investigation of a matter or case was held is not to vote upon a decision with regard to it; but, if necessary to arrive at a conclusion, a reinvestigation, with that member present, may take place, and thus he may bestow his vote.

1253....The junior member of a board is to be the recorder of its transactions, but the senior member is to draw the final reports, based upon the opinions of a majority, and these reports are to be signed by all the concurring members, and to have appended, over their signatures, the reasons of dissenting members.

1254....Members of a board are not to leave the vicinity of the place at which they are assembled unless authorized by the officer ordering it, or his superior.

1255....As distinct rules are framed for the Naval Academy, the above are not to apply to the boards held thereat, except when composed of officers not attached to it, or partly by such officers and partly by those who are attached to it.

ARTICLE XXXIII.

United States Naval Asylum.

1256___.The Naval Asylum having been placed under the supervision and direction of the Bureau of Yards and Docks, subject to the immediate control of the Secretary of the Navy, the following regulations have been adopted for its government :

1. The object of the Asylum is to provide a comfortable home for "disabled and decrepit naval officers, seamen, and marines," who shall be entitled to the benefits of the institution.

2. The officers shall consist of a Governor, not below the grade of a Captain in the Navy, and a Commander. a Lieutenant, a Surgeon, and a Chaplain, to be taken from their respective ranks, together with a Secretary to the institution, a Master-at-Arms, a Matron, and such officers and laborers, embracing watchmen, cooks, laundresses, and attendants, as the department from time to time shall authorize.

3. Applicants for admission into the Asylum will be required to produce evidence of twenty years' service in the Navy. They must state their age, birth-place, and physical condition, the vessels in which they have served, the names of the Captains, and the dates of such service. They will also be required to produce a naval surgeon's certificate, stating that the applicant is not able to support himself by manual labor ; and in cases where pensioned applicants desire to commute their pension for places in the Asylum, similar certificates will be required ; nor will these regulations be deviated from except under extraordinary circumstances, or the written permission of the Secretary of the Navy.

4. In consideration of the liberal provision which has been made for the beneficiaries in the Asylum, they will be required,

United States Naval Asylum.

at the discretion of the Governor or Commanding Officer, to perform such duties, for their benefit and that of the institution, as their age, physical abilities, and condition will allow.

5. For misconduct, (of which drunkenness, fighting, abusive and profane language may be enumerated as foremost,) or for any conduct subversive of good order and discipline, beneficiaries will be subjected to punishment by stoppage of their pocket-money and tobacco, confinement in the cells, and curtailment of the ration, at the discretion of the Governor or Commanding Officer, and to dismission from the Asylum, with the sanction of the Secretary of the Navy.

6. The Governor will administer the affairs of the institution, receive the daily reports of the subordinate officers, make the required returns to the Bureau of Yards and Docks, submit annual estimates for the probable wants of the institution, and transmit the same so as to reach the Bureau on or before the 1st October in each year. He will also cause a diary to be kept and forwarded annually to that Bureau. The diary will also contain a list of absentees, punishments, and misdemeanors of every kind.

7. The allowance to each beneficiary for clothing is not to exceed $3 per month, or $36 per annum.

8. In consideration of their good conduct, and the faithful performance, from time to time, of such duties in and about the Asylum as may be directed by the Governor or Commanding Officer, each beneficiary shall receive $1 per month. For any violation of the regulations, however, this gratuity may be stopped for such period as the Governor may deem expedient.

9. As a reward for meritorious conduct, the Governor or Commanding Officer shall form a corps of petty officers and watchmen (not to exceed eight in each class) of the best behaved and most efficient of the pensioners, who shall wear a suitable badge of office. It shall be the duty of the petty officers to set and relieve the watchmen on their respective beats, to attend to the hoisting and lowering of the colors, to report-

ing delinquents, and to the performance of such general duties as the Governor or Commanding Officer may direct. They shall hold their office for the term of three months, may be reappointed at the discretion of the Governor, and shall be allowed *two dollars* per month, *including* the monthly allowance of one dollar, for pocket money.

10. The products of the grounds shall be expended for the benefit of the institution, at the discretion of the Governor or Commanding Officer.

11. No liquors of any kind will be allowed the inmates of the institution, nor will they be permitted within its enclosures. A violation of this regulation will be deemed a sufficient cause for dismission from the Asylum.

12. The colors shall be hoisted and struck daily at the hours usually observed in the Navy.

13. During the summer months the fires will be extinguished as early after meals as practicable. The lights will be extinguished at 10 p. m. In the winter the fires and lights, with the exception of the furnaces and such others as the Commanding Officer may deem necessary, will be extinguished at 11 p. m. The gates and doors shall be closed and locked at 10.30 p. m., in winter, and 11 p. m. in summer, and shall not be opened until daylight, without permission from the Commanding Officer.

14 No beneficiary will be allowed to leave the Asylum without the permission of the Executive Officer, and no leave for a longer period than a week to be granted without the sanction of the Bureau; and if, when on leave, they break their liberty without a satisfactory explanation to the Governor, they will not be permitted to return, except by an or cr from the Bureau.

15. Any beneficiary who shall sell or otherwise dispose of his clothing shall have the value thereof deducted from his allowance of pocket-money and tobacco, and shall be restricted to the limits of the Asylum for a period of not less than three months.

16. All complaints shall be referred to the Governor or Commanding Officer, in the same respectful manner as the usage of the service requires on shipboard. Under no circumstances, however aggravated, will a resort to any other method be tolerated, except it be a respectful appeal to the Secretary of the Navy, through the Bureau of Yards and Docks.

17. Divine service will be performed on Sunday at 10 a. m., at which hour the beneficiaries will be required to attend, except in cases of sickness, or permission to the contrary having been obtained in writing from the Executive Officer.

ARTICLE XXXIV.

Arms of the United States.

1257....*Arms:* Paleways of thirteen pieces, argent and gules; a chief azure; the escutcheon on the breast of the American eagle displayed, proper, holding in his dexter talon an olive branch, and in his sinister a bundle of thirteen arrows, all proper; and in his beak a scroll, inscribed with this motto: "*E Pluribus Unum.*" For the *crest:* Over the head of the eagle, which appears above the escutcheon, a glory breaking through a cloud, proper, and surrounding thirteen stars, forming a constellation, argent, and on an azure field.

Flags and Broad Pendants.

1258....The flag of the Secretary of the Navy is to be blue, 10.25 feet in hoist, and 14.40 feet in length of fly, with a white foul anchor, three feet in extreme length, placed vertically in the centre; the storm flag of the Secretary of the Navy will be similar to the above, but only 5.40 feet in hoist, and 7.60 in length of fly, with the foul anchor eighteen inches in extreme length. These flags are to be displayed at the main to designate his presence on board. The flag of a Vice Admiral is to be plain and rectangular, with three five-pointed stars arranged as an equilateral triangle eighteen inches from centre to centre, with the upper star eighteen inches from the head, and twenty-seven inches from the tabling.   The flag of a Rear Admiral is to be similar to the above, but having only two stars arranged vertically, eighteen inches from centre to centre, and eighteen inches from the tabling, with the upper star eighteen inches from the head ; in boat and night flags, the distances between stars will be proportionately less than the above ; the color of these stars will be white when the flag is blue or red, and blue when the flag is white.   The broad pendants of Commodores will be, in colors and dimensions, as indicated in the book of allowances for vessels, with, however, only *one* star placed in the centre thereof.

APPENDIX.

Commanders-in-Chief and the Commanding Officers of vessels will see that the following returns are made :

Periodical Returns.

When to be sent.	By whom to be sent.	Subject.	Reference.	To whom to be sent.
Annually	Commanders of vessels	Sailing qualities of ship	Appendix form No. 1	Navy Department
	Do.	Copy of remark-book	Paragraph 459	....do....
	Surgeons	Expenditure book	Instructions to Surgeons	Bureau of Medicine, &c.
Semi-annually	Commander-in-chief	Inspection of efficiency	Ordnance instructions	Bureau of Ordnance
	Commanders of vessels	....do....	....do....	....do....
	Navigating officer	Copy of log-book	Paragraph 458	Bureau of Navigation
Quarterly	Commander-in-chief	Standing and attainment of officers	....do....296	Navy Department
	Do.	Fees of bills of purchase	....do....285	....do....
	Do.	Cond'n of steam machin'y & hrs	....do....311	Bureau of Steam Enginr'g
	Comd'rs of squadrons	Efficiency and prepara'n for battle	....do....316	Commander-in-chief
	Commanders of vessels	Punishments	Appendix form No. 7	Navy Department
	Do.	The returns	Ordnance instructions	Bureau of Ordnance
	Do.	Returns of all firing, giving numbers and mks of guns.	Ordn'ce fir Nv.5,'63	....do....
	Do.	Target practice	Ordnance instructions	....do....
	Do.	Steam log	Paragraph 397	Bureau of Steam Enginr'g
	Do.	Descriptive muster-rolls	Form Bu. of Equipment.	Bureau of Equip't, &c.
	Do.	Number and rating of crew	Appendix form No. 20	Commander-in-chief
	Do.	Conduct and list of chrs	....do....do.26 & 27	....do....
	Chief Engineer	Abstract of stores expended	Paragraph 670	....do....
	Do.	Cond'n of steam machin'y & hrs	....do....514	Bureau of Steam Enginr'g
	Fleet Surgeon	Synopsis of sm log and report.	Appendix form No. 2	....do....
	Surgeon	Aggregate of diseases and ? cases	Instrns to Surgeons	Bureau of Medicine, &c.
	Do.	Report of sick	....do....	....do....
	Do.	Bills of articles pud	....do....	....do....

Periodical Returns—Continued.

When to be sent.	By whom to be sent.	Subject.	Reference.	To whom to be sent.
Quarterly	Paymaster	Provisions, clng, &c., on hand, &c.	Instructions to Paymas'rs	Bureau of Provisions, &c.
	Do	Aggregate am't of cloth'g exp nded	do	do
	Do	Muster and pay rolls	do	Fourth Auditor
	Do	Articles condemned by board	do	Commanding Officer
	Chaplain	Duties performed	Paragraph 577	do
	Prof. of Mathematics	Attendance and proficiency of ... under instructions.	do 579	Navy Department
Monthly	Commander-in-chief	Condition and employm't of vessels	do 999	do
	Paymaster	Expenditure of provisions, &c.	do 561	...ng Officer
	Do	Summary statement.	do 1180	Fourth Auditor
Weekly, (fitting out)	Commander-in-chief	When fleet will be ready for sea	do 278	Navy Department
Weekly	Commanders of vessels	Condition, deficiencies, &c., before sailing.	do 331	Secretary of the Navy

Incidental Returns.

When to be sent.	By whom to be sent.	Subject.	Reference.	To whom to be sent.
Before sailing	Commander-in-chief	Stores, &c., required for fleet	Paragraph 280	ms
	Commanders of vessels	Descriptive muster-roll	Act of ...ss 17th July, 1862, 16th section, and form No. 3 Appendix.	Navy Department
	Do	List of passengers	Appendix, form No. 10.	do
	Do	Description of deserters	Purag'h 795 & form No. 4	Bureau of Equipment
	Do	List of absentees	Appendix, form No. 9	do
	Surgeon	Receipt of public property	Instructions to Surgeons	Bureau of ...
	Paymaster	Muster-roll	Instructions to Paymas'rs	Fourth Auditor

When	Commanders of vessels	Defects or deficiencies	Paragraph	Command't of Navy Yard.
When fitting out....	...er-in bd..	Defects or deficiencies	Paragraph 328	Navy Department........
After action	Do......	1 ...ct in ...n	do....290	do......
	...of ...ls	Events in action......	do....291	do......
		Recommendations for ...idals of honor.	do....798	......
When occurring	Commander-in-chief..	Transfers ...ps of ...ficers	do....294	Bureau of Construction..
	Do......	Expenditures abroad	Inst. from Constrm'n	Proper bureaus ......
	Do......	...les of bills of purchases....	Paragraph 1124	Commander-in-chief......
	Fleet Captain......	...et or ...die of ...drs.	do....323	Navy Department......
	...rs of ...ls	...his of invalids sent from foreign ...ts.	do....786	......
	Do......	...his of men discharged in foreign p...rts.o	do....774	do......
	Do......	Disasters	do....365	do......
	Do......	...is suggested	do....361	do......
	Do......	Losses of ...flag, by i...ngck or capture.	do....361	do......
	Do......	Passengers carried......	do....366	do......
	Do......	Collisions	do....372 & 373	do......
	Do......	...ps of bills of purchases....	do....1124	Proper bureaus ......
	Do......	Inspection on transfer of ...maml	do....381	Navy Department......
	Do......	...ry of property take ...ut of a ...pe.	do....720	Navy Department and U. S. District Judge.
	Do......	...hes of vessels within signal ... line at ...nte of ...pt.	do....723	do......
	Do......	Sales of ...he property	do....721	U. S. District Judge......
	Do......	Log-book ...nd papers d ...pzo ves...ls	do....719	do......
	Do......	Errors in ...ns	do....452 & 627	Navy Department, &c......
	Do......	...hen in port......	do....346	Navy Dep't & Com-in-chief
	Do......	Grounding of vessels, injury to hull or spars.	do....371	Bureau of Construction......
	Fleet Surgeon......	Casualties in ...the......	do....533	Commander-in-chief......
	Surgeon......	......do......	do....538	Commanding Officer and Fleet Surgeon.
When necessary	Commander-in-chief..	Suggestions for alterations in navy yards, ships, &c.	do....301	Navy Department......
	Do......	Reports and diagrams of service..	do....292 & 293	do......
	Commanders of vessels	Prize lists......	do....724	do......
	Do......	Reports and diagrams of service..	do....379	do......
	Fleet Surgeon......	Health of the fleet......	do....523	Bureau of Medicine, &c.

Incidental Returns—Continued.

When to be sent.	By whom to be sent.	Subject.	Reference.	To whom to be sent.
On rejoining comm'd	Commanders of vessels	No. of hours under steam and sail	Paragraph 391	Commander-in-chief
On transfer'g comm'd	Commanders of vessels	Qualities, &c., of vessels	do....345	Navy Dep't and successor
End of cruise	Commander-in-chief	List of ... the	do....300	Navy Department
	Commanders of vessels	Remark-book	do....356	do
	Do	list of men ...to an honor-able.	do....779	do
	Do	Log-book and ...	do....458 & 460	Bureau of Navigation
	Do	Book of ...	do....461	do
	Do	Yeoman's ...	do....595	Proper bureaus
	Do	Duplicate reports of injuries	do....371	Bureau of Construction
	Surgeon	All public property on hand, &c., with aggregate ... and ex...	Instructions to Surgeons	Bureau of Medicine, &c.
	Do	Surgeon's register	do	do
	Do	... of allotments and	do	do
	Paymaster	... of allotments and	Paragraph 799	Fourth Aud. & Pay Agent.
	Chaplain	Duties ...	do....577	Commanding Officer

The Commanding Officers of Stations and Navy Yards will see that the following returns are made :

Periodical Returns.

	By whom	Subject	Reference	To whom
Annually	Chief Engineer	Engines and boilers made, &c.	Paragraph 881	Commandant
	Surgeon	Expenditure-book and return of property.	Instructions to Surgeons	Bureau of Medicine, &c.
	Paymaster	Day's labor and cost	Inst. from Bu. of Const'n	Bureau of Construction

Semi-annually	Naval Constructor	Report of estimates, plans, and expenditures.	Paragraph 906	Commandant and Bureau of Construction.
	Civil Engineer	....do....	Instructions from Bureau Yards & Docks.	Bureau of Yards & Docks.
	Storekeeper	Stores on hand, receipts, and expenditures.	Instructions from Bureau Construction.	Bureau of Construction ..
	Inspector of Timber	Timber on hand.	....do....do....	
Semi-annually	Commandant	Record of apprentices.	Instructions from Bureau Yards & Docks.	Bureau of Yards & Docks.
	Storekeeper	Statement of transfers.	....do....do....	....do....
Quarterly	Ordnance Officer	Abstract of ...	Ordnance instructions	Bureau of Ordnance.
	Chief Engineer	...	Instructions from Bureau	Bureau of Steam Enginr'g.
	Surgeon	List of patients, (at ho ...)	Instructions to Surgeons	Bureau of Provisions ....
	Do	Bills of articles procured	....do....	Bureau of ...
	Do	... of ...	....do....	....do....
	Paymaster	... returns	Instruct's to ...	... of Provisi...
	Do	...r's ... units	... 181 ...	...
	Inspector-in-charge	... returns	...	Bureau of Provisi...
	Storekeeper	Sales of condemned wood and chips.	... Bureau Yards & Docks.	Bureau of Yards & Docks.
	Do	Returns of open purchase	P ... 958	Proper Bureau.
Monthly	...ndant	Officers attached to station.	Instructions from Bureau Yards & Docks.	Bureau of Yards & Docks.
	Do	List of bills approved	....do....	....do....
	...e Officer	Work ... for ordnance	Ordnance instructions	Bureau of Ordnance.
	Do	...	....do....	....do....
	N...on Officer	... on ..., received and ...	... Bureau	Bureau of Navigation.
	...ef Engineer	Work ... and boilers	... 882	Commandant.
	Do	Summary ...	Instru ...s from bureau	Bureau of Steam Enginr'g.
	...r	... rat...	... 89	Navy Department.
	Do	....do....	....do.... 180	Fourth Auditor.
	Do	Estimate of ...	... Bureau Construction.	Bureau of Construction ..

16

Periodical Returns—Continued.

When to be sent.	By whom to be sent.	Subject.	Reference.	To whom to be sent.
Monthly	Inspector-in-charge	Inspector's returns	Instructions from Bureau Provisions.	Bureau of Provisions
	Naval Constructor	Dock report, (Mare Island)	Instructions from Bureau Yards & Docks.	Bureau of Yards & Docks.
	Do	Condition of vessels in ordinary	Instructions from Bureau Construction.	Bureau of Construction
	Civil Engineer	Report of expenditures	Instructions from Bureau Yards & Docks.	Bureau of Yards & Docks.
	Storekeeper	Stores on hand, receipts and expenditures.	Bureau of Construction.	Bureau of Construction
	Do	do	Instructions from Bureau Yards & Docks.	Bureau of Yards & Docks.
	Do	do	Instructions from Bureau Equipment.	Bureau of Equipment
	Do	do	Instructions from Bureau Engineering.	Bureau of Yards & Docks.
	Clerk of Yard	Writers attached to station	Bureau Yards & Docks.	
	Do	Pay-roll summary	do........do	do
	Do	do....do	Bureau from Bureau.	Bureau
	Comd'r Recv'g Vessel	Report of exercises	Paragraph 050	Navy Department.
Semi-monthly	Commandant	Inspecting Engineer's report on machinery.	Bureau from Bureau Engineer'g.	Bureau of Engineering
	Chief Engineer	Expenditure of labor and materials	Paragraph 880	Bureau San Engineering.
	Naval Constructor	do	Bureau from Bureau.	Bureau of Construction.
	Do	Condition of vessels	do....do	do
	Civil Engineer	Report of expenditures	Bureau from Bureau Yards & Docks.	Bureau of Yards & Docks.
Weekly	Ordnance Officer	Ordnance returns	do	Bureau of
	Do	Inspection of magazines	do	do

	Inspector-in-charge	Inspector's returns	Instructions from Bureau Provisions.	Bureau of Provisions
	Recruiting Officer	Recruits enlisted	Parag'h 1038 & form 13.	Bureau of Equipment
	Do	Money on hand	Paragraph 1033	do
	Comd'r Recv'g Vessel	Changes in recruits	Parag'h 1060 & form 14.	do
		Recruits, prize crews, paroled prisoners, &c., on board.	Instructions from Bureau Equipment.	
Daily	Master Workmen	Labor performed	Paragraph 933	Clerk of Yard and Chief of Department.
	Do	Timber expended	......do...937	do

Incidental returns.

Be ...	...at ...	Inspection of outfit	Ordnance instructions	Bureau of Ordnance
	Do	Plans of stowage	Paragraphs 330 and 840.	Commander of Vessel
When fitting out	O...ce Officer	Copy of invoice of ordnance stores	Ordnance instructions	Bureau of Ordnance
When shipped	N...on Officer	Invoice of navigation stores	Instructions from Bureau Navigation.	Bureau of Navigation
When delivered	do	...s...	...do...do	do
When sent	Gnt	...f...	Paragraph 811	Navy Department
When made	do	...	...do...807 & 808.	do
	Do	Survey of ...	...do...837	Bureau of Construction
	Do	Survey of a ...	...do...1041	Bureau of Equipment
	Surgeon	...	...do...887	Proper Bureau
	S	...	Instructions from Bureau of Construction.	Bureau of Construction
When occurring	S...gn	...in of service at ...	Paragraph 890	Navy Department
On receipt and completion.	Gnt	Time consumed in repairing a vessel.	...do...838	Bureau of Construction
When completed	...do	Cost of building, &c	...do...841	Proper Bureau
When discovered	Naval Constructor	Defects, &c	...do...905	Commandant and Bureau of Construction.
When necessary	Civil Engineer	Plans and estimates	...do...920	Bureau of Yards & Docks.
End of cruise	Commandant	Ordnance Ledger	Ordnance instructions	Bureau of Ordnance

The Governor of the Naval Asylum will see that the following returns are made:

Periodical Returns.

When to be sent.	By whom to be sent.	Subject.	Reference.	To whom to be sent.
Yearly	Governor	List of beneficiaries	Instructions from Bureau Yards & Docks.	Bureau of Yards & Docks.
Quarterly	Do	Clothing, tobacco, & money exp'd	do	do
	Do	Miscellaneous articles expended	do	do
July	Do	Muster-roll of pensioners	do	do
	Do	Officers and employés	do	do
	Do	Pensioners received	do	do
	Do	Deaths	do	do
	Do	Changes	do	do
	Do	Absentees	do	do
Weekly	Do	Subsistence report	do	do

FORM No. 1.

———— STATION, ⎱
U. S. S. ⎰

COMPLEMENT OF MEN ————.

A report of the sailing and other qualities of this ————, ascertained under various circumstances, and from strict observation, between the —— of ————, 186-, and the —— of ————, 186-.

		Feet.	Inches.
The draught of water found, on trial, to be her best sailing trim, with —— weeks' provisions and stores, and —— tons of coal on board	{ Forward		
	Aft		
The draught of water found, on trial, to be her best sailing trim, with as much provisions, coals, and stores on board as she can conveniently stow	{ Forward		
	Aft		
The rake of her masts from a perpendicular	{ Foremast		
	Mainmast	in 6 feet	In.
	Mizenmast		

Tons.

The quantity of iron ballast on board, and where stowed......

Proposed quantity of iron ballast, if an alteration is considered desirable......

The quantity of water she stows, excluding the weight of tanks......

The quantity of coals (for steaming) she stows......

                                       Feet. Inches.

{ In iron tanks......
  In casks......
  In bunkers......
  In other places......

For'n service.

With —— weeks' provisions, —— weeks' stores, and —— tons of coals on board......

  Draught of water...... { Forward, Aft

  Height of port...... { Foremost, Midship, Aftermost

With as much stores, provisions, and coals on board as she can conveniently stow......

  Draught of water...... { Forward, Aft

  Height of port...... { Foremost, Midship, Aftermost

How many days' consumption of the following articles can she conveniently stow for her complement of men...... { Provisions, Bread, Water, Fuel, (if a sailing ship)

Description of guns.	Number.	Pounders, or calibre.	Weight.	Length.
			Cwt. qrs.	*Ft. inches.*

How armed*...... { On lower deck...... On middle deck...... On main deck...... On upper deck...... On poop......

* The number, weight, and description of rifled guns to be inserted separately.

FORM No. 1—Continued.

Sailing and other qualities.

NOTE.—Since the object of this form is to obtain full particulars respecting the qualities of the ship, under all circumstances of wind and sea, when under sail alone, and under steam alone, and under steam and sail combined, the Captain is to transmit with it a detailed account of any particular circumstances he may deem of importance, and also to suggest any alteration which, in his opinion, would improve the qualities of the ship.

	Degrees.	Force of wind.	1
1. Does she ride easy at her anchors?			
2.			
3. U			
4. U			
5. U			
6. U			
7. U			
8.			
9.			
10. How			
11. Does			
12. Stating			
13.			
14. With all sails			
15. With			
16. Under			
17. Under			
18. How does she steer off the wind?			
19. How			
20. In			
21. In			
22. Is			
23. Is			
24. How			

Inclinat'n of ship.

ship after a trial of —— months.

	Under sail alone. Knots.	Under steam and sail. Knots.

Close hauled with smooth water. { 25. 26.
Close hauled with a head sea. { 27. 28.
Wind on the beam.. { 29. 30.
31.
32. In
33. In
34. In a gale
35.
Wind on the quarter { 36. In
37. In a gale
38. In

Character of the

Close hauled with smooth water.
Close hauled with a head sea.
Wind on the beam..
Wind on the quarter
Before the wind ....

How does she behave in a
What is her best point of sailing
43. Is she,
44. Has she
45. If she has,
46.
47. If the ship be of iron,
48. How
49. Remarks, all

39. She has run per hour by the log or by known or calculated distance with as much wind as she could safely carry sail to.
40.
41.
42.

gallant sails
topgallant sails.
royals.
with all sails set.
sails, topgallant sails, and studding sails
weather, with royals and studding sails
studding sails
with all sails set.

45 ... the report
46 ... and on what sta-
47 ... been on, the state of the
48. If so, state full thereof.
49 ... as differ from ... in the last report, and any

FORM NO. 2.

the steam log of the United States steamer ———, during employed

ENGINES.								Mean temperatures in degr's, Fahr.					TIME.		REVOLUTIONS.	
ngine.	Number of cylinders.	Diameter of cylinder, in inches.	Stroke of piston, in feet.	Mean point of cutting off the steam, from commencement of stroke of piston, in inches.	Mean number of holes of throttle valve open.	Mean vacuum in condensers, in inches of mercury.	Mean steam pressure in boilers, in pounds, per inch above the atmosphere.	Of engine-room.	On deck.	Of injection-water.	Of discharge-water.	Of feed-water.	Total time the fires were lighted, in hours and minutes.	Total time the engines were in operation, in hours and minutes.	Total number.	Mean number per minute.

d, ——— ———,
Commanding.

FORM No. 2.

the three months ending ———, 18—, the vessel during that period being ———.

SPEED.		COAL.				STORES			DRAUGHT OF WATER.			PADDLE-WHEEL					SCREW		
Total number of knots.	Mean number of knots per hour.	Total weight of coal consumed, in tons of 2,240 pounds.	Total weight of refuse from coal, in tons of 2,240 pounds.	Total weight of coal consumed while the engines were in operation, in tons of 2,240 pounds.	Mean number of pounds of coal consumed per hour while the engines were in operation.	Total number of gallons of oil consumed.	Total number of pounds of tallow consumed.	Total number of pounds of wiping stuff consumed.	Greatest draught, forward and aft, in feet and inches.	Least draught, forward and aft, in feet and inches.	Average draught for the whole steaming, in feet and inches.	Diameter to outside of paddles, in feet and inches.	Number of paddles in each wheel.	Length of each paddle, in feet and inches.	Breadth of each paddle, in inches.	Deepest immersion of lower edge of paddle, in feet and inches, when the vessel is at the average draught for the whole steaming.	Multiple of gearing.	Diameter, in feet and inches.	Pitch, (mean,) in feet and inches.

——————, *Chief Engineer.*

Form No. 3.

Complete descriptive muster-roll of the crew of the

[To be transmitted to the Bureau of Equipment and Recruiting at the com

Ship's number.	NAMES. (Alphabetically arranged, without regard to ratings, with surnames to the left.)	Rating.	DATE OF ENLISTM'T.			Where enlisted.	Term of enlistment.	Place or vessel from which received.
			Year.	Month.	Day.			

Recapitulation of crew remaining on board at date of muster-roll.

Petty officers..
Seamen ....
Ordinary seamen..
Landsmen ....
Apprentices..
Musicians ....
Firemen ....
Coal-heavers ....
Contrabands ....

       Total............................ ....

NOTE.—Care must be taken that every column be correctly filled, and that all casu
dates of various changes, where transferred, &c. The names of the men thus reported
by the printed headings cannot be otherwise obtained, obtain it from the men them
are requested to keep themselves supplied with blanks by application to the Bureau

FORM NO. 3.

*U.*ᐟS. ——, *on the* —— *day of* ——, 186—.

mencement of a cruise, and on the 1st of January, April, July, and October.]

WHERE BORN.		State of which a citizen.	PERSONAL DESCRIPTION.								REMARKS.
City, town, or county.	State.		Age.	Occupation.	Eyes.	Hair.	Complexion.	Height.			
			Years.					Feet.	Inches.		

Approved this —— day of ——, 186—.

Certified to be correct by ——————— ————.

Received at the Navy Department ——.

——————— ———————.

——————— ———————, *Paymaster.*

alties or transfers which have occurred during the quarter are duly noted, reporting to be entered in common with those remaining on board. If the information required selves, making notes to that effect in the column for remarks. Commanding officers of Equipment and Recruiting, or Fleet Paymaster.

FORM No. 4.

Description of deserters and men absent without leave from the U. S. S.
——, 18—.

Name.	Rating.	Where born.	Age.	Height.	Hair.	Eyes.	Marks on person.	Complexion.	Reward offered.	Remarks.

—— ——, *Commanding.*

FORM No. 5.

Register of orders given, or of letters written, and of reports or letters
received.

(For commander-in-chief, flag captain, or principal aid.)

| When— | | | | Where, or place at noon. | Substance of orders or letters received. | Substance of orders given and of letters written. | From whom or to whom. | Remarks. |
Year.	Month.	Day.	Hour.					

FORM No. 6.

Register of signals.

(For commander-in-chief, flag captain. or principal aid.)

When—				Where, or place at noon.	Signal Nos. made from the ship.	Signal Nos. made by other vessels.	From what vessel.	To what vessel.	Remarks.
Year.	Month.	Day.	Hour.						

FORM No. 7.

Quarterly return of punishments on board the U. S. S. ——, from —— to ——, 18—.

Names.	Rating.	Offence.	Punishment, its mode and duration.	Remarks.

—— ——, *Commanding.*

To be sent in duplicate to commander-in-chief, who will forward one copy to the department.

Form No. 8.

U. S. S. ———, } List of men, &c., belonging to this vessel sick at hos-
at ———.   } pital, and who are not likely to return on board before
Date ———.   } the sailing of the vessel.

Name.	Rating.	Disease.	When and to whom the necessary papers have been sent.

——— ———, *Commanding.*
——— ———, *Surgeon.*

Form No. 9.

U. S. S. ———, } List of persons absent without leave from this ship,
at ———.   } and from any other cause except sickness in hos-
Date ———.   } pital.

Name.	Rating.	Reward offered.	Date of absence.	Cause of absence.

——— ———, *Commanding.*

NOTE.—Descriptive lists and accounts of absentees to be sent herewith.

Form No. 10.

Passengers.

List of officers, or others about to sail as passengers in the U. S. S.
———. Dated at ———, the ——— day of ———.

Name.	Rank.	To join what ship, &c.	Remarks.

——— ———, *Commanding.*

Form No. 11.

Transcript list.

U. S. (rendezvous or vessel, as the case may require.)

(Month and day,) 18—.

Name, (in full.)	Year, month, and day of enlistment.	Term or period for which enlisted.	Whether enlisted for general or special service.	Date of honorable discharge under which re-enlisted.	Name of vessel from which such honorable discharge was received.	Rating held as expressed on such honorable discharge.	Rating under present enlistment.	Wages per month under present enlistment.	Wages advanced.	Bounty paid.	Name of surety, (if any.)

NOTE.—If sent from a rendezvous, it is to be signed by the commanding officer; but if sent from a receiving or other vessel, it is to be signed by the paymaster and the commanding officer.

Form No. 12.

Descriptive list.

U. S. (rendezvous or vessel, as the case may require,)

(Month and day,) 18—.

Name, (in full.)	Previous naval service, and capacity when last discharged.	Place of birth.	Age.	Trade or occupation.	Color of eyes.	Color of hair.	Complexion.	Height.	Permanent scars or marks about the person.

NOTE.—If sent from a rendezvous, it is to be signed by the commanding officer; but if sent from a receiving or other vessel, it is to be signed by the executive and the commanding officer.

FORM No. 13.

ENLISTMENTS AT ———, IN 186—.

Return of the United States naval rendezvous at ———, *for the week ending Saturday,* ———, 186—.

☞ As this sheet will become the reference record at the Navy Department, great care must be taken that the information called for under the several headings is correctly given and plainly written. If the number of enlistments exceeds the capacity of this sheet, do not paste an addition to the bottom of it, but carry forward to a new sheet—dating and certifying each sheet.

NAMES OF RECRUITS. (In alphabetical order of surnames to the left.)	ENLISTED.			State whether for "general service" or "Coast Survey."	State name of ship, rate, and date of "HONORABLE DISCHARGE," under which the re-enlistment is made.	Previous naval service.	WHERE BORN, AND PERSONAL DESCRIPTION.								Height.		FUTURE HISTORY. (To be filled up at the Navy Department.)
	When.	Term.	Rating.				City, town, or county.	State.	Age.	State of which a citizen.	Occupation.	Eyes.	Hair.	Complexion.	Feet.	Inches.	

RECAPITULATION, &c., 186——.

	Musicians.	Firemen.	Coal-heavers.	Seamen.	Ordinary sea-men.	Landsmen.	Apprentices.	Boys.	Total.
Shipped this week, ending Saturday, ——, 186 , for general service...									
Shipped this week, ending Saturday, ——, 186 , for Coast Survey....									
Whole number of enlistments at this rendezvous since first day of January, 186 , (including the above)....									
Total number of re-enlistments under "honorable discharge," (act of March 2, 1855,) counting from the first entry under the law....									

FAILED TO APPEAR ON THE RECEIVING SHIP; ENLISTMENT NOT PERFECTED.

NAMES. (In alphabetical order, surnames to the left,)	Where born.	Age.	Date of enlistm't.	Rating.

REJECTED AT RECEIVING SHIP.

NAMES. (In alphabetical order, surnames to the left,)	Rating.	Date of rejection.	Date of enlistm't.	Where born.	Age.

UNITED STATES RENDEZVOUS, BOSTON, ——, 186—.

I certify that I have carefully examined the recruits agreeably to the regulations of the navy, and find that, in my opi ion, they are free from all bodily defects and mental infirmity which would in any way disqualify them from performing the ꓨꓦes for which they are intended.

———, *Examining Surgeon.*

I certify that this return shows the names of all persons who have enlisted at this rendez ꓦus for the week ending at the date hereof; also the names of such as have failed to appear at the receiving ship to perfect their enlistment, or who l we b en rejected at the rꙩv ng ship; that I did inspect the recruits previously to enlistment, and that they were not in ꙩd hen ꙩ bd; that, to the best of my judgment and belief, they were of lawful age, or, being minors, had lawful consent; and that, in accepting them, I ꙩve strictly observed the regulations which govern the recruiting service.

Forwarded by——

———, *Commandant.*

———, *Recruiting Officer.*

To the CHIEF OF BUREAU OF EQUIPMENT AND RECRUITING.

17

Form No. 14.

RETURN OF THE RECEIVING SHIP AT ————, IN 18—.

☞ As this sheet will become the reference record of the Navy Department, great care must be taken that the information called for under the several headings is correctly given and plainly written. The names must be alphabetically arranged, surnames to the left; and they must exactly correspond with those given at the rendezvous. Dates of enlistment must, in each and every case, be distinctly and correctly stated.

Return of recruits on board the United States receiving ship ————, at ————, for the week ending Saturday, ————, 18—.

Petty officers.	Musicians.	Firemen.	Coal-heavers.	Seamen.	Ordinary sea-men.	Landsmen.	Apprentices.	Boys.	Total.

Whole number of recruits on board at this date..............

Number unfit for duty..............

Exact number of each grade available for general service at this date, and ready for immediate transfer..............

Exact number of each grade available for Coast Survey, or duty other than "general service"..............

DEATHS.

NAMES.	Date of death.	What disease or accident.	Where deceas'd.	Latest service, &c.	ENLISTMENT.			WHERE BORN.		Age.
					When.	Where.	Rating.	City, town, or county.	State.	

DISCHARGES.

NAMES.	Date of discharge.	CAUSE. (Expiration of term, disability, own request, in disgrace, or otherwise.)	Latest service, &c.	ENLISTMENT.			WHERE BORN.		Age.
				When.	Where.	Rating.	City, town, or county.	State.	

DESERTIONS.

NAMES.	Date of desertion.	From what ship or duty.	Latest service, &c.	ENLISTMENT.			WHERE BORN.		Age.
				When.	Where.	Rating.	City, town, or county.	State.	

FORM No. 14—Continued.

DESERTERS APPREHENDED OR SURRENDERED.

NAMES.	Date of arrest.	Date of surrender.	By whom arrested.	Whence deserted.	ENLISTMENT.			WHERE BORN.		Age.
					When.	Where.	Rating.	City, town, or county.	State.	

I certify that this return shows all the changes of recruits that have occurred on board this receiving vessel, whether by deaths, desertions, discharges, apprehensions, surrenders, or transfers, during the week ending at the date hereof.

Forwarded by—————————— , *Paymaster.*
—————————— , *Commanding Officer.*

To the CHIEF OF BUREAU OF EQUIPMENT AND RECRUITING.

LIST OF TRANSFERS, 18—.

☞ When the number of transfers exceeds the capacity of this sheet, carry forward to the head of a new sheet. The length of this must not be added to.

NAMES. (Names in alphabetical order, surnames to the left.)	Date of enlistment.	Where enlisted.	Term.	Rating.	Age.	From what place rec'd.	TO WHAT PLACE TRANSFERRED.		Date of transfer, 18—.	Remarks.
							Name of ship intended for.	Name of navy yard or station.		

Forwarded by—

—————————— , *Commandant.*

—————————— , *Paymaster.*
—————————— , *Commanding Officer.*

Letter to be given to Prize Master by a Commanding Officer making a seizure or capture.

U. S. S. ————————,

OFF ——————,

————————.

Sir : You will take charge of the ————, captured on the —— day of ————, 186 , by ————, and proceed with the said prize to the port of ————, and there deliver her, with the accompanying papers, (which were all that were found on board,) and the persons sent as witnesses, to the Judge of the United States District Court or to the United States Prize Commissioners at that place, taking his or their receipt for the same. You will not deliver either the vessel, the papers, or the witnesses to the order of any other person or parties, unless directed to act otherwise by the Navy Department or Flag Officer commanding the squadron to which you are attached.

On your arrival at ———— you will immediately report in person to the Commanding or Senior Navy Officer of the navy yard or station thereat, and show him these instructions ; and you will report also, by letter, to the Secretary of the Navy, stating in full the particulars of your passage home, and transmit to him, through the Commandant or Senior Officer, the names of the officers and men composing your prize crew, and any communications for the Department with which you may be charged. You will, on your arrival, allow no person to leave the vessel without permission from the Commandant of the station, nor go on shore yourself except on your necessary duty. You will not sleep out of the vessel while in charge, nor allow any but official boats to approach, and only official persons on duty to come on board.

You will, without delay, after reporting, call upon the United States District Attorney at ————, show him these instructions, which are issued by order of the Secretary of the Navy, and give him all the information in your power respecting the circumstances connected with the capture of the ————.

You will then report, and show these instructions to the Naval Prize Commissioner of the district, who is hereby directed to ascertain and notify you of the earliest date at which your attendance shall no longer be required by the court, and to indorse the notification on this paper. You will, on being discharged from attendance, if not in the mean time instructed, and whenever you need instructions respecting yourself, officers, or prize crew, immediately report to the Commandant of the nearest yard or station or Senior Officer for such instructions.

You will particularly bear in mind and strictly observe the injunctions of the law and of the Department respecting captured property or persons under your charge, and recollect that you will be held rigorously responsible for any mismanagement of the trust confided to you.

You, your officers and prize crew, are hereby detached from the ———, and you will be careful to apply for and take with you their pay accounts and your own, to be presented to the Paymaster of the yard or station at or nearest to the port to which you are ordered.

The sea-pay of yourself and officers will continue while in charge of the prize or under the orders of a Flag Officer or Senior Navy Officer afloat; but your name will not be borne on the books of the vessel from which you are detached, and you will not be entitled to share in prizes made by such vessel after your detachment.

Commanding the U. S. ———.

To ——— ———,

——— ———,

——— ———.

CIRCULAR.

The attention of Commanding Officers in the Navy is called to the following extract, in relation to their duties, from the 25th article, section 16th, of the act of July 16, 1862, for the better government of the Navy:

"He shall, whenever he orders officers and men to take charge of a prize and proceed to the United States, and whenever officers and men are sent from his ship, for *whatever cause*, take care that each man be furnished with a complete statement of his account, specifying the date of his enlistment and the period and terms of his service, which account shall be signed by the Commanding Officer and Purser."

These requirements must be strictly complied with, and, in addition, duplicate statements must be forwarded to the Paymaster of the vessel or station to which the men are sent, together with a descriptive list of the men sent, according to the form here annexed:

NAMES OF CREW.	ENLISTED.			WHERE BORN AND PERSONAL DESCRIPTION.								Height.	
	When.	Term.	Rating.	City, town, or county.	Date.	Age.	Occupation.	Eyes.	Hair.	Complexion.		Feet.	Inches.

FORM No. 16.

Letter of application for an examination.

—— —— 186 .

To THE SECRETARY OF THE NAVY :

I respectfully make application for an examination as to my qualifications for appointment as °—— in the United States Navy. I was — years of age on the — day of ·——, 186 . I was born in ——, county of ——, and State of ——, and I reside in ——, county of ——, and State of ——.· I forward herewith testimonials of moral and physical qualifications.

Very respectfully,

—— ——.

* This blank to be filled up with the position the applicant desires to obtain, as Master's Mate, Sailmaker, Carpenter, Gunner, Boatswain, Third Assistant Engineer, Assistant Civil Engineer, Assistant Naval Constructor, Assistant Paymaster, or Assistant Surgeon. No professional examination being required of candidates for the office of Chaplain, or Professor of Mathematics, except at the Naval Academy, their application will be the same as the above, striking out the words, " examination as to my qualifications for."

FORM No. 17.

Letter of acceptance.

———— ————, 186 .

To THE SECRETARY OF THE NAVY :

I hereby acknowledge the receipt of an appointment (or warrant or commission) as ——— in the Navy of the United States, dated ———, 186 , and inform the Department of my acceptance of the same. I enclose herewith the oath of allegiance, duly signed and certified.

Very respectfully,

———— ————,

——— *U. S. Navy.*

———

Be it enacted by the Senate and House of Representatives of the United States of America in Congress assembled, That hereafter every person 'elected or appointed to any office of honor or profit under the Government of the United States, either in the civil, military, or naval departments of the public service, excepting the President of the United States, shall, before entering upon the duties of such office, and before being entitled to any of the salary or other emoluments thereof, take and subscribe the following oath or affirmation :

" I, A. B., do solemnly swear (or affirm) that I have never voluntarily borne arms against the United States since I have been a citizen thereof; that I have voluntarily given no aid, countenance, counsel, or encouragement to persons engaged in armed hostility thereto ; that I have neither sought, nor accepted, nor attempted to exercise the functions of any office whatever, under any authority or pretended authority in hostility to the United States ; that I have not yielded a voluntary support to any pretended government, authority, power, or constitution within the United States, hostile or inimical thereto. And I do further swear (or affirm) that, to the best of my knowledge and ability, I will support and defend the Constitution of the United States against all enemies, foreign and domestic ; that I will bear true faith and allegiance to the same ; that I take this obligation freely, without any mental reservation or purpose of evasion ; and that I will well and faithfully discharge the duties of the office on which I am about to enter. So help me God.''

Which said oath, so taken and signed, shall be preserved among the files of the court, house of Congress, or department to which the said office may appertain. And any person who shall falsely take the said oath shall be guilty of perjury, and on conviction, in addition to the penalties now prescribed for the offence, shall be deprived of his office and rendered incapable forever after of holding any office or place under the United States

Form No. 18.

Article of agreement for ———.

I do hereby agree to enter the Navy of the United States as ———, and to repair on board such vessel and at such time as may be ordered, and to remain in said capacity till the expiration of the service of the vessel, unless sooner discharged by the proper authority, or under the provisions of paragraph No. 250 of the Regulations of the Navy.

I do oblige and subject myself during my service as ——— to comply with and be obedient to such laws, regulations, and discipline of the Navy as are or that may be established by Congress or other competent authority.

——— ———.

Witness .

——— ———.

Note.—The Medical Officer will testify (on the reverse) to the physical fitness of the person selected ; or, if he exhibit defects, they are to be noted.

Form No. 19.

Surveys.

U. S. S. ——— ———,

———, 18 .

Sir : I respectfully request that a survey may be ordered upon the below-mentioned articles in my department, which I believe to be ———.

Respectfully,

——— ———.

To ——— ———,
    Commanding.

U. S. S. ——— ———,

———, 18 .

Gentlemen : You will hold a strict and careful survey on the articles above mentioned, in the ——— department, and report to me, in triplicate, their condition. If, in your judgment, they are unfit for use, you will state the particulars in which they are so, and the probable cause which has made them so ; and you will include in your statement the names of the contractor and inspector, if they can be obtained by marks or otherwise, and the invoice prices of the articles, together with your recommendation as to their disposition.

Respectfully,

——— ———,

Commanding.

To ——— ———.

——— ———.

——— ———.

U. S. S. ——— ———,

———, 18 .

Sir : In obedience to your order of the ———, we have held a strict and careful survey on the articles in the ——— department therein mentioned, and report that in our opinion ———.

Respectfully,

——— ———.

——— ———.

——— ———.

To ——— ———,

Commanding.

Approved :

——— ———,

Commanding.

I certify that the foregoing articles recommended to be ——— were so disposed of in my presence.

Form No. 20.

Quarterly return of the number and rating of the crew of the U. S. S. —— —, 18—, with the number whose term of service expires in each month.

Complement allowed.

Officers ....
Petty officers ....
Seamen ....
Ordinary seamen ....
Landsmen ....
Boys ....
Firemen.............
Coal-heavers.........
Musicians............
Marines ....
——

Year.	Month.	Boatswain's mates.	Gunner's mates.	Carpenter's mates.	Sailmaker's mates.	Ship's stewards.	Surgeon's stewards.	Master-at-arms.	Ship's corporals.	Armorer.	Ship's cook.	Cooper.	Quartermasters.	Quarter gunners.	Captains of forecastle, tops, and after-guard.	Armorer's mates.	Painter.	Captains of hold.	Officers' stewards and cooks.	Seamen.	Ordinary seamen.	Landsmen and boys.	Musicians.	Coal-heavers.	Firemen.	MARINES. Orderly sergeants.	MARINES. Sergeants.	MARINES. Corporals.	MARINES. Musicians.	MARINES. Privates.
		The number whose term of service expires in each month.																												
18—.	January																													
	February																													
	March																													
	April																													
	May																													
	June																													
	July																													
	August																													
	September																													
	October.........																													
	November																													
	December........																													

Total on board.

Officers ....
Petty officers ....
Seamen ....
Ordinary seamen.
Landsmen ....
Boys ....
Firemen.........
Coal-heavers ....
Musicians .. ..
Marines ....
——

—— ——, *Paymaster.*

Approved: —— ——, *Commanding.*

FORM No. 21.

Return of persons enlisted at the United States naval rendezvous ——— during the week ending at the hour of closing, Saturday, ———, 18 .

	White.	Colored.
Seamen...		
Ordinary seamen...............................		
Landsmen......................................		
Coal-heavers..................................		

	Class.				
	1st.	2d.	3d.		
Firemen........................					
Musicians.....................					
Boys...........................					
Total......................					

——— ———,
Commanding Rendezvous.

To ——— ———,
Commanding U. S. Naval Station.

FORM No. 22.

Discharge.

This is to certify that No. ———, a ———, has this day been discharged from the United States ——— and from the naval service.
Dated this ———.

——— ———,
Paymaster.

Approved:

——— ———,
Captain.

NAME.	ENLISTED.			WHERE BORN AND PERSONAL DESCRIPTION.								Height.	
	When.	Term.	Rating.	City, town, or county.	Date.	Age.	Occupation.	Eyes.	Hair.	Complexion.		Feet.	Inches.

FORM No. 23.

Honorable discharge from the United States Navy.

This is to certify that No. ——— enlisted ———, 18 , at ———,
for three years, ——— years of age, ——— feet ——— inches high,
——— eyes, ——— hair, ——— complexion, has ———, born at
———, "as a testimonial of fidelity and obedience," is this day
"honorably discharged" from the United States ——— and from the
naval service of the United States. Now, according to the provisions
of the second section of the act approved March 2, 1855, if within
three months from this date the above-described ——— ——— shall
present this his "honorable discharge" at any United States naval
rendezvous, and if found physically qualified, and shall re-enlist for
three years or longer, then he shall be entitled to pay during the said
three months equal to that to which he would have been entitled if
he had been employed in actual service.

——— ———,
Paymaster.

Approved :

——— ———,
Commanding Officer.

FORM NO. 24.

SURGEON'S OFFICE, NAVY YARD,

—— ·——, 186 .

SIR : I have examined, [state the name in full,] who states that he
was born in, [name of town and State,] on the —— day of ———,
18 , and find that he is [not] physically qualified to perform the
duties of a [name the grade] in the Navy of the United States, [if not
qualified add,] because he has [state the disability.]

I am, very respectfully,

—— ———,

Surgeon.

To —— ———,

Commanding U. S. Naval Station.

FORM No. 25.

Report of commanding officers of squadrons, divisions, and vessels belonging to the ———— fleet, commanded by ————, for the quarter ending ————.

Name.	Rank.	COMMANDING—			IMPRESSIONS AS TO—			CONDITION AND EFFICIENCY OF—			Qualifications for command.	Professional skill and attainments.	Remarks.
		Squadron.	Division.	Vessel.	Conduct.	Morals.	Health.	Squadron.	Division.	Vessel.			

————, Commanding.

FORM No. 26.

Report of line officers attached to the U. S. S. ———, commanded by ———, for the quarter ending ———, 186—.

Name.	Rank.	IMPRESSIONS AS TO GENERAL QUALIFICATIONS.			IMPRESSIONS AS TO PROFESSIONAL APTITUDE.				IMPRESSIONS AS TO APTITUDE FOR—		Languages spoken.	Remarks.	Recommendations.
		Conduct.	Morals.	Health.	Seamanship.	Steam.	Navigation.	Gunnery and ordnance.	Infantry drill & evolutions.	General information.			

———, Commanding U. S. ship ———.

FORM No. 27.

Report of staff officers attached to U. S. S. ———, commanded by ———, for the quarter ending ———, 186—.

Name.	Rank.	IMPRESSIONS AS TO GENERAL QUALIFICATIONS.			IMPRESSIONS AS TO—				Languages spoken.	Remarks.	Recommendations.
		Conduct.	Morals.	Health.	Professional aptitude.	Capacity.	Zeal.	General information.			

———, Commanding U. S. ship ———.

18

CIRCULAR.

NAVY DEPARTMENT,
August 9, 1864.

The following course of examination will be required for all officers of the Volunteer Naval service, for entering that service, or for promotion in it. The Commanding Officers of squadrons will, upon recommending an officer of the Volunteer Naval service for promotion, forward at the same time to this Department a report of his qualifications, in accordance with these regulations. And should a Volunteer Officer be reported by his Commanding Officer as incompetent to discharge the duties assigned him, he will be subjected to this examination, a report of which will be forwarded to the Department.

In the examination of candidates for the position of Mate, there being but three years' sea service required, a proficiency in seamanship and navigation is not to be expected. It is desirable to ascertain the general intelligence of the candidate and his aptitude for the duties of the position :

IN SEAMANSHIP.—Such ordinary routine of ship duties and knowledge of seamanship as any one may acquire in three years at sea.

NAVIGATION.—Observing and working the meridian altitude of the sun for latitude, and dead reckoning.

Acting Ensign.

Will be examined in—

SEAMANSHIP —General routine of rigging ship and stowing hold ; bending, unbending, reefing and furling sails ; working anchors, cables, and hawsers ; tacking, wearing, and the ordinary evolutions ; hand and deep-sea lead lines.

NAVIGATION.—Log-line, compass and its corrections ; dead reckoning, use and adjustments of sextant and quadrant ; observing and working meridian altitude and longitude by chronometer.

GUNNERY.—Stationing men at gun and gun exercise ; loading and use of tangent sight and fuzes ; small-arm drill and broad-sword exercise.

The examination in Gunnery is only to be required in candidates for promotion who have served as Mates, and not for original appointments to Acting Ensigns.

Acting Master.

SEAMANSHIP.—Rigging, and stowing hold, as practiced in the naval service; naval routine of bending and unbending sails; crossing and sending down yards; working ship and sails under all circumstances, and working anchors and cables.

NAVIGATION.—Log-line, compass and its corrections; dead reckoning; use of sextant, with corrections and adjustments; observing and working meridian altitude, single and double altitudes; longitude by chronometer and lunar distances; amplitude and azimuth; latitude by polar star; treatment of and rating chronometer; use of barometer and thermometer, and use of charts.

GUNNERY.—Stationing men at guns; broadside and pivot gun; small-arm and broad-sword exercise; use of tangent sight; mounting and dismounting guns; exercise of boat and field howitzer; stowing magazine and shell-room and working powder division; use and adjustment of fuzes, and general use and management of rifle guns.

In addition, the candidate will be examined and a report made as to his proficiency in the ordinary branches of English education—reading, writing, arithmetic, and geography—specifying any accomplishments which the candidate may possess.

Acting Volunteer Lieutenant.

The examination will consist of that specified for Acting Master, with the addition in—

SEAMANSHIP.—Watching, and stationing crews for all evolutions, and requiring a greater proficiency in all naval routine, and the management of a vessel under sail and steam.

GUNNERY.—A good knowledge of Ordnance Manual.

Acting Volunteer Lieutenant Commander and Acting Volunteer Commander.

The examination the same as for Acting Volunteer Lieutenant, but to be conducted with more precision, and with a view to ascertain the qualifications of the candidate for separate command, and ability for conducting correspondence, &c. All the requirements are to be strictly complied with.

Board for examination for MATE will consist of one Acting Volunteer Lieutenant, or Master, and two Acting Ensigns.

For ACTING ENSIGN, will consist of one regular officer and two volunteer, not below the grade of Master.

For ACTING MASTER, will consist of one regular officer and two Volunteer Lieutenants.

For ACTING VOLUNTEER LIEUTENANT, will consist of two regular officers and one Acting Volunteer Lieutenant.

For ACTING VOLUNTEER LIEUTENANT COMMANDER, will consist of two Commanders and one Lieutenant Commander.

For ACTING VOLUNTEER COMMANDER, will consist of one Commodore, or Captain, and two Commanders.

GIDEON WELLES,
Secretary of the Navy.

CIRCULAR.

Regulations for the admission and advancement of Volunteer Line Officers in the United States Navy.

Mates are to be between the ages of eighteen (18) and thirty-five (35,) and have seen three (3) years service at sea, before the mast or as an officer, and be able to work a dead reckoning and latitude by meridian altitude of the sun, and pass an examination in seamanship.

Commanders of squadrons, or of single ships acting independently, may fill any vacancies in this grade occurring within their commands, subject to the approval of the Department.

Acting Ensigns are to be between the ages of twenty-one (21) and thirty five (35,) and have seen eight (8) years sea service before the mast or as an officer.

Abroad, vacancies to this grade may be filled by the Commanders of squadrons or Commanders of vessels acting singly, from the most worthy Mates, after due examination, subject to the approval of the Department.

Acting Ensigns, who have served as such at least six months, may be recommended to the Department by Commanders of squadrons for promotion to the grade of Acting Master, for professional skill, zeal in the performance of duty, and good character.

Acting Masters, who have served as such at least one year, may be recommended to the Department, by Commanders of squadrons, for promotion to the grade of Acting Volunteer Lieutenant for highly meritorious services.

Acting Volunteer Lieutenants, who have served as such at least one year in command of a vessel, and received the special commendation of a Commander of a squadron in public despatches, for meritorious services against the public enemy, and for having his vessel in an efficient state of discipline, may be promoted to the grade of Acting Lieutenant Commander.

Acting Lieutenant Commanders, who have served as such for two years, will be examined for the grade of Acting Commander, and a proportion of the whole number of Acting Lieutenant Commanders will be advanced according to their record in the service, and the merit of their examination.

NAVY DEPARTMENT, 18C4.

CIRCULAR.

Regulations for the admission and advancement of Volunteer Line Officers and Engineers in the Mississippi squadron.

Mates are to be between the ages of nineteen (19) and thirty (30) years. If from the Atlantic States, to have seen three (3) years service at sea as an officer or before the mast. If from the inland States, to have seen one (1) year's service on steamers on the lakes or western rivers, or in the army. The Commander of the squadron will make all such appointments as vacancies occur.

Acting Ensigns are to be between the ages of twenty-one (21) and thirty-five (35.) If from the Atlantic States, to have seen eight (8) years service at sea as an officer or before the mast. If from the inland States, to have seen three (3) years service on the rivers or lakes before the mast or as a line officer on board of steamers, or been three (3) years in the army, and been honorably discharged. The Commander of the squadron will make appointments of Acting Ensigns according to the above rule, subject to the approval of the Department.

Appointments to Acting Second and Third Assistant Engineers will be made by the Commander of the squadron, from such competent and experienced persons as he shall designate, according to rules for examination which he will prescribe.

Promotions above the grade of Ensign and Second Assistant Engineer to be recommended to the Department, when vacancies occur, by the Commander-in-Chief. No appointments to be made to these or any other office in the gift of the Commander-in-Chief, unless the party shall first file evidence of his citizenship, place of nativity, fair English education, proof of loyalty and sobriety, and have passed a physical examination. No foreigner can be appointed a line officer.

No person formerly of the Naval School can be appointed a line officer without the previous authority of the Navy Department.

The qualifications of all appointments in the Mississippi squadron must be forwarded to the Department for record.

NAVY DEPARTMENT, *December* 27, 1864.

U. S. NAVY REGULATION CIRCULAR No. 1.

The following alterations and additions are hereby made to the Regulations, published for the government of all persons attached to the United States naval service, under date of April 18, 1865, and will be obeyed accordingly:

Every person subject to the control of the Navy Department will preserve this circular in his book of regulations.

1.... Paragraph 126, page 22. The first clause is annulled, so as to conform to paragraph 1258, pages 233, 234.

2.... Paragraph 173, page 30, omit the word "important."

3.... Hereafter every official letter and communication from any officer of the Navy to any department of the government, or to the heads of any of the subordinate bureaus or offices, must pass through and be indorsed by his Commanding Officer.

4.... Paragraph 261, page 46, is annulled.

5.... Paragraph 386, page 69, is annulled, and the following is substituted therefor: "Steam will only be used, in entering or leaving port, when the vessel cannot be managed under sails alone, and under other circumstances where an urgent necessity may exist, which renders it necessary for the performance of the service, if a specified time for its performance has been directed by proper authority."

6.... Paragraph 387, page 70, is annulled, and the following is substituted therefor: "Whenever steam is used the Commanding Officer of the vessel must enter in the steam log-book, in red ink, over his own signature, the reasons why he ordered it, and he will be held to a strict accountability for the sufficiency of his reasons. In no case will he use steam without a necessity so strong that the public interests would obviously be materially injured by not using it. The Bureau of Steam Engineering will examine the steam log-books as they arrive, and report to the department the amount of steaming done and the reasons given therefor."

7.... Paragraph 422, page 74, is modified so as to leave the keys of the Paymaster's storerooms under the charge of that officer.

8.... Paragraph 565, page 100, is changed so as to read, "Officers' messes of ships in commission may be allowed to draw from the ship any one or more of the component parts of the ration: *Provided*, That the aggregate quantity of any article issued to a mess during a quarter shall not exceed twice the quantity which such mess would have been entitled to had none of the rations of the officers and the servants in the messes been commuted: *And provided further*, That all articles so issued shall be used exclusively by the officers' messes on board ship. Officers are not to be permitted to draw the full allowance of any article while the crew are upon short allowance of that article. Issues of provisions to officers' messes, to the medical and other departments of the ship, and to vessels in distress, will be charged at the prices given in the ration table."

9....Paragraph 632, page 119, is rescinded, the law providing that the Boatswain, Gunner, Carpenter, and Sailmaker shall be called warrant officers.

10....Paragraph 839, page 150, the last clause is altered so as to read hereafter as follows: " All decks even with or below the water-line will be covered with shellac, paint, oil, or varnish, to avoid holy-stoning, which is forbidden on such decks."

11....Paragraph 900, page 159, is amended by the following addition to the end thereof: "But articles of clothing and small-stores which have been in any degree injured by use will not thus be received."

12....Paragraph 1019, page 179, is to be regarded as unconditional, so that every person re-enlisting, at an Atlantic port, in the naval service of the United States must produce his discharge therefrom. If the discharge is said to be lost, the Recruiting Officer will refer the case to the Bureau of Equipment and Recruiting.

13....Paragraph 1083, page 193, is amended, so that hereafter the aggregate of leaves of absence granted by Commanding Officers within the United States, to any one under their command, shall not exceed one month in any one year; and it is to be understood that, except in special cases, to be judged of by the department, a leave of one month in a year is to cover all of the time which an officer may be absent from his post or station.

14....Paymasters performing their legitimate duties as Pay Agents, Purchasing Agents, and Disbursing Agents, will take care to affix their rank only to all official papers, as required by paragraph 1099, page 196, and will not permit themselves to be addressed by any other title.

15....Paragraph 1122, page 199, is modified so as to require Officers making reports of the misconduct of those under their command to fur-. nish the accused with a copy of the report, and afford him an opportunity to make any written explanations he may have to offer, which will be forwarded with the report to the Secretary of the Navy.

16.... Paragraph 1163, page 209, is amended in the first clause, so that for the future, when an Officer is ordered to a vessel preparing for sea, his sea pay and sea service will only begin when the vessel is regularly put in commission, which date will be indorsed on the orders of the Officer by the Commandant of the station, and reported to the Bureau of Navigation.

17.... Paragraph 1177, page 211, is annulled.

18.... Paragraph 1199, page 216, to the end thereof the following is to be added : "Paymasters of shore stations will be allowed, after detachment, the necessary time for the settlement of their accounts, not exceeding the following :

Paymasters of navy yards at New York and Boston, 60 days.

Paymasters of navy yards at Portsmouth and Philadelphia, 40 days.

Paymasters of navy yards at Washington and Mare Island, 40 days.

Paymasters of other navy yards and stations, 30 days.

Inspectors at New York and Boston, 40 days.

Inspectors at other stations, 30 days.

Paymasters of receiving ships at New York and Boston, 60 days.

Paymasters of receiving ships at other ports, 40 days."

19.... Paragraph 1228, page 223, is so far modified that the Judge Advocate will not be required to read over aloud the entire record after the reading of the defence, but only such portions of it as may be indicated by members of the Court.

20.... Paragraph 1260, page 345, is so far modified as not to apply to Medical Stores.

21.... The monthly return of "Officers attached to stations," page 241, will be sent to the "Bureau of Navigation, Office of Detail," as well as to the Bureau of Yards and Docks.

22.... Form No. 10, page 254, will be considered as applying to passengers arriving in the United States, as well as those "about to sail."

23.... Clerks or Stewards duly appointed, and proceeding to join their vessels or stations, under orders to that effect, will be allowed travelling expenses within the United States, at the rate of three cents per mile, the amount not to be paid, nor credited to them, until they shall have entered upon the discharge of their duties. When proceeding by sea to join their vessels or stations, travelling expenses will not be allowed them without the special direction of the Navy Department.

24.... When a vessel is to be laid up, or put out of commission, the orders detaching the Officers, for leaves of absence or waiting orders, will not be delivered by the Commandant of the station until the stores of the vessel shall have been landed, her crew transferred or paid off, and the vessel ready to be turned over to the station, and all regulations relative to a vessel arriving from sea fully complied with.

25.... Before sailing, the Commanding Officers of squadrons, and of each vessel, will make a special report to the Secretary of the Navy, as to whether or not every regulation of the Department and its Bureaus required previous to sailing has been complied with.

26.... It is especially the duty of all Commanding Officers to examine into the complaints of enlisted persons, to correct them so far as they are reasonable, and to direct their Paymasters to use all diligence in obtaining their accounts. Letters are constantly being received, and personal applications at the Department made by sailors touching their accounts, descriptive lists, prize money, terms of enlistment, &c., which ought to have been attended to by Commanding Officers and Paymasters as a sacred duty, and thus keep the men from placing their affairs with the Department and Bureaus in the hands of brokers.

27.... Coast or general Pilots on board of a United States vessel do not relieve the Commanding Officer from the responsibility placed upon him by paragraph 1200, page 216. A regularly licensed harbor or river Pilot in charge of a United States vessel, within the limits for which he is licensed, is responsible for keeping the vessel off the bottom, but Commanding Officers will see that the rules about collisions are strictly observed by the Pilots.

28.... The Commanding Officer of a vessel arriving at any port in the United States is to see that a requisition is forwarded, the day of his arrival, for money to pay off all the crew who may be ordered to be discharged, or whose terms of service have expired; and none of the crew to be discharged will be allowed to go on shore until paid off, without special permission from the Secretary of the Navy. Commanding Officers of vessels, under the orders of the Commandant of a station, will not give liberty to officers or men without the authority of said Commandant first obtained.

29.... Commanding Officers of squadrons, and of naval stations, are directed to investigate immediately, by a Court of Inquiry, or if the

Regulation Circular No. 1.

matter is of less importance, and a court impracticable, then by a board of three officers, all accidents, occurrences, and transactions, which it is necessary the Department should have full information upon, and forward the same to the Secretary of the Navy, in such a complete and concise form that action may be taken thereon without referring the case back again. Commanding Officers of vessels, acting singly, will, so far as practicable, conform to the above order.

30....A written order from the Department to an officer to leave his domicile for duty, fixing no date and not expressing haste, will be obeyed by leaving within four days after receipt; if the order reads "without delay," he will leave within forty-eight hours; if "immediately," then within twelve hours; and all Officers are required to indorse on their orders from the Department the date and hour of receipt.

31....Hereafter the Office of Detail will be attached to the Bureau of Navigation, and the Chief of that Bureau will, "by direction of the Secretary of the Navy," sign the orders and documents referring to detail. All papers connected with the detail will be addressed to the "Bureau of Navigation, Office of Detail."—See paragraph 1115, page 198.

32....A vessel of the Navy, under orders to go to sea, will be considered under sailing orders from the time the powder is taken on board, and no person will then be permitted to leave the ship, except on duty.

33....Paymasters entitled to Clerks or Stewards will be allowed to retain them in service during the time allowed them for settling their accounts.

34....Masters and Ensigns of the regular Navy, and Midshipmen serving on board any naval steamer, will hereafter be taught thoroughly the duty of steam enginery. They will be divided into four watches on deck, and the same number in the engine and fire-rooms, and will serve alternately on deck and below whenever steam power is used. Quarterly reports, according to Form No. 26, page 272, will be made, under the heads of "Steam" and "Remarks," showing the proficiency and reliability of each officer in steam enginery, and these reports will be used at the examination of the above-mentioned officers. After the first day of January, 1866, no Master nor Ensign of the regular Navy, nor any Midshipman, will be promoted until he has passed an examination in steam enginery. Commanders of squadrons, Commanders of steam vessels, and the Superintendent of the Naval Academy, are charged with the faithful execution of this regulation.

35.... Officers having men sent to them without their accounts will report immediately to the Secretary of the Navy the names and rates of such men, and all other information which can be obtained, and which may be necessary to enable the Department to ascertain the name of the Officer who has been guilty of this violation of law.

36.... Officers are prohibited from borrowing money. accepting deposits from, or having any pecuniary transaction with, enlisted men or appointed Petty Officers in the naval service. The Pay Officer of the vessel is the proper person to receive deposits. Such deposits are at the risk of the depositors in all cases, and it must be so stated in the memorandum of deposit which the Paymaster is authorized to give.

37.... Commanding Officers, when issuing general orders to carry into effect instructions given by a Bureau of the Navy Department, will always say, "In accordance with orders from the Navy Department," &c. See paragraph 1115, page 198.

38.... Inspectors at naval stations are charged with grave duties, and they will be held to a very strict accountability for the reception of any inferior articles. Under the direction of the appropriate Bureau they will provide their offices with facilities for testing the purity and quality of all articles which are offered for reception at their stations; where more accurate determinations are required, the proper Bureau will authorize scientific analyses. Every Inspector will keep a book, which shall be an official register of his examinations of articles offered for delivery; it will contain the names of the contractors or vendors, the articles passed or rejected, with the dates of passage or rejection, and the daily indorsement of the Inspector. The rejected articles will be placed by themselves, and the Commandant will cause them to be removed from the yard within forty-eight hours after rejection, or report to the proper Bureau when such immediate removal is impracticable On the last day of every month, Inspectors, whether regularly or specially charged with such duties, will make an abstract report of all their transactions, under this regulation, to the respective Bureaus, and the Chiefs of the different Bureaus will be vigilant in perfecting a rigid and impartial system of inspection of all articles furnished, either under contract or open purchase, and will require reports of all articles rejected, with the names of the persons offering them, and the origin analyses in cases where analyses have been made. Every article of supply for the Navy must be thoroughly inspected before reception, and every officer charged with this duty of examination, whether a regular Inspector, or specially detailed for the occasion, will make out and forward his reports in accordance with these instructions.

39.... In accordance with the 15th section of the act approved July 17, 1862, which provides, "That every person who shall furnish supplies of any kind to the Army or Navy shall be required to mark and distinguish the same with the name or names of the contractors so furnishing said supplies, in such manner as the Secretary of War and the Secretary of the Navy may, respectively, direct, and no supplies of any kind shall be received unless so marked and distinguished," hereafter all articles furnished for the use of the Navy must be marked and distinguished with the name or names of the contractors supplying the same.

40.... All requisitions for purchases to be made in open market must, before any such purchases are made, be submitted to the appropriate Bureau for its action. The requisitions must be in duplicate and accompanied by an explanation of the uses of, and the necessity for, such purchases.

41.... Whenever it shall be deemed necessary, upon the report of the Medical Officer, to destroy the clothing, or other personal effects of officers or men, to prevent the spread of disease, the Commanding Officer will direct a survey to be held on the articles to be destroyed, and the report of survey, approved by him, will be transmitted to the Department, and will contain a descriptive list of the articles, with an estimate of their value.

42.... Paragraph 425, page 74. The first clause of this paragraph is altered to read as follows: "He will keep a correct muster-roll of the crew and a descriptive list, and will have prepared by the ship's writers copies of this roll, to be transmitted, approved by the Commanding Officer, to the Navy Department; and the correctness of the descriptive muster-roll [Form No. 3, pages 250 and 251] will in future be certified by the Executive Officer instead of the Paymaster, and he will have charge of the liberty and conduct books."

43.... When pilots are employed, care will be taken that none but such as exhibit evidence of their authority to act as such are permitted to pilot a man-of-war.

Regulation Circular No. 1.

44.... Hereafter the columns for "conduct," "health," and "morals," with the other columns under the general heads of "impressions," in Forms 26 and 27, pages 272 and 273, will be filled up by numbers, so that No. 5 shall be equivalent to "excellent," No. 4 to "very good," No. 3 to "good," No. 2 to "indifferent," and No. 1 to "bad," and these reports will be sent to the Bureau of Navigation.

45.... After the first of June, 1866, neither Ensigns, Masters, nor Lieutenants will be promoted to the next higher grades, respectively, until they have established to the satisfaction of a board of examining officers, or other duly appointed board, that they possess a sufficient knowledge of the French or Spanish languages to speak the same with a fair degree of fluency.

46.... Commanding officers of squadrons, single ship, navy yards, and naval stations, will forward to the Department, at the end of each month, reports of all suspensions, arrests, or confinements of officers under their command, made out in accordance with the annexed form.

UNITED STATES NAVAL STATION,

186 .

Monthly report of all officers who have been placed under suspension, arrest, or in confinement, within the limits of this station, for the month ending

Name.	Rank or rate.	Suspension, arrest, or confinement, and if the latter, its nature.	By whose order.	Date.	Remarks.

——— ———,

Commanding Station.

——— ———, *Secretary of the Navy,*
Washington City.

Regulation Circular No. 1.

47....No officer will remove from where he may be reached by the regular United States mails without the permission of the Secretary of the Navy.

48....Commanding officers of vessels will deliver to their successors a list of such three years' men as are entitled to honorable discharges, and when any such men are transferred to a hospital, to a station, to any other vessel. or to any other duty, such lists shall always accompany their transfer. Officers receiving men without such lists will immediately report the fact to the Bureau of Equipment and Recruiting, with the name of the officer who transferred the men in violation of this regulation.

49....Hereafter neither fleet surgeons, fleet paymasters, nor fleet engineers, will be detailed for service to any squadron in which the aggregate number of officers and men attached to such squadron is less than twenty-five hundred.

50....All modifications which may have been granted during the late insurrection in regard to the allowance for "sea-service" will cease from and after the first day of September next, from which date paragraph 191 will be the rule governing sea-service.

51....Commanding officers will, before leaving port, send to the Bureau of Navigation, if it has not been previously done, a report containing the compass corrections, due to local attraction, which have been discovered by swinging their ships, and thereafter similar reports will be forwarded by them whenever they may deem it necessary to swing their vessels for the same object.—*See paragraph* 459.

52....All correspondence with private parties on public business by any official of a navy yard or station, except the Commandant thereof, is prohibited.

GIDEON WELLES,
Secretary of the Navy.

NAVY DEPARTMENT, *August* 1, 1865.

2 N. R.

INDEX.

A.

C.

20

No. of paragraph.

N.

21

O.

22

U.

V.

OMISSION.

Paragraph 1259....The salute to a Vice-Admiral is fifteen guns; in other respects the military honors will be the same as those for Rear-Admirals.

ERRATA.

Page 88. For paragraph "294," read "494."

Page 88. On second line from bottom, for "breech," read "breach." .

Page 111. On second line from top, for "foremost," read "foremast."

Page 129. On fourteenth line from top, insert "him" after "require."

Page 185. On seventh line from top, for "other," read "clothes."

Page 237. "Sailing qualities of ships," Form No. 1, should be sent to the Bureau of Construction and Repair, and not to the Department.

Page 240. "Qualities, &c., of vessels," paragraph 345, should be sent to the Bureau of Construction and Repair, and successor.

Page 328. On line twenty-nine of Index, insert "not" after "is," so as to read, "is not permitted."

ADDENDUM.

Paragraph 1260....With the single exception of turpentine, no explosive oils nor inflammable liquids will be allowed on board vessels of the Navy; all such materials must be carefully tested as to their inflammability before being received on board, and all the turpentine required must be kept in sound, safe tanks, securely stowed in the most convenient place on the spar-deck, and none of it ever taken below.

George W Adamson

U. S. NAVY REGULATION CIRCULAR No. 1.

The following alterations and additions are hereby made to the Regulations, published for the government of all persons attached to the United States naval service, under date of April 18, 1865, and will be obeyed accordingly:

Every person subject to the control of the Navy Department will preserve this circular in his book of regulations.

1....Paragraph 126, page 22. The first clause is annulled, so as to conform to paragraph 1258, pages 233, 234.

2....Paragraph 173, page 30, omit the word "important."

3....Hereafter every official letter and communication from any officer of the Navy to any department of the government, or to the heads of any of the subordinate bureaus or offices, must pass through and be indorsed by his Commanding Officer.

4....Paragraph 261, page 46, is annulled.

5....Paragraph 386, page 69, is annulled, and the following is substituted therefor: "Steam will only be used, in entering or leaving port, when the vessel cannot be managed under sails alone, and under other circumstances where an urgent necessity may exist, which renders it necessary for the performance of the service, if a specified time for its performance has been directed by proper authority."

6....Paragraph 387, page 70, is annulled, and the following is substituted therefor: "Whenever steam is used the Commanding Officer of the vessel must enter in the steam log-book, in red ink, over his own signature, the reasons why he ordered it, and he will be held to a strict accountability for the sufficiency of his reasons. In no case will he use steam without a necessity so strong that the public interests would obviously be materially injured by not using it. The Bureau of Steam Engineering will examine the steam log-books as they arrive, and report to the department the amount of steaming done and the reasons given therefor."

7....Paragraph 422, page 74, is modified so as to leave the keys of the Paymaster's storerooms under the charge of that officer.

8....Paragraph 565, page 100, is changed so as to read, "Officers' messes of ships in commission may be allowed to draw from the ship any one or more of the component parts of the ration: Provided, That the aggregate quantity of any article issued to a mess during a quarter

shall not exceed twice the quantity which such mess would have been
entitled to had none of the rations of the officers and the servants in the
messes been commuted : *And provided further,* That all articles so issued
shall be used exclusively by the officers' messes on board ship.   Officers
are not to be permitted to draw the full allowance of any article while
the crew are upon short allowance of that article.   Issues of provisions
to officers' messes, to the medical and other departments of the ship, and
to vessels in distress, will be charged at the prices given in the ration
table."

9....Paragraph 632, page 119, is rescinded, the law providing that
the Boatswain, Gunner, Carpenter, and Sailmaker shall be called warrant officers.

10....Paragraph 839, page 150, the last clause is altered so as to read
hereafter as follows : " All decks even with or below the water-line will
be covered with shellac, paint, oil, or varnish, to avoid holy-stoning,
which is forbidden on such decks."

11....Paragraph 900, page 159, is amended by the following addition
to the end thereof: "But articles of clothing and small-stores which
have been in any degree injured by use will not thus be received."

12....Paragraph 1019, page 179, is to be regarded as unconditional,
so that every person re-enlisting, at an Atlantic port, in the naval service
of the United States must produce his discharge therefrom.   If the discharge is said to be lost, the Recruiting Officer will refer the case to the
Bureau of Equipment and Recruiting.

13....Paragraph 1083, page 193, is amended, so that hereafter the
aggregate of leaves of absence granted by Commanding Officers within
the United States, to any one under their command, shall not exceed
one month in any one year; and it is to be understood that, except in
special cases, to be judged of by the department, a leave of one month
in a year is to cover all of the time which an officer may be absent from
his post or station.

14....Paymasters performing their legitimate duties as Pay Agents,
Purchasing Agents, and Disbursing Agents, will take care to affix their
rank only to all official papers, as required by paragraph 1099, page 196,
and will not permit themselves to be addressed by any other title.

15....Paragraph 1122, page 199, is modified so as to require Officers
making reports of the misconduct of those under their command to furnish the accused with a copy of the report, and afford him an opportu-

nity to make any written explanations he may have to offer, which will be forwarded with the report to the Secretary of the Navy.

16.... Paragraph 1163, page 209, is amended in the first clause, so that for the future, when an Officer is ordered to a vessel preparing for sea, his sea pay and sea service will only begin when the vessel is regularly put in commission, which date will be indorsed on the orders of the Officer by the Commandant of the station, and reported to the Bureau of Navigation.

17.... Paragraph 1177, page 211, is annulled.

18.... Paragraph 1199, page 216, to the end thereof the following is to be added : "Paymasters of shore stations will be allowed, after detachment, the necessary time for the settlement of their accounts, not exceeding the following :

Paymasters of navy yards at New York and Boston, 60 days.

Paymasters of navy yards at Portsmouth and Philadelphia, 40 days.

Paymasters of navy yards at Washington and Mare Island, 40 days.

Paymasters of other navy yards and stations, 30 days.

Inspectors at New York and Boston, 40 days.

Inspectors at other stations, 30 days.

Paymasters of receiving ships at New York and Boston, 60 days.

Paymasters of receiving ships at other ports, 40 days."

19.... Paragraph 1228, page 223, is so far modified that the Judge Advocate will not be required to read over aloud the entire record after the reading of the defence, but only such portions of it as may be indicated by members of the Court.

20.... Paragraph 1260, page 345, is so far modified as not to apply to Medical Stores.

21.... The monthly return of "Officers attached to stations," page 241, will be sent to the "Bureau of Navigation, Office of Detail," as well as to the Bureau of Yards and Docks.

22.... Form No. 10, page 254, will be considered as applying to passengers arriving in the United States, as well as those "about to sail."

23.... Clerks or Stewards duly appointed, and proceeding to join their vessels or stations, under orders to that effect, will be allowed travelling expenses within the United States, at the rate of three cents per mile, the amount not to be paid, nor credited to them, until they shall have entered upon the discharge of their duties. When proceeding by sea to join their vessels or stations, travelling expenses will not be allowed them without the special direction of the Navy Department.

24.... When a vessel is to be laid up, or put out of commission, the orders detaching the Officers, for leaves of absence or waiting orders, will not be delivered by the Commandant of the station until the stores of the vessel shall have been landed, her crew transferred or paid off, and the vessel ready to be turned over to the station, and all regulations relative to a vessel arriving from sea fully complied with.

25.... Before sailing, the Commanding Officers of squadrons, and of each vessel, will make a special report to the Secretary of the Navy, as to whether or not every regulation of the Department and its Bureaus required previous to sailing has been complied with.

26.... It is especially the duty of all Commanding Officers to examine into the complaints of enlisted persons, to correct them so far as they are reasonable, and to direct their Paymasters to use all diligence in obtaining their accounts. Letters are constantly being received, and personal applications at the Department made by sailors touching their accounts, descriptive lists, prize money, terms of enlistment, &c., which ought to have been attended to by Commanding Officers and Paymasters as a sacred duty, and thus keep the men from placing their affairs with the Department and Bureaus in the hands of brokers.

27.... Coast or general Pilots on board of a United States vessel do not relieve the Commanding Officer from the responsibility placed upon him by paragraph 1200, page 216. A regularly licensed harbor or river Pilot in charge of a United States vessel, within the limits for which he is licensed, is responsible for keeping the vessel off the bottom, but Commanding Officers will see that the rules about collisions are strictly observed by the Pilots.

28.... The Commanding Officer of a vessel arriving at any port in the United States is to see that a requisition is forwarded, the day of his arrival, for money to pay off all the crew who may be ordered to be discharged, or whose terms of service have expired; and none of the crew to be discharged will be allowed to go on shore until paid off, without special permission from the Secretary of the Navy. Commanding Officers of vessels, under the orders of the Commandant of a station, will not give liberty to officers or men without the authority of said Commandant first obtained.

29.... Commanding Officers of squadrons, and of naval stations, are directed to investigate immediately, by a Court of Inquiry, or if the

Regulation Circular No. 1.

matter is of less importance, and a court impracticable, then by a board of three officers, all accidents, occurrences, and transactions, which it is necessary the Department should have full information upon, and forward the same to the Secretary of the Navy, in such a complete and concise form that action may be taken thereon without referring the case back again. Commanding Officers of vessels, acting singly, will, so far as practicable, conform to the above order.

30.... A written order from the Department to an officer : to leave his domicile for duty, fixing no date and not expressing haste, will be obeyed by leaving within four days after receipt; if the order reads "without delay," he will leave within forty-eight hours ; if "immediately," then within twelve hours; and all Officers are required to indorse on their orders from the Department the date and hour of receipt.

31.... Hereafter the Office of Detail will be attached to the Bureau of Navigation, and the Chief of that Bureau will, "by direction of the Secretary of the Navy," sign the orders and documents referring to detail. All papers connected with the detail will be addressed to the "Bureau of Navigation, Office of Detail."—See paragraph 1115, page 198.

32.... A vessel of the Navy, under orders to go to sea, will be considered under sailing orders from the time the powder is taken on board, and no person will then be permitted to leave the ship, except on duty.

33.... Paymasters entitled to Clerks or Stewards will be allowed to retain them in service during the time allowed them for settling their accounts.

34.... Masters and Ensigns of the regular Navy, and Midshipmen serving on board any naval steamer, will hereafter be taught thoroughly the duty of steam enginery. They will be divided into four watches on deck, and the same number in the engine and fire-rooms, and will serve alternately on deck and below whenever steam power is used. Quarterly reports, according to Form No. 26, page 272, will be made, under the heads of "Steam" and "Remarks," showing the proficiency and reliability of each officer in steam enginery, and these reports will be used at the examination of the above-mentioned officers. After the first day of January, 1866, no Master nor Ensign of the regular Navy, nor any Midshipman, will be promoted until he has passed an examination in steam enginery. Commanders of squadrons, Commanders of steam vessels, and the Superintendent of the Naval Academy, are charged with the faithful execution of this regulation.

35.... Officers having men sent to them without their accounts will report immediately to the Secretary of the Navy the names and rates of such men, and all other information which can be obtained, and which may be necessary to enable the Department to ascertain the name of the Officer who has been guilty of this violation of law.

36.... Officers are prohibited from borrowing money, accepting deposits from, or having any pecuniary transaction with, enlisted men or appointed Petty Officers in the naval service. The Pay Officer of the vessel is the proper person to receive deposits. Such deposits are at the risk of the depositors in all cases, and it must be so stated in the memorandum of deposit which the Paymaster is authorized to give.

37.... Commanding Officers, when issuing general orders to carry into effect instructions given by a Bureau of the Navy Department, will always say, "In accordance with orders from the Navy Department," &c. See paragraph 1115, page 198.

38.... Inspectors at naval stations are charged with grave duties, and they will be held to a very strict accountability for the reception of any inferior articles. Under the direction of the appropriate Bureau they will provide their offices with facilities for testing the purity and quality of all articles which are offered for reception at their stations; where more accurate determinations are required, the proper Bureau will authorize scientific analyses. Every Inspector will keep a book, which shall be an official register of his examinations of articles offered for delivery; it will contain the names of the contractors or vendors, the articles passed or rejected, with the dates of passage or rejection, and the daily indorsement of the Inspector. The rejected articles will be placed by themselves, and the Commandant will cause them to be removed from the yard within forty-eight hours after rejection, or report to the proper Bureau when such immediate removal is impracticable On the last day of every month, Inspectors, whether regularly or specially charged with such duties, will make an abstract report of all their transactions, under this regulation, to the respective Bureaus, and the Chiefs of the different Bureaus will be vigilant in perfecting a rigid and impartial system of inspection of all articles furnished, either under contract or open purchase, and will require reports of all articles rejected, with the names of the persons offering them, and the origin analyses in cases where analyses have been made. Every article of supply for the Navy must be thoroughly inspected before reception, and every officer charged with this duty of examination, whether a regular Inspector, or specially detailed for the occasion, will make out and forward his reports in accordance with these instructions.

39.... In accordance with the 15th section of the act approved July 17, 1862, which provides, "That every person who shall furnish supplies of any kind to the Army or Navy shall be required to mark and distinguish the same with the name or names of the contractors so furnishing said supplies, in such manner as the Secretary of War and the Secretary of the Navy may, respectively, direct, and no supplies of any kind shall be received unless so marked and distinguished," hereafter all articles furnished for the use of the Navy must be marked and distinguished with the name or names of the contractors supplying the same.

40.... All requisitions for purchases to be made in open market must, before any such purchases are made, be submitted to the appropriate Bureau for its action. The requisitions must be in duplicate and accompanied by an explanation of the uses of, and the necessity for, such purchases.

41.... Whenever it shall be deemed necessary, upon the report of the Medical Officer, to destroy the clothing, or other personal effects of officers or men, to prevent the spread of disease, the Commanding Officer will direct a survey to be held on the articles to be destroyed, and the report of survey, approved by him, will be transmitted to the Department, and will contain a descriptive list of the articles, with an estimate of their value.

42.... Paragraph 425, page 74. The first clause of this paragraph is altered to read as follows: "He will keep a correct muster-roll of the crew and a descriptive list, and will have prepared by the ship's writers copies of this roll, to be transmitted, approved by the Commanding Officer, to the Navy Department; and the correctness of the descriptive muster-roll [Form No. 3, pages 250 and 251] will in future be certified by the Executive Officer instead of the Paymaster, and he will have charge of the liberty and conduct books."

43.... When pilots are employed, care will be taken that none but such as exhibit evidence of their authority to act as such are permitted to pilot a man-of-war.

Regulation Circular No. 1.

44....Hereafter the columns for "conduct," "health," and "morals," with the other columns under the general heads of "impressions," in Forms 26 and 27, pages 272 and 273, will be filled up by numbers, so that No. 5 shall be equivalent to "excellent," No. 4 to "very good," No. 3 to "good," No. 2 to "indifferent," and No. 1 to "bad," and these reports will be sent to the Bureau of Navigation.

45....After the first of June, 1866, neither Ensigns, Masters, nor Lieutenants will be promoted to the next higher grades, respectively, until they have established to the satisfaction of a board of examining officers, or other duly appointed board, that they possess a sufficient knowledge of the French or Spanish languages to speak the same with a fair degree of fluency.

46....Commanding officers of squadrons, single ship, navy yards, and naval stations, will forward to the Department, at the end of each month, reports of all suspensions, arrests, or confinements of officers under their command, made out in accordance with the annexed form.

UNITED STATES NAVAL STATION,

186 .

Monthly report of all officers who have been placed under suspension, arrest, or in confinement, within the limits of this station, for the month ending

Name.	Rank or rate.	Suspension, arrest, or confinement, and if the latter, its nature.	By whose order.	Date.	Remarks.

————— —————,

Commanding Station.

————— —————, *Secretary of the Navy,*
Washington City.

Regulation Circular No. 1.

47....No officer will remove from where he may be reached by the regular United States mails without the permission of the Secretary of the Navy.

48....Commanding officers of vessels will deliver to their successors a list of such three years' men as are entitled to honorable discharges, and when any such men are transferred to a hospital, to a station, to any other vessel, or to any other duty, such lists shall always accompany their transfer. Officers receiving men without such lists will immediately report the fact to the Bureau of Equipment and Recruiting, with the name of the officer who transferred the men in violation of this regulation.

49....Hereafter neither fleet surgeons, fleet paymasters, nor fleet engineers, will be detailed for service to any squadron in which the aggregate number of officers and men attached to such squadron is less than twenty-five hundred.

50....All modifications which may have been granted during the late insurrection in regard to the allowance for "sea-service" will cease from and after the first day of September next, from which date paragraph 191 will be the rule governing sea-service.

51....Commanding officers will, before leaving port, send to the Bureau of Navigation, if it has not been previously done, a report containing the compass corrections, due to local attraction, which have been discovered by swinging their ships, and thereafter similar reports will be forwarded by them whenever they may deem it necessary to swing their vessels for the same object.—*See paragraph 459.*

52....All correspondence with private parties on public business by any official of a navy yard or station, except the Commandant thereof, is prohibited.

GIDEON WELLES,
Secretary of the Navy.

NAVY DEPARTMENT, *August* 1, 1865.

2 N. R.

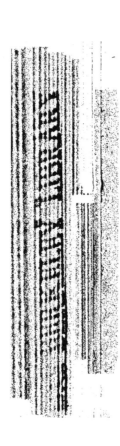

U. S. NAVY REGULATION CIRCULAR No. 2.

The following alterations and additions are hereby made to the Regulations published for the government of all persons attached to the United States naval service, under date of April 18, 1865, and will be obeyed accordingly:

Every person subject to the control of the Navy Department will preserve this circular in his book of regulations.

1.... Paragraph 52, page 8, in the second line after the word "follows," insert: "The Boatswain will attend the side with eight side boys; the side shall be piped."

2.... Paragraph 61, page 9, at the end add: "A vice-consul, consular agent, or commercial agent, shall be saluted with five guns."

3.... The following paragraphs, designated as *a*, *b*, *c*, and *d*, will immediately precede paragraph 62, page 10:

a. When a Vice-Admiral shall go on board of his flag-ship to assume command, the side shall be attended by the Boatswain, with eight side boys. He shall be received by all the officers of the vessel in full-dress uniform, and the crew, in clean mustering clothes, arranged on the side opposite to that on which he enters. The marine guard shall be paraded. He shall be received at the gangway by the Commanding Officer and such other officers of the vessel as may be designated by the Commander. The officers and men shall uncover their heads; the guard shall present arms; the drums shall give three ruffles, and the music on board shall then play a march. When the Vice-Admiral orders his flag to be hoisted, a salute of fifteen guns shall be fired—the flag to be unfurled at the firing of the first gun.

b. When a Vice-Admiral shall make a visit of ceremony or inspection to any vessel of the fleet under his command, the same honors shall be paid to him, and the same ceremonies observed, as in the case of his assuming command, with the exception that, if saluted, the salute shall be fired immediately after he comes on board.

c. When a Vice-Admiral relinquishes his command afloat, the ceremonies prescribed for his first reception shall be observed; and after he shall have disembarked the salute shall be fired, and his flag lowered down at the firing of the last gun of the salute.

d. When a Vice-Admiral leaves his flag-ship with the intention of soon returning on board, the side shall be attended by the Boatswain, with eight side boys. He shall be entitled to a full guard, which is to present arms as he passes in front of it, and the drums will give three ruffles. He is to be attended to the gangway by the line officer on board next in rank to himself, and by all the line officers of his staff other than those who are to accompany him. The officer of the deck and junior officers of the watch will also be in attendance. The same ceremonies are to be observed on his return to the ship. If absent at night and with the intention of returning, four white-light lantern lights are to be hoisted perpendicularly at the peak. The top lights of all flag-ships are to be lighted at night while in port.

4....Paragraph 62, page 10, in the second line after the word command, insert: "The side shall be attended by the Boatswain and six side boys."

5....Paragraph 66, page 10, amended so as to apply to a Vice-Admiral's flag also.

6....Paragraph 73, page 12, is rescinded, and the following substituted: "The side may be piped and attended by side boys for all commissioned officers visiting and leaving vessels of the Navy. When commanding officers visit or depart from vessels of the Navy, they shall be received at the gangway on arriving, and attended to the gangway on departing, by the Commander of the vessel, if the visiting Commanding Officer is of the same or higher rank; otherwise, by the executive officer. The officer of the deck for the time being will receive at the gangway on the arrival, and attend at the gangway at the departure, of all commissioned officers. Warrant Officers will receive and see over the side of the ship all Warrant Officers visiting or departing from the same."

7....Paragraph 74, page 12, in next to the last line, read "one light for two lights."

8....Paragraph 75, page 12, insert in the first line after a and before Rear, the words, "Vice or."

9....Paragraph 81, page 13, is rescinded.

10....Paragraph 82, page 13, in the first and second lines, insert the words, "Vice or," before the word Rear, in each case.

11....Paragragh 83, page 13, is modified as follows: "As accidents may occur during the firing of salutes in vessels, from the haste with which the guns are necessarily reloaded, no vessel of the Navy mounting

Regulation Circular No. 2.

less than ten guns is in future to fire a salute that may require the re-loading of the guns. If necessary, in order to avoid giving offense to official persons abroad, she may, however, fire a return salute; but under no circumstances shall a transport, store-ship, or surveying vessel fire a salute.

12....Paragraph 84, page 13, is altered to read ten guns instead of six guns.

13....Paragraph 91, page 14, omit the words "or less," in the first line.

14....Paragraph 103, page 17, at the end add, "unless such honors have been tendered and declined."

15....Paragraphs 166 and 167, page 29, are hereby rescinded.

16....Officers not on duty, or on leave of absence, are to keep the Department at all times advised of their particular address in the State or Territory in which they reside.

17....The residence of an officer is within the State or Territory which he habitually makes his home when off duty, and the appropriate column in the Navy Register will designate whatever State or Territory officers may select as their residence. No officer making such selection will afterwards change it or his residence without the authority of the Secretary of the Navy.

18....No officer under arrest or suspension, or on furlough, will leave the State or Territory of which he is a resident, or visit the Navy De-partment, without the authority of the Secretary of the Navy.

19....No officer whose residence is without the District of Columbia will come within the limits of the same without the permission of the Secretary of the Navy. Every officer applying for permission to visit the District of Columbia will state the object which induces his appli-cation, and the period and length of his intended visit.

20....Paragraph 178, page 31. The following is substituted for the last clause of said paragraph: "In case of officers who are required to furnish testimonials on presenting themselves for examination, such testimonials may be written by those whose province it is to do so; but they shall be directed to and sent to the Navy Department, and certified copies of them given to the individuals to whom the testimonials are due

Regulation Circular No. 2.

21....Paragraph 179, page 31, add the words, "excepting such as are authorized in the preceding amended paragraph."

22....Paragraph 448, page 78, is amended so as to read after the word "Navigator," (in the second line,) "and Ordnance Officer;" and he will, in addition to his duties as Navigator of the vessel, have charge of, and be responsible for, the expenditure, care, preservation, and safe-keeping of all ordnance equipments and stores, and of all receipt and account books and returns, under the orders and instructions of the commander of the vessel, and in conformity to the prescribed regulations and instructions in the Ordnance Manual. All returns, receipt and expenditure of ordnance equipments and stores, will be made by the "Navigator and Ordnance Officer," in conformity to the regulations and instructions in the Ordnance Manual.

23....Paragraph 459, page 82, add to the paragraph the following: "He will keep and transmit to the Bureau of Navigation an abstract of the meteorological observations recorded in the log-book, according to the prescribed form.

24....Paragraph 460, page 82, is rescinded, and the following is substituted: "The Navigator shall prepare, and, after it shall have been approved by his Commanding Officer, transmit to the Bureau of Navigation, from time to time, if practicable, otherwise, at the end of the cruise, a skeleton chart of the cruising ground, showing distinctly the track or tracks of the vessel, with the day, month, and year, noted during the entire cruise or period of time the vessel was absent from port or the United States; to which must be appended remarks and notes bearing upon the winds, weather, currents of the ocean, and other phenomena of value to nautical science."

25....So much of paragraphs 478 to 491, inclusive, (pages 84 to 86,) which relate to the duties of Gunner, and are in conflict with the amended paragraph 448, are rescinded in respect to that officer; but are hereby made applicable to, and remain in full force and effect in regard to, the duties of the "Navigator and Ordnance Officer" of the vessel. When a Gunner is attached to a vessel having a "Navigator and Ordnance Officer" on board, the duties of the Gunner, in connection with the battery, magazines, and ordnance equipments in charge of the "Navigator and Ordnance" Officer, will be prescribed by the commander of the vessel, but not in conflict with the amended paragraph 448.

26.....Paragraph 553, page 99, is so far modified as to dispense with sending to the Department copies of all bills or accounts.

27.....Paragraph 665, page 116, add the words: "When the cases are simple, and there is but one medical officer attached to the vessel, the Surgeon's steward may be directed to accompany them."

28.....Paragraph 1084, page 193, is rescinded, and the following is substituted: "Commandants of navy yards, stations, or senior officers in charge of duty of any kind, by order of the Department, in the United States, shall not go beyond the limits of their respective commands, stations, or specified duty, for a longer period of time than 48 hours, without the permission of the Secretary of the Navy, except in cases of pressing emergency which will not admit of sufficient delay to communicate with and receive a reply from the Department. In cases of such pressing necessity as hereinbefore mentioned, it shall be the duty of the before-mentioned officers to report to the Department, without unnecessary delay, a detailed statement of the facts and circumstances which induced them to leave their station.

29.....Paragraph 1146, page 205, is rescinded, and the following is substituted: "In all cases where transportation is furnished at the public expense to an officer of the Navy traveling under orders, the charge, cost, or value of such transportation shall be deducted from his mileage."

30.....Paragraph 1162, page 208, is so far modified as to read: "The pay of all promoted officers (modified by the laws in relation to the pay of officers subject to examination before promotion) commences, &c., as prescribed in said paragraph 1162."

31.....No. 16 of U. S. Navy Regulation, Circular No. 1, is rescinded, and paragraph 1163, page 209, "Regulations for the Navy," is amended to read as follows: "When ordered on sea service, officers are entitled only to 'shore' or 'other-duty' pay from the day they leave their domicils, in obedience thereof, to the date they report for such service at the place where the vessel to which they are ordered is lying, if the vessel is in commission for sea-service; but if the vessel to which they are ordered is not in commission for sea-service at the time of their reporting, then until the vessel is regularly commissioned for sea-service. Sea-service and sea pay and rations of officers will only commence from the date of reporting for and joining a vessel in commission for sea-service. The duty pay of an engineer officer is the same, whether employed on shore duty or at sea, and it commences from the date of his leaving his domicil in obedience to orders for duty, though only entitled to credit for sea-service and allowance of rations from the date of joining a vessel in commission for sea-service."

32....Paragraph 1164, page 209, add after the word "accordingly," at the end of the paragraph: "But it is not to be understood that this allowance of 'other-duty pay' is to apply to officers returning to the United States under the sentence of a court martial."

33....Paragraph 1165, page 209, add: "When an officer on other duty than 'sea-service' enters a naval hospital for treatment, he shall continue to receive duty pay, unless detached, but not for a longer period of time than two months."

34....Commanders of squadrons, stations, and vessels acting singly, will endorse upon the orders of all officers reporting for duty the dates thereof.

35....Commanders of vessels will report the dates on which the vessels under their commands are regularly put into commission, to the Bureau of Navigation, and transmit, at the same time, correct lists of all the officers then and there present on board for duty.

36....Officers ordered to duty on board a vessel already in commission for sea-service, will, immediately after reporting for duty and joining that vessel, report the facts and date to the Bureau of Navigation.

37....All communications to the Department, or which require the action or consideration of the Department, from officers not on duty or not under orders, will be transmitted by them directly, and not through persons holding any civil office or other position under the Government, with a view to the influence of such persons; and officers are admonished that such attempts to avail themselves of influence will be regarded as an evidence of the weakness of their claims.

38....Commandants of navy yards and stations will promptly report to the Department the departure of vessels from, or their arrival within, the limits of their command, stating the destination of the vessel or the quarter from which it came, as the case may be, and the Commanding Officer thereof.

Regulation Circular No. 2.

39.... Commandants of navy yards and stations, Commanders of of squadrons, and Commanders of vessels, will communicate to the appropriate Bureau every three months, and oftener should the importance of the matter demand it, any faults in the Book of Allowances, as ascertained from its actual use, and any suggestions that, in their opinion, would tend to its perfection.

40.... Commandants of navy yards and of naval stations at which vessels may be laid up in ordinary, will make reports at the end of every month to the Bureaus of Construction and of Steam Engineering on the condition of the hulls and machinery, as follows:

To the Bureau of Construction—the condition of the hull of each vessel, and the probable time required to make it fit for service.

To the Bureau of Steam Engineering—the condition, separately, of the engines, boilers, screw propellers, or paddle-wheels, and appurtenances not included under those heads, of each vessel, and the probable time required to make them fit for service.

The Commandants will make such suggestions, in these reports, as they deem will conduce to the better or more economical preservation of the hulls and machinery.

41.... No vessel will be reported by the Commandant of a yard or station as ready for officers until she is in a condition to receive them on board to mess.

42.... A supply of all General Orders and Circulars of the Department will be forwarded to the Commandants of stations and Commanders of squadrons, who are required to distribute them to each and every officer under their respective commands.

43.... Commandants of stations will post, for at least three months after their date, in the most conspicuous place within the limits of their command, a copy of each of the General Orders and Circulars received by them.

44.... All officers on duty are required to apply, in writing, monthly, to the Commandant of the station or the squadron under whose command they are serving, for such General Orders and Circulars as they have not received; and all officers not on duty will make similar application to the Navy Department, such application to specify the numbers or dates of the General Orders or Circulars they have not received, or the number and date of the last one received by them.

Regulation Circular No. 2.

45.... Vessels under steam will never use more than two-thirds of their boiler power unless in an emergency, which must be fully entered and explained upon the Log, and a special report of the same made to the Bureau of Steam Engineering.

46.... In reporting to the Department deaths, desertions, and personal casualties of whatever description, the name and rank or rating of the person will invariably be given.

47.... Public property in the custody of officers of the Navy will not be loaned for private use, except under special authority from the Navy Department. ·

48.... Whenever a court martial shall impose a sentence including forfeiture of pay upon any person in the Naval service, it shall be the duty of the court, in the case of commissioned officers, to state the rate of pay and time of such forfeiture, and in all other cases to fix the amount of pay so forfeited, stating it in dollars and cents.

49.... Such of the forms, indicated in the Book of Regulations, as shall not be furnished in blank by the Department or its Bureaus, are to be prepared in manuscript by or under the direction of those who are required to use them.

50.... Neither open purchases of bunting nor the flags prescribed in the Book of Allowances will be made except upon requisitions which have been submitted to the Bureau of Navigation and received its approval.

51.... When requisitions for open purchases are returned, approved by the proper Bureau, the purchasing paymaster will procure only those items the estimated cost of which is under one hundred dollars, reserving the remainder until the 25th of the month, on which day, monthly, he will advertise in at least two commercial newspapers for three successive days for proposals for furnishing such supplies, and will forward a printed copy or slip of the advertisement to each Bureau having articles contained in it. On the 1st day of the succeeding month the bids will be opened and the lowest bidders notified to make immediate deliveries, unless the prices are so exorbitant as to make it advisable to reject the bids altogether; which will be done if it is apparent that they are much above the market price.

52.... The Chiefs of Bureaus will carefully scrutinize requisitions for open purchases, and will decline to approve those that are considered unnecessary, or where the variation from the contract article is so trivial that the latter will serve the purpose instead.

53....No requisition for an open purchase will be approved until it has the endorsement of the Naval Storekeeper that the articles required are not in the public store and are not due upon an existing contract.

54....No requisition will be made for articles under contracts which have expired, nor after the close of the fiscal year; and no deliveries upon any contract will be received unless requisition for the same shall have been made on the date of or prior to said expiration or termination and previous to the receipt of articles upon a new contract.

55....Requisitions for stores, furniture, and articles that are perishable, or can be readily purchased, will not be made for vessels that have been ordered to be repaired and placed in ordinary, but only for vessels that have been ordered to be fitted for immediate service at sea; nor will requisitions be made without first ascertaining that there are no suitable articles for the purposes for which they are needed on hand.

56....Requisitions for purchasing at the cost of defaulting contractors, in accordance with paragraph 964, page 171, must be submitted to the proper Bureau and receive its approval before the purchase be made.

57....There must not be any serviceable articles at a navy yard or station that are not on charge and subject to requisition. All such articles must be on the Storekeeper's books at a fair and proper valuation.

58....The assessing and taxing of the workmen or other employés in the navy yards for party or political purposes is forbidden. Attempts to exact money from such persons for such purposes, is, in every point of view, reprehensible, and is to be wholly and absolutely prohibited. Any master workman, or other appointee of the Navy Department, employed in the navy yards, who shall levy, or participate in the levying of, contributions on persons in Government service, for party purposes, will render himself liable to removal. Committee men, or the representatives of political parties, will not be permitted to visit the yards to make collections for any political party whatever.

59....The employment of extra hands preceding warmly-contested elections, with the view of advancing the interests of any political party, is expressly forbidden. No more persons shall be employed or retained in a navy yard than the public service actually requires. Party gatherings and party discussions are at all times to be avoided within the navy yards.

60....Application to fill the position of Master Workman in any of the navy yards will hereafter be addressed to the Chief of the Bureau of Yards and Docks, stating the name, age, and residence of the applicant, with testimonials as to his character, habits, professional skill and competency, and physical ability.

61....Whenever a vacancy shall occur in the office of Master Workman, a board will be convened at the navy yard where such vacancy exists, under the direction of the Secretary of the Navy, and a selection will be made from the qualified candidates, who shall have passed a satisfactory examination, irrespective of locality—no district or State being entitled to preference for these positions.

62....All nominations of persons to office in navy yards, which require the approval of the Department, must be accompanied by testimonials of character, habits, and competency, and a statement as to whether the nominee has served in the military or naval service during the war, and, if so, how long and in what capacity.

63....In the employment of mechanics and others in navy yards, at naval stations, or elsewhere in the service of the Navy Department, preference is to be given to such as have been honorably discharged from the Navy and Marine Corps, and especially to those who have been wounded or disabled, provided they are capable of performing satisfactorily the duties required of them.

64....The Bureaus of the Navy Department will not pass bills for work performed that are not properly approved by the Commanding Officer who has been authorized to incur the indebtedness for, and has had charge of, such work.

65....The Commanders of coast survey vessels, or other vessels having officers and crews belonging to the Navy, will transmit to the Department muster rolls and make the other returns required by the Regulations, so far as applicable.

66....The following form will be used in making return of persons honorably discharged, required by paragraph 779, page 136, Navy Regulations:

Regulation Circular No. 2.

LIST AND DESCRIPTION OF MEN *Honorably Discharged from the U. S. ——, 18—.*

Ship's No.	Names.	Rating.	Enlisted.		From what vessel received.	Where born.		Age.	Eyes.	Hair.	Complexion.	Height.		Permanent Marks, &c.	Date of Discharge.
			When.	Where.		City or County.	State.					Feet.	Inches.		

——— ———,
Paymaster.

Approved

——— ———,
Commanding Officer.

Regulation Circular No. 2.

67.... The following is substituted for Form No. 3, on pages 250 and 251:

FORM No. 3.

Complete Descriptive Muster Roll of the Crew of the U. S. ——— on the ——— day of ———, 18—.

[To be transmitted to the Bureau of Equipment and Recruiting at the commencement of a cruise, and on the 1st of January, April, July, October, and at the expiration of a cruise.]

NAMES. (Alphabetically arranged, without regard to ratings, with the surnames to the left.)	Ship's No.	Rating.	Date of enlistment.			Where enlisted.	Term of enlist'm't.	Place or vessel from which received.	When received on board.	Where born.		Personal Description.							Height.		T. D. R. D. D.	REMARKS. Where and when.
			Year.	Month.	Day.					City, town, or county.	State.	Age. Yrs.	Occupation.	Eyes.	Hair.	Complex'n.			Ft.	In.		

Recapitulation of *Crew remaining on board at date of Muster Roll.*

Petty Officers ----------
Seamen ----------
Ordinary Seamen ----------
Landsmen ----------
Boys ----------
Apprentices ----------
Musicians ----------
Firemen ----------

Total ----------

Approved this ——— day of ———, 18—, at ———.

——————,
Commanding Officer.

Certified to be correct, and that all casualties, transfers, deaths, desertions, and discharges that have occurred since the date of last Muster Roll are duly noted.

——————,
Executive Officer.

Received at the Navy Department ———.

NOTE.—Care must be taken that every column be correctly filled, and that all casualties, transfers, or discharges which have occurred during the quarter, or to date of roll, are duly noted, reporting dates of various changes, where transferred, &c. The names of the men thus reported to be entered in common with those remaining on board. If the information required by the printed headings cannot be otherwise obtained, obtain it from the men themselves, making notes, showing the portions thus obtained, in the column for remarks. Commanding officers are requested to keep themselves supplied with blanks by application to the Bureau of Equipment and Recruiting, or Fleet Paymaster.

Regulation Circular No. 2.

68.... The following is substituted for Form No. 4, on page 252:

FORM No. 4.

DESCRIPTION OF DESERTERS AND MEN *Absent without Leave, from the U. S. S.* ———, 18—.

Name.	Rating.	Enlisted.		Where born.	Age.	Eyes.	Hair.	Complexion.	Height.		Permanent Marks, &c.	Date of Desertion.	Reward offered.	Remarks.
		When.	Where.						Feet.	Inches.				

———— ————,
Commanding.

69.... The following is substituted for section 1236, page 225: "The officer by whose order a general court martial, summary court martial, or court of inquiry, has been convened, is the only proper person to dissolve the court. When, therefore, any court shall have concluded the trial of all cases actually referred to it, and transmitted, severally,

Regulation Circular No. 2.

the records of its proceedings in each to the officer by whose order it was convened, it will await the further orders of that officer, whose duty it shall be, so soon as such records are received, to revise the same, and either to return them to the court for its reconsideration or to dissolve the court; and, after having dissolved the court, to forward such records to the Department as soon as practicable.

70....Steam may be raised on board vessels of the Navy for the purpose of dispelling damp and unwholesome air or drying the ship, whenever, in the opinion of the Commanding Officer, it is necessary.

GIDEON WELLES,
Secretary of the Navy.

NAVY DEPARTMENT,
January 30, 1866.

U. S. NAVY REGULATION CIRCULAR No 3.

The following alterations and additions are hereby made to the Regulations published for the government of all persons attached to the United States Naval Service, under date of April 18, 1865, and will be obeyed accordingly:

Every person subject to the control of the Navy Department will preserve a copy of this circular in his book of regulations.

1....In foreign ports where a paymaster in charge of stores is stationed—whether on shore or on board a stationary storeship—all requisitions for stores will be made upon him, and all purchases in open market will be made by him, unless otherwise directed by the commander of the squadron for reasons to be stated to the Department.

2....The descriptive lists attached to certificates of death, certificates of ordinary disability, and certificates of pension, are always.to be signed by the paymaster in charge of the accounts of the person in whose case the certificate issues.

3....Whenever a vessel-of-war visits a foreign port where there is a consular representative of the United States, the commanding officer of such vessel will consult with such representative with regard to procuring coal or other supplies of which the vessel may stand in need, and will give due consideration to his suggestions, and act upon them, if it shall appear to the interest of the naval service to do so. In receiving the suggestions of such consular representatives, and availing themselves of their local knowledge, commanding officers are not thereby in any degree relieved from the duty and responsibility of making diligent personal inquiry themselves, with the view of protecting and doing the best for the government.

4....Attempts to influence the legislative branch of the government, or any member thereof, touching measures connected with naval affairs, are often productive of embarrassment, and are therefore disapproved, excepting when the opinion of an officer is requested, in writing, by a member or members.

5....A committee of Congress officially visiting a navy yard or station will be saluted with fifteen guns.

6....The following is substituted for paragraph 163, page 29:

Regulation Circular No. 3.

When any commissioned or warrant officer, seaman, marine, or other person belonging to the navy, shall be accused of a capital crime, or of having used violence, or committed any offense against the person or property of any citizen of any of the United States, such as is punishable by the known laws of the land, the commanding officer and officers of every vessel, naval station, or command to which the person or persons so accused shall belong, are hereby required, upon applications duly made by or in behalf of the party or parties injured, to use their utmost endeavors to deliver over such accused person or persons to the civil magistrate, and likewise to be aiding and assisting to the officers of justice in apprehending and securing the person or persons so accused, in order to bring him or them to trial.

7....Article II, pages 2 and 3, is amended as follows:

LINE OFFICERS.

Midshipmen, who have finally graduated, shall rank next after Ensigns.

Boatswains next after Midshipmen who have finally graduated.

Gunners next after Boatswains.

Midshipmen, who have not finally graduated, next after Gunners.

Mates next after Midshipmen who have not finally graduated.

STAFF OFFICERS.

3d Assistant Engineers. } To have assimilated rank with Midshipmen who have not finally graduated.
Clerks................ }

Carpenters .... } To have assimilated rank with Mates.
Sailmakers............ }

8....The second clause of paragraph 178, page 30, having been superseded by paragraph 20, page 359, Regulations Circular No. 2, the first or remaining clause is hereby rescinded.

9....Reports in full of the character and qualifications of officers having been provided for by forms 25, 26, and 27, pages 271, 272, and 273, and paragraph 44, page 354, Regulation Circular No. 1, all other testimonials or certificates to persons either in or out of the naval service are forbidden, excepting the following mentioned:

Those that are authorized by paragraph 20, page 359, Regulation Circular No. 2, which, however, must not be given if the official association or intercourse between the two has been for a less period than three months.

Such cases of exceptional good conduct as may require special report. Those that are authorized by paragraph 969, page 172.

To *enlisted* persons who are then, or who shall have been, in the Navy, who can receive the benefit of a letter of recommendation as to character and service from any officer acquainted with them.

And *appointed* persons, who can receive commendatory letters or certificates from those by whom they were appointed or under whom they immediately served, countersigned by the commanding officer; but such letters or certificates are not to be given except at the termination of the appointment, nor unless the service of the persons shall have exceeded three months.

10.... Forms 26 and 27, pages 272 and 273, and paragraph 44, page 354, Regulation Circular No. 1, will hereafter apply to commandants of yards and stations, who will make quarterly returns in accordance therewith of officers attached to the yard or station.

11.... Commanding officers of vessels will see that the steam heaters placed on board be not removed from their positions during warm weather, as the practice of taking them down and storing them in the hold rapidly destroys them.

12.... Paragraph 364, page 65, is amended by adding to it the following words: this report will be forwarded to the Bureau of Construction and Repair.

13.... Page 237, report of "sailing qualities of ship," according to form No. 1, page 246, to be sent to the Bureau of Construction and Repair, instead of the Navy Department.

14.... The attention of all persons in the naval service is particularly called to the following law, any violation of which will be considered as an offense against the naval regulations, in addition to the penalty imposed by the law:

AN ACT reducing the duty on imports, and for other purposes.

SEC. 10. *And be it further enacted,* That no officer or other person connected with the navy of the United States shall, under any pretense, import in any ship or vessel of the United States, any goods, wares, or merchandise liable to the payment of any duty.

Approved July 30, 1846.

15....In all cases of trial by courts martial of any person in the naval service, where the accused has no legal adviser, he will be permitted to select some officer within reach to defend him; and in case he does not select any one, the authority convening the court will detail an officer, who shall faithfully advise and assist the accused to the best of his ability.

16....Officers who have chronic disorders not likely to be benefited by medical treatment, will not be retained in a medical hospital over four months; and no officer will be a second time received into a hospital on account of any disease or disability for which he has already had the advantage of medical treatment in a naval establishment for the period above named.

17....In case of robbery, or on the discovery of the loss of money or other public property, the person responsible for the safe custody of the same will immediately report the occurrence to the senior officer present, who will thereupon order a board of three suitable officers to investigate the alleged robbery or loss, and to report fully and impartially all the circumstances connected therewith, so far as they can ascertain, which report will be forwarded to the Secretary of the Navy, and a copy of it to the chief of the appropriate bureau.

18....Paragraph 45, page 364, Regulation Circular No. 2, is so far modified that when paddle-wheel steamers are running long distances in the trades, with the wind free, the paddles in the water are to be removed and the vessel navigated under sail alone. Under other circumstances, steam may be used according to the said paragraph.

19....Paragraph 1199, page 216, Naval Regulations, and paragraph 18, page 349, Regulation Circular No. 1, give ample time to pay officers for rendering their accounts in all ordinary cases Therefore, when any pay officer shall fail to render his final accounts for settlement promptly within the prescribed period, he will be considered as delinquent, and will be placed on furlough until further orders. The usual time necessary for packages to reach the Department by express from any given point will be allowed, in addition to the time given by the above-mentioned regulations; but no increase of pay will be granted for this additional time. In extraordinary cases, the Department may suspend the operation of this rule upon application of the officer and satisfactory evidence that the delay was unavoidable.

Regulation Circular No. 3.

20....The commanding officer of each vessel under repairs or fitting out at a navy yard or station, will report to the Secretary of the Navy, through the commandant of the yard or station, on the 1st and 15th of the month, what progress is being made in the preparation of the vessel for sea, what important work remains to be done, and when the same will probably be completed; what changes of consequence have been made, and the reasons therefor; and will make any suggestions which he thinks would facilitate the preparation of the vessel for sea, if adopted.

21....On the 1st of each month commandants of navy yards or shore stations will forward to the Secretary of the Navy a report of the vessels of the Navy repairing or fitting for sea at such yard or station, which report will embrace, in separate columns, the name of the vessel, her rate, probable time of completion of hull, probable time of completion of machinery, when ready for officers to mess on board, when ready for sea, name and rank of commanding officer, and any remarks that may be deemed necessary. This report will be in lieu of the weekly one heretofore required, and will also embrace the names, &c., of the vessels on service connected with the yard or station.

22....So far as the public service will permit, and supplies can be procured, commanding officers of squadrons will require their vessels to visit alternately all the places within the limits of their squadrons where American commerce extends, unless otherwise directed by the Secretary of the Navy. The vessels will take advantage of the great wind currents, and thus economize in the use of coal.

23..... Lengthy anchorage in ports where no public exigency requires the presence of a vessel is forbidden; also the wintering of the vessels of a squadron in port.

24....Commanders of squadrons and of vessels on special service abroad will cause the Secretary of the Navy to be furnished quarterly with a cruising report in the following form:

Vessel.	Rate.	Commanding Officer.	Ports visited, and date.	Days at Sea.	Days in Port.	Remarks.

Regulation Circular No. 3.

25....Masters-at-arms, yeomen, surgeons, and paymasters' stewards, appointed to a vessel ordered on distant, service, will be allowed an advance of pay for the. usual term, upon. condition that the officers by whom they are respectively appointed consent to become responsible for such advance, which will be made by the paymaster of the vessel..

26....Paragraph No. 975, page 173; is so modified;. in the last line of the same, as to read: "yearly pay."

27....Persons deserting from the naval service forfeit. all claim to any balances, including prize money, due to them at the time of desertion, unless sentenced to other punishment, or acquitted by a general court martial, or unless the mark of: desertion is erased by competent authority.

28....Paragraph 422, page 74. is so far modified as to leave the keys of the medical store-rooms in charge of the surgeon of the vessel.

29.....Whenever a person is enlisted on board ship, or elsewhere than at a rendezvous, a complete descriptive list must be made and returned quarterly; with the shipping articles, signed by the recruiting officer and the surgeon. The form will be that found on page 256 of the Naval Regulations, substituting the name of vessel or place for "Naval Rendezvous," and quarter in place of the word "week." The recapitulation on. page 257, is not required;. but the certificate at the foot of this page, is to be adopted; leaving out the second line of the second paragraph, viz: "also the names, &c., &c., who have been rejected at the receiving ship." Printed blank forms will always be forwarded with the muster rolls and shipping articles.

30....Attention is called to paragraph 49, page 364, Regulation Circular No. 2. The omission to forward the required returns and reports is not excusable because of the want of printed blank forms.

GIDEON WELLES,
Secretary of the Navy.

Navy Department,
April 30, 1866.